The National Trust
Book of the
Coast

Clare Gogerty

Acknowledgements

The author would like to thank the following people:

Sean Adams, Grant Berry, Max Bell, Henry Bexley, Katie Bond, Jane Cecil, Mike Collins, Robin Cottrell, Phil Dyke, Sian Evans, Amy Fieldman, David Fincham, Tony Flux, Simon Garner, Cathy Gosling, Adrian Harrison, Reuben Hawkwood, Michaela Hinton, Marc Hoskins, Rob Joules, Kate Martin, Alison Moss, Richard Neale, Matthew Oates, Alex Reece, Robert Sonnen, John Stachiewicz, David Steel, Peter Taylor, Ajay Tegala, Tony Tutton, Sally Williams, Gareth Wilson, Greg Wilson. And John Gogerty who always loved to be by the sea.

This page: Aldeburgh

The old Aldeburgh Lifeboat Station on the Suffolk coast, built in the mid 19th century.

Previous page: Bedruthan Steps

A beautiful sea thrift-topped cliff and beach near Newquay in Cornwall.

First published in the United Kingdom in 2015 by National Trust Books, 43 Great Ormond Street London WC1N 3HZ
An imprint of Pavilion Books Group Ltd

ISBN: 978 1 90988 137 2

A CIP catalogue record for this book is available from the British Library

Colour reproduction by Mission Productions, Hong Kong
Printed and bound by Leo Paper Products Ltd, China

Design by Lee-May Lim
Layout by Blok Graphic

This book can be ordered direct from the publisher at the website www.pavilionbooks com, or try your local bookshop. Also available at National Trust shops and www.nationaltrustbooks.co.uk

Contents

Foreword

One serene, damp October morning, I swam out at Mother Ivey's Bay near Padstow and, looking across to Harlyn and Trevone with Stepper Point in the distance, I noticed the blowhole was spurting even though there was only a gentle swell. Some of the loveliest stretches of the coast between Trevose Head and Hartland Point are owned by the National Trust, and are where many of my happiest childhood memories were made. My family had a house on Trevose Head and, as a boy, I would love to watch bigger waves blown into the sky forced up by the pressure from the blowhole.

My swim also made me think how little that coast has changed in the last 50 years and how much other parts of the world I have visited have. On our over-crowded island, we are lucky enough to have a mature enough economy to preserve a great deal of our precious coastline for posterity. And we are lucky to have the National Trust's Neptune Coastline Campaign to help. The British coast is like a well-loved teddy bear, its fur worn down by the affection of its many visitors, which is why Neptune is so important in funding coastal protection. In 2000, I did a programme about the great seafood available around our coast called The Seafood Lover's Guide to Great Britain and Ireland. We filmed many beautiful, soaring aerial shots, which drove home to me what a great coastal heritage we have; how unspoilt it is, and how much we owe to the National Trust's Neptune Coastline Campaign.

Rick Stein

Opposite: Seacombe Ledge

The late winter sun warms Seacombe Ledge at low tide, Purbeck, Dorset.

Introduction

A Place of Escape

Many of our happiest memories are made at the coast. And little wonder – whether we head there for a bucket-and-spade holiday, a blustery walk along a coastal path or a day's sailing around a choppy headland, the British coast has plenty of opportunities for mood-boosting pleasure. It's where we go to get away from the frenetic pace of modern life, to stare at the horizon and stride out on a long stretch of sand, a dog scampering before us.

This place of escape, adventure and tranquility has been rediscovered in recent years. Once neglected in favour of foreign holidays with their guarantee of warmer weather, the British seaside is a holiday destination once more. As air travel becomes more tiresome and costly, more coastal paths are opened up and accommodation and restaurants improve, we are once again heading to the sea. And it's not difficult to reach: none of us is ever further than 75 miles from the coast.

What the 11,000 miles of our coast (double that length if you include the 1,000 or so islands) has to offer is a huge variety of landscape and wildlife habitat, from teetering chalky cliffs, to lonely saltmarsh and rolling dunes, sandy beaches and secret coves. This coastline is a dynamic environment, forged and shaped by the effects of tides, waves and weather. Its distinctive features – sand bars, spits, mud flats, arches, stacks and caves – are a direct result of the deposition and erosion of the shoreline through the agencies of wind, sea, frost and ice. The constantly evolving shore is not only fascinating but diverse, and suits many moods and activities.

At the National Trust we want to encourage people to make the most of their coast. We want to reverse the trend that shows that children today spend 60 per cent less time outdoors than their parents did at the same age. We want to encourage people to believe that days spent outside, and at the seaside, are not just memorable, they are fun. Figures from our 2005 and 2010 Coastal Values Surveys show that the appetite is there: 63 per cent of people questioned regarded visiting the seaside as important to their quality of life, and 31 per cent considered their happiest childhood memory as being by the sea.

This book, produced as part of the celebrations of 50 years of the National Trust's Neptune Coastline Campaign, is packed with ideas for days out, walks and adventures, from rock pool rambles to coastal walks and wildlife spotting. We hope it will trigger many more trips to the coast and generate many more memories.

Right: Tennyson Down

A glorious view of Tennyson Down across the white cliffs at Freshwater Bay on the Isle of Wight. Tennyson Monument can just be seen on the highest point.

Below: Morston Quay

Morston Quay is found just within the shelter of Blakeney Point in Norfolk. The salt marshes of the Point form a wonderful backdrop to the quay.

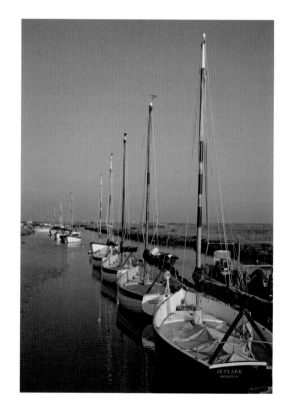

The National Trust and care of the coast

The coast has been central to the National Trust right from our beginnings. The first piece of land given to us was 1.82 hectares (4.5 acres) of gorse-covered cliff top at Dinas Oleu, overlooking Cardigan Bay in Wales, in 1895 by landowner and philanthropist Mrs Fanny Talbot. Mrs Talbot donated the land on the understanding that the newly founded National Trust would never 'vulgarise it, or prevent wild nature from having its way'. Octavia Hill, one of our founders (along with Sir Robert Hunter and Canon Hardwicke Rawnsley) had created the organisation 'to preserve land and buildings of beauty or historic interest for the benefit of the nation', and could assure her that it wouldn't. She pondered that Dinas Oleu was, 'Our first piece of land. I wonder if it will be our last.' It wasn't: 70 years later, we had care of 186 miles of coastline including the Gower Peninsula in Wales, the Farne Islands in Northumberland and Baggy Point in North Devon.

These days, the National Trust cares for 742 miles of coastline in England, Wales and Northern Ireland, representing nearly 10 per cent of the total. (Not all of this is coastline: 8,000 hectares (19,768 acres) of National Trust estate is marine, meaning below Mean High Water, the highest spring tide.) The region with the most National Trust-owned coastline is the South West, with 295.08 miles – 1 in 3 miles of the coast.

Some of our busiest properties are by the sea: Giant's Causeway, Northern Ireland, Rhossili, South Wales, and Studland, Dorset, each attract in excess of 1 million visits each year. We look after four World Heritage Sites, three of them coastal: Giant's Causeway and the Causeway coast, Dorset and East Devon Coast, and Cornwall and West Devon Mining Landscapes. There are also nine lighthouses under our ownership.

And it doesn't stop there: we keep a weather eye on land coming up to purchase; if we are best placed to buy and protect it. It is reassuring to know that once we have acquired a stretch of coastline it becomes inalienable, meaning it cannot be bought or sold except by an Act of Parliament.

'...we help ensure our future coast remains a great place for wildlife to thrive.'

Having so much coastline to look after comes with responsibilities and challenges. The biggest of these is monitoring changes and assessing how best to deal with them. Coastline change is inevitable, driven by rising sea levels and the impact of storms. But other changes, such as inappropriate or damaging tourist and urban development, can be contested and stopped. At the National Trust, we cannot tame the sea or control the effects of climate change, but by careful management we help ensure our future coast remains a great place for wildlife to thrive. Over 200 coastal rangers are employed by us to do just that, and together with thousands of volunteers, they ensure that these coastal places are protected forever, for everyone to enjoy.

The Neptune Coastline Campaign

In the late 1950s and early 1960s, the UK coastline was rapidly changing due to public holidays, growth in car ownership and leisure time. Caravan and holiday parks sprang up, and oil refineries, car parks and urban sprawl consumed the coastline. In 1964, Dr John Whittow, a lecturer at Reading University, got his students to map the coastline for the National Trust to chart what was happening. The results revealed that, through development or neglect, land was disappearing at the rate of 6 miles or more a year.

We decided that it was time to act. Under the patronage of the Duke of Edinburgh, we launched Enterprise Neptune on 11 May 1965, with the purpose of raising funds to stop the despoiling of the British shoreline, and set an initial fund-raising target at £2 million. Since then, the Neptune Coastline Campaign has a broader scope and includes our management work and communication with people about coastal matters. Our donors' generosity has amounted to £65 million, along with gifts of land, and we now care for 742 miles of coast and thousands of acres inland. Popular beauty spots, including Rhossili Beach on the Gower Peninsula and Golden Cap in Dorset, have been saved for future generations. Donations to Neptune have been spent on many things: helping staff on the Farne Islands monitor the migratory habits of sea birds by fitting them with tiny geo-locators; aiding the clean-up operation in Devon when *Napoli*, a container ship, ran aground there in January 2007; and picking up the cost of removing a beached sperm whale washed up at Brancaster in Norfolk, in 2006.

Now, with much of the coastline in good hands, the challenge is to face the future, adapting our coast to natural processes, particularly the threat posed by climate change. Cash must now be spent on future-proofing the coast – moving car parks and cafés back from eroding shorelines, working in partnership with other organisations, and ensuring people have more and better access to the coast that they love.

The changing coastline: the National Trust and climate change

Since 1919, sea levels in the UK have risen by nearly 20cm. Predictions suggest that climate change will lead to continued sea-level rise and increased storminess, in turn accelerating the scale and pace of coastal change. This has major implications for the shape of the coastline, with coastal places changing in our lifetimes.

This presents serious challenges for us. Over the next 100 years, 377 miles of National Trust-owned coastline will be affected by increased flooding and erosion. Around 60 per cent of the land that we care for on the coastline is at risk of erosion in the twenty-first century – with 15 per cent of these sites potentially losing more than 100m of land to the sea. This means that 160 of our properties could lose land by erosion over the next 100 years, and 126 of our coastline properties are at risk from tidal flooding.

The twin pressures of rising sea levels and extreme weather, as witnessed during the winter storms of 2013/14, when, among other casualties, the rock arch at Porthcothan Bay, Cornwall, and the great stack on the south side of Portland in Dorset, were destroyed by the raging sea, mean that we have had to fast-forward decisions about land and buildings in our care. Changes that that we thought we had a decade to plan for have happened pretty much overnight.

We have had to look at how to adapt coastal places in the months ahead, rather than years or decades. The future is inherently unpredictable, even more so with climate change and a dynamic coastal environment, so that we need to be flexible. We aim to have adaptation strategies in place for our 79 coastal places most at risk of erosion or flooding by 2020.

These strategies include, where possible, working with nature rather than against it. Areas must be created where the coastline can realign as the sea levels rise. Natural habitats such as sand dunes and saltmarshes

'Areas must be created where the coastline can realign as the sea levels rise.'

Right: Newlyn Harbour

High tide and a Force 12 gale combine to bombard Newlyn on the Cornish coast, one of many coastal communities now in the front line of rising sea levels and increasingly severe storms.

Below: Rhossili Bay

Part of the cliff face collapsed on 22 January 2014, taking with it the bottom steps that lead down to the beach on the Gower Peninsula.

Left: Beach clean-up

The National Trust works hard to care for the coast for the enjoyment of everyone, including cleaning up the beach at Branscombe, Devon, after the cargo of the *Napoli* wreck came ashore.

Below: Birling Gap

Demolition work begins on vulnerable cliff-top buildings at Birling Gap on the East Sussex coast, after seven years' worth of erosion occurred in just a few weeks early in 2014.

can act as buffers absorbing the impact of storms and very high tides. Hard coastal defences will always have their place, but the winter storms have provided a valuable reminder that they have a limited life.

There is a need to shift from our natural instinct to defend the land from the power of the sea towards a more holistic approach where adaptation is at the heart. If we begin this process now and start the conversation, we can find solutions to living with a changing coastline.

The National Trust looks after some of the most spectacular areas of coast for the enjoyment of all of us. We need your support to help us continue our work to cherish the countryside and provide access to our beautiful and refreshing landscapes. To find out more about how you too can help our work as a volunteer, member or donor please go to www.nationaltrust.org.uk.

In the meantime, we hope that some of the beautiful places and expansive shoreline featured in this book will encourage you to pack a picnic and head to our wonderful, life-enriching coast.

The National Trust Coast

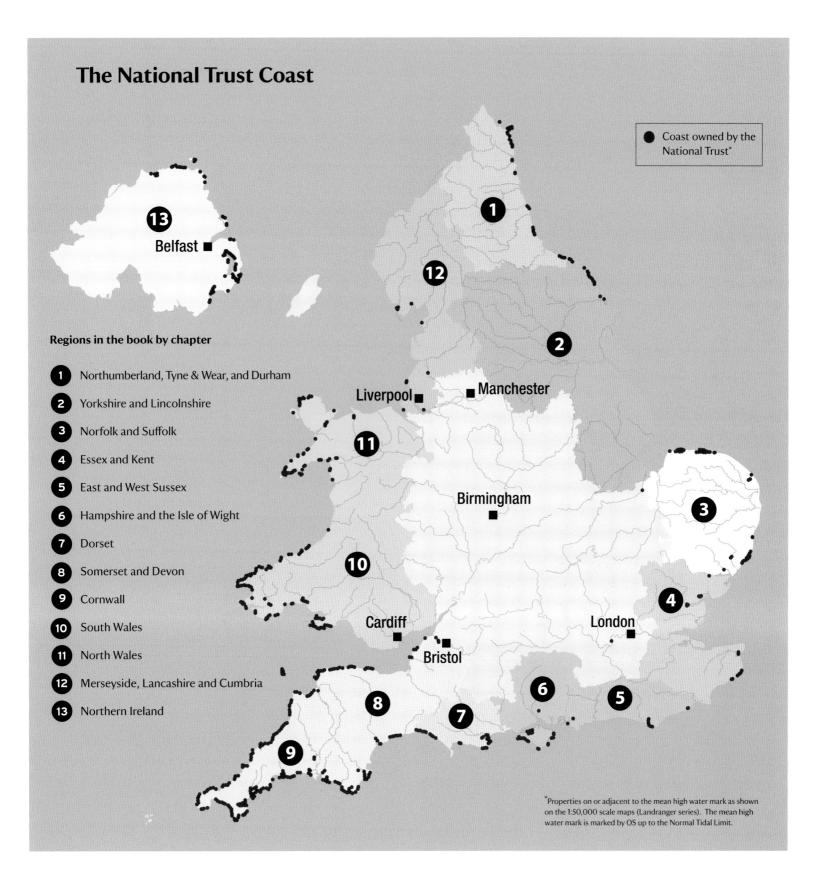

Coast owned by the
National Trust*

Belfast ■

Regions in the book by chapter

1 Northumberland, Tyne & Wear, and Durham

2 Yorkshire and Lincolnshire

3 Norfolk and Suffolk

4 Essex and Kent

5 East and West Sussex

6 Hampshire and the Isle of Wight

7 Dorset

8 Somerset and Devon

9 Cornwall

10 South Wales

11 North Wales

12 Merseyside, Lancashire and Cumbria

13 Northern Ireland

Liverpool ■   ■ **Manchester**

Birmingham ■

Cardiff ■   **London** ■

■ **Bristol**

*Properties on or adjacent to the mean high water mark as shown on the 1:50,000 scale maps (Landranger series). The mean high water mark is marked by OS up to the Normal Tidal Limit.

Things to know

Throughout this book we offer suggestions for making the most of your time at the coast, whether it is on your own, or with friends and family. However, conditions at the coast can be unpredictable, so we have included our tips for enjoying coastal activities safely and responsibly.

Please help us look after the coast by leaving it as you found it, and following the countryside code: www.gov.uk/government/publications/the-countryside-code.

Advice for walkers

- Staying safe is your own responsibility. Please look after yourself and other members of your group.
- Wear sensible shoes and be prepared for all weather.

- Stay away from the base of cliffs – rockfalls can happen at any time.
- Keep back from cliff edges.
- If you are intending to explore the coastline always check the tide timetables beforehand.
- Look out for signs marking places it might be unsafe to go, and ask at the property if you are not sure.

The fossil code

- There are a few rules that all fossil hunters need to follow.
- As long as you are not in a protected area you can pick up small fossils that are lying on the ground to get a closer look.
- If you are in a Site of Specific Scientific Interest, please follow any rules they might have.

Opposite left: Walking the coast path

A couple make the steep climb on the South West Coast Path near Pencarrow Head, Cornwall.

Opposite right: A treasured find

A child reveals the fossil she has discovered on a Yorkshire beach.

Left: Kayaking

A group of kayakers explore the cliffs at sea level near Old Harry Rocks in Dorset.

- If you find something rare, please report it to closest museum or visitor centre.
- The best, and safest, place to look for fossils is on the beach where the sea has washed them out and left them for you to find.
- Please do not collect or remove any fossils from, or hammer into, the cliffs, fossil features or rocky ledges.

At the beach safety tips

- Always swim or surf at a beach patrolled by lifesavers or lifeguards.
- Swim between the red and yellow flags. They mark the safest areas to swim.
- If the red flag is flying, do not swim there.
- Avoid swimming alone.
- Float with a rip current or underflow, don't swim against it.

Kayaking and canoeing safety tips

- Before boarding a canoe, you should be able to swim at least 50m. Here are some other considerations.
- Do you have appropriate clothing? As well as your buoyancy aid, always wear shoes with a good grip. Also consider wearing a hat and layering clothes that can be removed easily.
- Check the weather forecast before you set off: **www.metoffice.gov. uk/; www.bbc.co.uk/weather/.**
- Look up the tide times. Going up river with an incoming (flood) tide and returning with the outgoing (ebb) is usually easiest.
- Be aware of the rules at sea and observe the navigation rules for the waterway you are travelling on.
- Check your equipment. You should have a buoyancy aid, bailer/ sponge, small first-aid kit, penknife, mobile phone in a waterproof bag, drinking water, sun cream, licence (as required).
- For more information see **www.gocanoeing.org.uk**

Northumberland, Tyne and Wear, and Durham

You can thank whippy North Sea winds for keeping the beaches of Northumberland unspoilt and unpopulated: even in the height of summer, chilly gusts can put off the less-hardy visitor. Which leaves this stretch of expansive, sandy coastline free for those sensible enough to put on an extra layer; those who appreciate its mile-upon-mile of empty beaches, rolling dunes, romantic castles and rocky headlands, and islands cloaked with seabirds.

The Northumberland coastline is an Area of Outstanding Natural Beauty (AONB) and it is clear why: the North Sea winds scour the long, white beaches, thousands of seabirds feed on the mudflats and nest in its islands' rocky crevices, and its extensive dune system is rich with flora and fauna.

Stretching for 40 miles from Amble to the Scottish border, the North Northumberland Heritage Coast exhibits impressive cliffs and headlands, formed through exposure of Carboniferous rock. Further south, beyond Amble, the coastline is gradually being rediscovered. Forgotten during its days as a dump for the colliery industry, it has been cleaned up and reborn as a landscape rich in wild flowers and grassland.

This is a stretch of coast in which to stride out purposefully, a dog at the heel, or to scramble up the battlements of a castle and reimagine its beleaguered past.

Previous Pages: St Aidan's Dunes run between Bamburgh and Seahouses village, Northumberland.

Left: Puffins on Staple Island, Inner Farne, part of the island group off the coast of Northumberland.

Northumberland: castles and holy islands

As well as chilly winds, the North Sea has also brought its fair share of invaders to the Northumberland coast. Its history is chequered with accounts of Border battles between the Scottish and English armies which raged for hundreds of years, and with tales of Viking and Norman invasions. The border town of Berwick-upon-Tweed, which sits on a peninsula between the sea and the River Tweed, alternated between Scottish and English rule during the Middle Ages, and was encircled by a stone wall during the reign of Elizabeth I.

The castles that were built to defend the coast – Bamburgh, Dunstanburgh (see page 28) and Warkworth – remain as dramatic silhouettes glowering over the sea, and give the coastline its romantic appeal.

Even the spiritually charged Holy Island has its own evidence of military occupation: its castle, Lindisfarne, was built in the sixteenth century and was a coastal defence for 300 years (see page 31). Cut off by the tide for most of the day, a trip to the island requires some planning and can feel like a pilgrimage. Visitors tread in the footsteps of St Aidan who founded a monastery here in the seventh century and St Cuthbert, the shepherd boy who became a reluctant bishop.

The Farnes are made from resistant Dolerite (subvolcanic rock) and would have once been connected to the mainland. Erosion and sea-level rises eroded the softer limestone rock that makes up most of the Northumberland coastline and created the islands following the last Ice Age. Dolerite is columnar in form, resulting in steep, vertical cliffs and stacks, perfect for nesting seabirds.

The much photographed Bamburgh Castle was built on the same seam of igneous rock, Whin Sill, as the Farnes, and rises 46m above the glorious stretches of beach that are Bamburgh Sands, Seahouses, Beadnell, and National Trust-owned Embleton Bay and Newton Links. The castle has had many manifestations since it was first built in the Middle Ages: it was destroyed by Vikings, rebuilt in the twelfth century by Normans, held by Henry II, governed by the Forster family of Northumberland before being bought by Victorian industrialist William Armstrong in 1894 and restored to splendour. (It still belongs to the Armstrong family who live in nearby National-Trust owned house Cragside.) Bamburgh village is also home to the museum dedicated to the county's most famous heroine: Grace Darling (see feature, page 30).

Right: Bamburgh Castle

Silhouetted against the dawn sky, the imposing walls of Bamburgh Castle stand firm against the blasts of North Sea winds.

Below: Holy Island Harbour

Looking across the harbour towards Lindisfarne Priory, founded by St Aidan in AD 635 and the original home of the Lindisfarne Gospels.

'Bamburgh, Dunstanburgh
and Warkworth remain
as dramatic silhouettes
glowering over the sea.'

Newbiggin-by-the-Sea, another former coal town, was reinvented in 2007 when more than 500,000 tonnes of sand were brought up from Skegness to replace the eroded beach. A breakwater was installed to try to protect the beach and a massive sculpture of two people standing on a platform looking out to sea entitled *Couple* by Sean Henry, was erected offshore.

Nearby, at Blyth, is the site of UK's first offshore wind farm, which lies half a mile off the coast. The nine original wind turbines were the most powerful in the world when Blyth Offshore Wind Farm opened in 2000. Now the National Renewable Energy Centre in the town tests and develops offshore renewable technologies.

The River Tyne divides the cities of Newcastle-upon-Tyne and Gateshead for 13 miles before flowing into the North Sea between South Shields and Tynemouth. Newcastle's position on the river and its proximity to the coalfields largely shaped it: from as early as the thirteenth century, ships left the port carrying coal for export. The large wooden staithes, built to load coal on to the ships in 1890, remain as a reminder of the city's past. The city was also one of the world's most important centres of shipbuilding, with islands and meanders in the river removed to accommodate it. Little remains of either of these industries: the quayside now bustles with bars, restaurants and offices, and regeneration has delivered an innovative tilting bridge, the BALTIC Centre for Contemporary Art and the Sage Gateshead music centre.

Left: Seahouses

Fishing boats in the village harbour on a misty morning. This is the place to board a boat for a trip to the Farne Islands.

South of the city stretch expanses of white sand, reached by Metro from the centre. Marsden Bay is lined with soft limestone cliffs that are particularly susceptible to erosion. Marsden Rock, in the centre of the bay, was once an arch but is now a solitary stack as time and tide has reduced it.

A rediscovered coastline

The coast south of the Tyne to the town of Amble has, until fairly recently, been a place to avoid rather than visit as a holiday destination. An industrial stretch of collieries and docks, it was very much a working coastline. The deposits left as a result of coal mining laid waste to the shoreline but since the closure of the last collieries in 1993, it has been reborn.

Sunderland, on the mouth of the River Wear, was a major port exporting coal and salt, and a shipbuilding centre. Both of these industries significantly declined during the second half of the

twentieth century leading to mass unemployment and a search for a new identity for the city. Regeneration has created two new beach resorts – Roker and Seaburn – and a marina, and visitors come to enjoy outdoor activities and the new clean beaches.

South of Wearmouth, the coastline of County Durham was similarly an industrial wasteland of colliery tips: Durham's mines extended 4 miles out to sea and their waste was scattered over a large area. Thanks to the work of the Turning the Tide initiative in 1997–2002, the area has been cleaned up and regenerated and wildlife has returned as habitats have become re-established.

The harbour town of Amble was where colliery wagons from pits north of Newcastle-upon-Tyne would bring the 'black diamond' for loading into sailing ships destined for ports further south. Now it is the place to watch yachts bob about in the marina and to catch a boat to nearby Coquet Island to see the puffins.

Explore National Trust places on the Northumberland, Tyne and Wear, and Durham coast

Druridge Bay

Stretching from Amble to Cresswell, this 7-mile stretch of beach is fringed by dunes, woodland and the 40.5-hectare (100-acre) Ladyburn Lake (popular with watersports enthusiasts). Lively winds and open space attract kite flyers, and bird watchers flock here to try to catch a glimpse of golden plovers, goldeneye snipe and purple sandpipers, among other birds. During the Second World War it was the site of anti-invasion defences including anti-tank blocks and pillboxes, the remains of which can still be seen.

Dunstanburgh Castle

One of the landmarks of the Northumberland coastline, Dunstanburgh Castle sits on a rocky crag overlooking Embleton Bay. Built in the fourteenth century by Thomas, Earl of Lancaster (the wealthiest nobleman in England at the time), it was once the largest fortification in Northern England. It fell into disrepair after he was executed for his role in a rebellion against Edward II, despite being modernised later by John of Gaunt. The romance of its ruin appealed to artists, including JMW Turner who captured it in a painting in 1798–1800.

The castle with its ruined twin-towered silhouette makes an exciting destination for a coastal walk from nearby Craster (pick up a Craster kipper, an oak-smoked herring, when you're there – a delicious local delicacy), accompanied by the sound of crashing waves and squawking seabirds. Alternatively, approach from Embleton Bay, a stretch of dunes and sand that runs from Low Newton. Take a picnic, and on arrival at the castle, tuck in, overlooking a spectacular vista of the sea and the dramatic Northumberland coastline. **Craster, Alnwick, Northumberland, NE66 3TT (01665 576231)**

Opposite: Dunstanburgh Castle

The dramatic ruins of Dunstanburgh Castle seen from the foreshore of Embleton Bay. Stride out from the village of Craster to really appreciate its isolated location.

What's so special about … dunes?

Constantly shifting and susceptible to the lightest gust of wind, dunes are one of our most fragile habitats. Despite their vulnerability to wind and sea, they are surprisingly rich in vegetation due largely to the hardiness of marram grass whose network of roots stabilise them. They are also important as a natural sea defence. But how are dunes formed? There are five stages:

1. The wind blows in from the sea bringing with it light, dry sand grains picked up off the exposed beaches.

2. The sand is dropped during a lull in the wind, or checked by obstacles such as pebbles or pieces of wood, and piles up in wave-like ridges and mounds.

3. The mounds are convex on the windward side and concave on the lee. A steady wind forms them into a crescent shape; variable winds convert them into shapeless heaps or ridges.

4. These mounds become colonised by pioneer plants such as sand couch grass and lyme grass, and salt-tolerant flowers including sea sandwort and sea rocket. These early dunes are fragile, constantly moving and at the mercy of tides. Pioneer plants with root systems (such as sand couch grass) help to bind the sand and stabilise the dunes.

5. As dunes merge and grow beyond the reach of the highest spring tide, the pioneer plants die out and marram grass becomes the dominant species. Marram grass stabilises the dune with its extensive root system and fertilizes the dune so that other species, such as red fescue, bloody cranesbill, viper's bugloss, mosses and lichens, can grow on it.

Few animals live in dunes: their shifting, open nature prevents habitation, but plant-eating and predatory insects such as grasshoppers, crickets and ground beetles are common. Sand wasps also nest in shallow burrows, stocking the nest with a paralysed caterpillar to provide larvae with fresh food.

Farne Islands

Over the centuries, these 20 or so volcanic outcrops (the number depends on the height of the tide) have been a retreat for hermit monks, a graveyard for drowned sailors, a refuge for seabirds and a breeding ground for grey seals. The National Trust has owned the islands since 1925 and runs them as a nature reserve. Boat trips from Seahouses take visitors to Inner Farne and Staple Island in the summer (the trip takes about an hour) where they can see some of the 23 species of seabird, including puffins who nest there. Visitors are allowed to land on Inner Farne (where there is a National Trust shop), Staple Island and Longstone, but landing on all other islands is prohibited to protect the wildlife.

There are over 80,000 pairs of seabirds, 4,000 grey seals and 11 National Trust rangers on the islands. The rangers are the only human inhabitants: they live in the old Pele Tower – a fortified keep – on Inner Farne and in one of three lighthouses on the islands, Brownsman. Alongside other duties, they monitor the dangers presented to the seabird population by erosion and climate change. Puffins, eider duck, arctic tern, kittiwakes and guillemots are all at risk from rising sea temperatures. A shortage of puffins' main food source, sand eel, as a result of over-fishing and warmer waters, has meant that the birds have started to eat snake pipefish. The lack of food combined with bad weather resulted in dozens of birds dying and being washed up along the coast of north-east England. However, a census taken by National Trust rangers on the Farne Islands in 2013 showed an 8 per cent increase in the number of birds since the last count in 2008 – there are now 39,962 pairs nesting on the Farnes, as opposed to 36,835 five years earlier – bringing hope that the puffin is adapting to the changes.

As well as seabirds and seals, the islands are famous for the heroism of Grace Darling who helped her father rescue survivors from the *Forfashire* in 1838 (see feature, right), and St Cuthbert, one of the most important medieval saints of Northern England. St Cuthbert lived in a simple stone and turf cell on Inner Farne, leaving to spend two years as bishop of Lindisfarne (see opposite), before returning to the island where he died in 687. He lived frugally in isolation, watching and caring for the birds. In 676 he introduced a law to protect the eider ducks and other seabirds nesting on the island; this is thought to be one of the earliest bird protection laws in the world. **Near Seahouses, Northumberland (01665 721099)**

Northumberland's Darlings

One of maritime history's most memorable events occurred over 175 years ago when a 22-year-old woman battled with wild seas and fierce storms to rescue a group of shipwrecked passengers. On 7 September 1838 at 4am, Grace Darling saw the 400-ton steamship *Forfarshire* crash on to Big Harcar Rock from her window in the Longstone lighthouse on the Farne Islands. The ship, which was the *Titanic* of its day and was kitted out with fine china and panelled rooms, had set off from Hull on 5 September carrying 52 passengers and crew. Nine of these (the sole survivors) now desperately clung to rocks.

Grace and her father William, who was the lighthouse keeper, set out in a 21ft wooden fishing boat (a coble) and rowed for almost a mile through the turbulent North Sea storm towards the unfortunate few. William leapt on to the rocks as Grace rowed the boat, and returned with five survivors. Grace then rowed back to the lighthouse and as William returned for the others, she stayed with her mother to care for the victims.

Although her heroism brought fame and acclaim, Grace kept out of the limelight, staying at the lighthouse with her parents until her death in 1842, aged 27, from consumption.

Grace Darling's nephew Robert was a lighthouse keeper at Souter Lighthouse (see page 33) for 24 years from 1873 to 1897. He followed in his family's footsteps: his father, grandfather and great grandfather were all lighthouse keepers at Longstone, and Robert was born there. However, he never knew his famous aunt as he was born in 1846, four years after Grace's death.

Lindisfarne Castle

It is easy to understand why wealthy Edwardian magazine magnate Edward Hudson fell in love with ruined Lindisfarne Castle. Perched on a high outcrop of rock on Holy Island, cut off from the mainland by tides for 11 out of 24 hours per day, the romance of it was irresistible. Built in the sixteenth century, Lindisfarne was originally a garrison manned by soldiers defending the coastline from intruders for 300 years. Edward Hudson first leased then bought the romantic ruins and corralled his friends, architect Edwin Lutyens and gardener Gertrude Jekyll, to fashion it to his tastes. It was reborn as an Arts and Crafts masterpiece and provided a holiday home for Hudson until the travelling and upkeep proved too much. He eventually sold it to financier Oswald Flak in 1921, with the National Trust taking ownership in 1944 after a gift by then-owner Sir Edward de Stein.

The castle, standing 30.5m above the sea, offers panoramic views of the coastline and the sea. Inside, its massive rooms, sandstone pillars and model of a ship, The Henrietta, hanging from the ceiling, are all well worth investigating, but don't forget to wander around outside.

Above: Lindisfarne Castle

Perched high on a volcanic mound known as Beblowe Craig, the castle can be seen from miles around.

The tidal pools are perfect for rockpooling, the nineteenth-century lime kilns are well preserved and a fascinating insight into a now defunct industry, and Gertrude Jekyll's garden, which she created in 1911, is especially colourful in July and August when it bursts into life with hollyhocks, sweet peas and heritage vegetables. **Holy Island, Berwick-upon-Tweed, Northumberland, TD15 2SH (01289 389244).** For a walk around Lindisfarne, see page 38.

 ## Holiday Cottage

St Oswald's Cottage, Holy Island, Berwick-upon-Tweed, Northumberland. For a chance to experience what Holy Island is like when the tide comes in and the visitors have gone, stay in this cottage, which is the last on the road to the castle. Built around 1911

by Edward Hudson, tenant of Lindisfarne Castle, it was designed by Edwin Lutyens who was working on the renovation of castle at the time. The Grade-II-listed stone cottage was given to the Trust in 1944 by Sir Edward de Stein and restored in 2009. Wake up to views of the harbour and castle and then go for a wander before the daytrippers arrive. For more information see www.nationaltrustcottages.co.uk

Seaton Delaval Hall

This masterpiece of English Baroque, situated inland from the harbour of Seaton Sluice, has had a colourful and unsettled history. Neither its architect, John Vanbrugh, nor his patron, Admiral George Delaval, lived to see its completion in 1728 as an imposing building built in the Palladian style with monumental columns and a dramatic staircase.

Funded by the mining of panned salt and coal, which was exported on ships from the Delaval-improved Seaton Sluice Harbour, this once modest manor house was only half completed when it was inherited by Francis Blake, Admiral George Delaval's nephew, who moved in with his wife and 12 children once it was finished.

Subsequent heirs lived there intermittently and whereas some were industrious, building up salt, coal and glass businesses, others were better known for their large and scandalous parties and pranks played on guests. The Trust bought the Hall in 2009 from Lord Hastings who had done much to restore its fabric and fortunes. **The Avenue, Seaton Sluice, Northumberland, NE26 4QR (0191 237 9100)**

Souter Lighthouse and The Leas

Standing proudly on the coastline midway between the Tyne and Wear, hooped in red and white, is Souter Lighthouse, the first lighthouse in the world to be powered by electricity. Commissioned in 1869 by Trinity House to prevent shipwrecks on the dangerous rocks off Whitburn and Marsden, it is a 23m tower surrounded by an engine house, workshop, storeroom and six houses for staff and families. Two black, trumpet-shaped foghorns stand separately in a field that is now a popular place for outdoor events (including pirate days) and for simply sitting with a cup of tea and a piece of cake.

Left: Seaton Delaval Hall

Seaton Delaval Hall was the work of architect Sir John Vanbrugh, one of the masters of English Baroque.

Why this place is special to me

Nick Dolan, General Manager, Souter Lighthouse and The Leas

'With a majestic view of the mouth of the Tyne, Souter Lighthouse and its coastline, The Leas, is an extraordinary place. From the coast road which borders the thin stretch of grassland, there are areas of close-cut grassland with locals walking dogs, cycling, flying kites, jogging…and generally enjoying their local green lung.

'Look closer and the taller grasses teem with wildlife. At the cliff edge, staying on the safe side of the barrier, the eroded coast darts in and out in erratic fashion with the layers of geology describing millions of years. Below, the sea is as turquoise as any Greek island retreat, or grey-brown and angry, as the tide, weather and mood takes her.

'Above all this, a perfectly proportioned lighthouse, hooped in red like a child's toy, and sparkling from its recent repaint, stands proud, no longer warning ships away from the cliffs, but beckoning people to come and enjoy a very special piece of coast – acquired with Neptune's help and vision.'

Although no lighthouse keeper has lived here since 1988 when it was decommissioned, it appears that some have never left: since the National Trust acquired it in 1989, staff have often been startled, but not threatened, by strange happenings – shadowy presences, the smell of strong tobacco and figures in old-fashioned uniforms. Objects have also been known to disappear, then reappear. Anything inexplicable is now attributed to 'Fred the Ghost' and no more is thought of it.

Visitors get a good idea of what life as a Victorian lighthouse keeper was like by looking around one of the keepers' houses, which has been restored by the National Trust. They can climb the 76 steps to visit the engine room at the top of the tower and witness an unchanging view.

Above: Marsden Rock

This is all that remains of the once great arch in Marsden Bay, Tyne and Wear, which succumbed to the sea in 1996.

They will also learn of the lost village of Marsden, once a self-sufficient mining village of 700 people, which was demolished in 1968 following the closure of Whitburn Colliery.

The Leas

This is the adjacent 2.5-mile stretch of cliffs, foreshore and coastal grassland. The Magnesian-Limestone-rich soil supports rich flora including thrift, scurvy grass and sea plantain, and kittiwakes nest in Marsden Bay. It includes Trow Quarry, a Durham Coast Site of Special Scientific Interest (SSSI), important for its geology, land forms, wild flowers and sea birds; Whitburn Coastal Park, a nature reserve situated on reclaimed mining land, with a bird observatory and wetland habitats for a variety of creatures, including pochard ducks; and Rocket Green, a clifftop meadow with the richest variety of rare wild flowers on this coast including the autumn gentian, bee orchid and dropwort.

Offshore is Marsden Rock, once a distinctive arch and local landmark that became the victim of erosion in 1996 when the arch collapsed into the sea, leaving behind two separate sea stacks. In 1997 the smaller stack was demolished for safety reasons, leaving a 30m tall lump of Periclase and Magnesian Limestone. Ninety-one metres from the main cliff face, it is reachable at low tide only, and home to seabirds including fulmars, kittiwakes and cormorants. (For more on sea stacks, see page 157.) **Coast Road, Whitburn, Sunderland, Tyne and Wear, SR6 7NH (0191 529 3161)**

The Durham Coast

Walk along the 11-mile Durham Coastal Footpath from Seaham to Crimdon, and you pass through land owned by the National

> '**Offshore is Marsden Rock, once a distinctive arch and local landmark that became a victim of erosion.**'

Trust including Beacon Hill, the highest point on the Durham coast. Magnesian Limestone bedrock laid down between 250 and 295 million years ago, has enabled a rare form of grassland to prosper here and created a habitat rich in wildflowers and animals. Blast Beach in Seaham, overlooked by local landmark Nose's Point had suffered from the dumping of colliery waste but a massive clean-up has transformed it into a clean and safe place to walk and enjoy. Look out for pieces of sea-buffeted glass, the remains of waste glass deposited into the sea from the London Bottleworks which closed down in 1921. The coastal gills, including Warren House Gill, which cut through the cliffs along the Durham Coast and run down to the sea, are also worth exploring. These small valleys were formed by rivers during the last Ice Age, and provide a rich habitat for birds such as redwings and field fares that feed on the berry-bearing bushes.

Enterprise Neptune and the Durham Coast

The Durham coastline has been disturbed and polluted by a century of waste tipping from the five collieries dotted along its length (Vane Tempest, Seaham, Easington, Horden and Blackhall). Today none of these are active but their influence is still visible. Waste that was dumped on to the beaches was first washed out to sea, then, with the action of the tide, made its way back on to the beaches and down the coast. This created huge piles of black and grey spoil.

Before Enterprise Neptune was launched in 1965, the National Trust conducted a survey of the 3,000 miles of coastline of England, Wales and Northern Ireland. Some coast was already protected by the Trust and other organisations, of the rest one third was judged to be developed, one third of little interest and one third to be of outstanding natural beauty. Entreprise Neptune was aimed at securing as much of this last category as possible.

Horden on the Durham coast, where coal mining had taken place under the sea and the slag was thrown up on the beach, wouldn't have fallen into the latter category but the Trust recognised that the area between the cliffs and high water mark contained a whole series of important habitats. In 1988 in a watershed moment, Neptune bought the coast at Horden from British Coal for £1. Now all is flourishing. Under a Countryside Stewardship Grant Scheme, the Trust took away the wheat fields above the beach to improve the wildlife and provide public access via a coastal path.

Shore-spotter's Guide

The **kittiwake** (*Rissa tridactyla*) population is declining in some areas but not in Marsden Bay. Thousands nest here and the number has steadily risen since they first appeared in the 1930s. It is now home to over 5,000 pairs. After breeding, the birds move out into the Atlantic where they spend the winter.

Sea plantain (*Plantago maritima*) is an herbaceous perennial with thick leaves, which is harvested and eaten, like samphire, in parts of Canada. It has fleshy leaves in a rosette form and the flowers are small and greenish-brown and grow in a spike. The Magnesian-Limestone-rich soil in The Leas supports rich flora including sea plantain, scurvy grass and thrift.

Larger than the common seal and with a less-curved profile and a longer muzzle the **Atlantic grey seal** (*Halichoerus grypus*) can reach lengths of 3 metres and weigh up to 190kg. They prefer rocky coastline to the sandbanks and estuaries favoured by the common seal. There is an important colony on the Farne Islands which has Europe's largest breeding population: 4,000 seals give birth to approximately 1,500 pups every autumn.

Often referred to as a 'clown among seabirds', the **puffin** (*Fratercula arctica*) is one of the coast's most charming creatures. It has a brightly coloured bill, bright orange legs and distinctive eye markings. Its black back and white underparts may have earned it its name – *fratercula* means little friar. It is most easily seen during its breeding season in March and April on the Farne Islands and Coquet Island.

5

The small **bee orchid** (*Ophrys apifera*) grows to about 45cm and flowers from May to July in dry grassland and dunes on Rocket Green, a clifftop meadow on The Leas. It produces up to 12 flowers on a spike and the markings on each three-lobed lip resemble a bumble bee.

6

One of the UK's rarest seabirds whose numbers have seriously declined, the **roseate tern** (*Sterna dougallii*) has a black cap and beak and long tail-streamers. It can be seen off the Northumberland coast during breeding season in the summer.

7

The **razorbill** (*Alca torda*) only comes ashore to breed, and winters in the northern Atlantic. Its numbers are threatened by declining fish stocks and fishing nets. Compact, with a heavy body, black and white colouring and a deep, blunt, black beak, the largest colonies are in northern Scotland but they can also be seen on Inner Farne and at Marsden Bay.

8

The **Durham argus butterfly** (*Aricia artaxerxes salmacis*), or Northern Brown Argus, is only found in northern England. Areas of the Durham coast such as Warren House Gill, where there is an abundance of its larval foodplant, common rock rose, offer a good chance to see them in June and July.

Lindisfarne Castle walk

BEGINNER
GRADE

Distance: 1 mile to 1.5 miles (1.6km to 2.4km)

Time: 20 to 40 minutes

Uncover Lindisfarne's often forgotten industrial past where a busy lime industry operated in the shadow of the castle in the late nineteenth century. Along with the massive lime kilns, networks of trackways remain leading to all parts of the island.

Terrain

Cobbled roads and a grass path which were former railway embankments. There is one flight of steps en route which can be avoided by taking the shorter route. Take care if the field north of the castle is flooded. Sheep are often in the field around the castle so can obstruct the route. The path to the walled garden can be muddy at times. Dogs are welcome in the castle grounds but are not permitted in the castle itself; please keep them on leads due to the livestock.

Directions

1 Enter the gate into the field, pausing to read the information board about the castle site before deciding on your next step. For the longer route, follow the road to the left which will take you on ground level towards the lime kilns. For a shorter route, which avoids steps, go up the hill to the right to the kilns past the castle entrance.

2 Another choice presents itself here. To your left is the path to the garden, but beware, the field can be very muddy or indeed totally flooded, hence its name The Stank. For a short detour, the steps to the right lead to the castle, or you continue straight ahead to point 3.

3 Here you will see a pond to your left, which certain species of newt are known to call home. If you are very lucky, you may see swans paddling among the reeds. At one stage, Edward Hudson wanted to flood this area and make an ornamental lake. This proved to be too costly and the Gertrude Jekyll garden was planted instead.

4 After the pond, you will arrive at a small bridge. By passing under it you can get to the kilns, although you will see it is possible to walk up

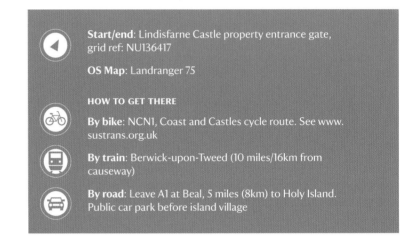

Start/end: Lindisfarne Castle property entrance gate, grid ref: NU136417

OS Map: Landranger 75

HOW TO GET THERE

By bike: NCN1, Coast and Castles cycle route. See www.sustrans.org.uk

By train: Berwick-upon-Tweed (10 miles/16km from causeway)

By road: Leave A1 at Beal, 5 miles (8km) to Holy Island. Public car park before island village

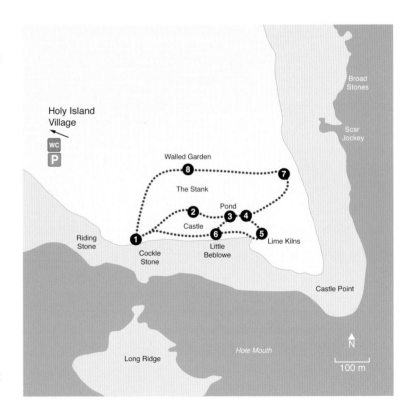

on to the wagonway itself. If you continue under the bridge, you will loop round and cross it later.

⑤ The massive lime kilns now appear on the right. There are six pots inside, where tonnes of limestone were roasted to produce the desired quicklime, which was then taken to the jetty for export. The scale of the industry and the finance behind it is evident from the sheer magnitude of the architecture. Take the steps to point 6.

⑥ Walk past the smaller Little Beblowe Crag, around which run several trackways and sidings. The route across the bridge follows the line of the trackway to the Nessend limestone quarry.

⑦ Go through the gate to the quarry, which is in the heart of the Nature Reserve, managed by Natural England. Various routes back to the village can also be followed. Following the inside line of the wall will lead to point 8 and the Gertrude Jekyll designed garden.

⑧ Enjoy the garden, which flowers in early summer (colour is there at other times of the year). Continue on the route back to the start.

Above: Lindisfarne Castle

View of the beach and castle taken from the causeway at low tide.

Right: Holy Island

One of the boat sheds located near the entrance to the castle. These were installed by Edwin Luytens as part of the major refurbishment of the castle, but hark back to the local tradition of using upturned old herring boats as storage sheds. Authentic examples can be seen near the harbour.

Coastal rock stars

By looking at the geology of the coast, says **Ronald Turnbull**, we can learn about what happened hundreds of millions of years ago. And pick up a few fossils while we're at it.

Within its small area, Britain is blessed with some of the richest and most varied rocks in the world. The coast in particular has a fine geological display. Not just the rocks and strata shown off in the sea cliffs, but also the beach pebbles polished by the sea displaying their beautiful colours and structure, and even the cliff falls that yield fresh fossils after every winter storm.

But more than that, the coastline itself is a demonstration of one of the first principles of geology. The Principle of Uniformity was worked out by Scotsman Charles Lyell in 1830. The rocks around us didn't come about by way of Noah's Flood or other one-off disasters, he suggested. The rocks came about by ordinary natural causes similar to ones happening now. And by looking around us, we can see what happened hundreds of millions of years ago.

A wave-cut landscape

At the coast, you are a spectator of one of the main rock-making forces. A glacier or a volcano might be more exciting but in terms of making (and unmaking) rocks and scenery, the sea is more important. When the gods of mythology battled the giants, they tackled them at the ankles, and this is exactly how the sea attacks the land. Waves, with their freight of abrasive sand and pebbles, slash into the narrow zone – just a few metres high – between the high-tide mark and the low. And so, as the tide goes out, we see wave-cut platforms: the rock cut off almost level by the sea.

At the base of the cliff there will be a wave-cut notch; above, cliffs may stand vertical until they're chopped away at the bottom and collapse. Where there's a fault or joint in the rock face, the sea carves inwards to make a cave – look in the roof of any sea cave, and you'll usually see the faultline that the sea took advantage of. Where a fault goes right through a headland, the sea can get in at both ends to make arches and sea stacks, but eventually it all falls down. The sea clears away the debris, and moves another 2m inland.

Watching the sea slicing into the cliff base, a pebble at a time, you wonder if one day it will carve right across England. If you're anywhere between Sidmouth in Devon and Golden Cap in Dorset, then it already did. An earlier England, of slightly slanted red sandstone and mudstone, has been sliced right across by the chalk sea of 100 million years ago – exactly as the sea is slicing into Dorset at the moment. Half way up the cliff, those older, red rocks abruptly stop. Above them lies Greensand, a type of sandstone, which actually looks yellow but mostly has trees growing out of it. This was the sea-bed that moved in across England from east to west. Above it lies the white chalk, a slightly more recent sea-bed.

A land created by the sea

Most of England's seaside cliff is stone originally made by the sea: sandstone, along with limestone. (Wales is more complicated and much of Highland Scotland is volcanic, or else the 'metamorphic' rock so mangled it scarcely matters what it started off as.) Leonardo da Vinci was one of the first to understand that sandstone is indeed former sand: that the odd seashell-like objects sometimes found in it are indeed seashells – despite the fact that some of them are thousands of metres above the sea. On every beach, the sea of today is making the sandstone of tomorrow.

Where sandstone formed originally in shallow seas, you can sometimes spot the beach ripples, just like those seen on the beaches. More often there'll be a scrambled-egg effect, caused by the burrowing of shrimps and worms millions of years ago. Sea-level rises and the sand gets finer, carried from what is now a more distant land. And then, as the sea comes clear and blue, pure white limestone is formed, full of the shells of the sea creatures.

Where sand formed in estuaries, you see the slanted layers of former sandbanks, alternating with muddy stagnant layers now coloured in bluish-grey. Sand from desert wadis shows pebbly layers, each the result of a single flash flood.

> "On every beach, the sea of today is making the sandstone of tomorrow."

The UK's unimaginably early history

The present is the key to the past. And in the rock pools, the barnacles and whelks are like – but not exactly like – the fossil shells of the Jurassic period. The corals in the three cliffs of Three Cliffs Bay are telling us that, at some time, Wales was a hot tropical island. Desert sand dunes entombed in the cliffs of Orcombe Point, chalk raised up on its edge at Durdle Door, no rock pools anywhere with live ammonites in – all these tell us important and surprising facts about the UK's unimaginably early history.

As for those fossils: the best way to find them is simply to walk along the beach quite slowly with an alert eye. Look at clean, sea-washed boulders: they're too big for the fossil-gathers to carry away. Small, portable fossils are more likely to be among the beach pebbles when the tide goes out very early in the morning, or in winter, or after an overnight storm. Or just sit on the beach sifting through the shingle.

The broken ammonites, partial seashells and crinoid bits – or the inksplodge corals, supposing you're in a Carboniferous bit of Britain – won't be nearly so perfect as the ones in the museum. But in another way they're much finer, when you've found them for yourself. Geology doesn't start with names and information out of books. Geology starts when you look at a pebble, or the cliff, and start wondering what its story is.

Ronald Turnbull is an author, walker and photographer. His publications include Sandstone and Sea Stacks, *a guide to Britain's coastal geology.*

Seaside things to do in Northumberland, Tyne and Wear, and Durham

❶ Tuck into traditional Tyneside food

The tearoom at the Souter Lighthouse offers a chance to sample some traditional local food. Try a plate of panckelty – layers of sliced meat and vegetables, originally made from leftovers from the Sunday lunch, but made here with corned beef and vegetables. Or you could sample a singin hinnie – a scone, which traditionally made a whistling or singing sound when it was on the griddle. Impatient youngsters who asked when it would be ready were told 'Soon – 'It's still singin' hinnie.' (Hinnie is a term of endearment.) To accompany your meal, a glass of Souter Lighthouse Best Bitter, an English copper-coloured best bitter made in local brewery Delavals, would slip down nicely. **Coast Road, Whitburn, Sunderland, Tyne and Wear, SR6 7NH (0191 529 3161)**

❷ Go puffin watching

Catch a boat trip to the Farnes during May–July and there is a very good chance you will see its puffin population (est. 37,000 pairs) during the breeding season. Puffins nest on Staple Island, which is also home to shags, guillemots and Atlantic grey seals. Don't forget your binoculars for close-up views of this most comical and entertaining bird, and a camera to record your experience.

A day in the life of ... *David Steel, Head Ranger, Farne Islands*

'The Farne Islands are arguably one of the best wildlife localities in the British Isles with 85,000 pairs of seabirds (including 40,000 pairs of puffins), 5,000 grey seals and plenty more aside. It's not only home to some spectacular wildlife; for nine months of the year, it's also home to the resident National Trust ranger team who live, work and breathe everything Farnes. The season starts in mid-March when winter gives way to spring and the ranger team moves onto the islands ready for an action-packed nine months. Island living has its own unique qualities as the team live between a fifteenth-century fortified Pele Tower and a nineteenth-century former lighthouse keepers' cottage, and with no running water or mains electricity, it's not for the faint hearted. However, it's home for nine months and we wouldn't swap it for the world!

'The islands are famous for its seabirds and by mid-April they have transformed into a spectacular seabird city with the trials and tribulations of life being played out on a daily basis. From thousands of puffins to a handful of ringed plovers, the 16 islands which make up this famous north-eastern archipelago are alive with the sights, sounds (and smells!) of seabirds getting on with their daily lives.

'The summer is a hectic time but once the onset of autumn approaches the seabirds depart for warmer climes and then the biggest visitor of them all takes over; the grey seal. The months of October–November will witness the birth of 1,500 seal pups on the rocky outcrops – England's largest colony – but even this will come to an end as December arrives. At this stage it's time to say goodbye for another year as the ranger team depart for the festive period but within three months, we will be returning to do it all over again.'

Above: The Farne Islands

Take a boat trip to the Farne Islands and enjoy getting close to the bird life, including Arctic terns (opposite) who swoop and dive-bomb visitors during the breeding season.

Left: Bamburgh Beach

The wide, long sandy beach at Bamburgh is the perfect place to let dogs run free.

③ Go for a rockpool ramble at Low Newton

Low Newton-by-the-sea, an eighteenth-century fishing hamlet, has a natural rock harbour and a sandy beach that is sheltered from the tides by an offshore reef. Perfect, then, for studying the fascinating marine life in rockpools. The National Trust runs regular rockpool rambles with a coastal ranger: see www.nationaltrust.org.uk for details. Eighty metres from the shore is a freshwater lagoon with a variety of wildlife to spot, some from bird hides reached via a path behind the village square.

Other National Trust places to rockpool: Holy Island, Northumberland; St Helens Duver, Isle of Wight; Birling Gap, East Sussex; Wembury, Devon; Glendurgan Garden, Cornwall; Port Mulgrave, Yorkshire.

④ Go on a 'pilgrimage' to Holy Island

During the summer, local company Shepherd's Walks, in association with the National Trust, runs two guided walks across the sand to Holy Island. These follow in the footsteps of the monks and pilgrims who have used the route for centuries and are an uplifting way to approach the island. A National Trust ranger accompanies the walk to point out interesting flora and fauna along the way.

⑤ Explore Durham's heritage coast

This 11-mile route from Seaham to Crimdon reveals the incredible transformation of this part of the coastline, once filthy with colliery spoil, now a grassland rich in plants and wildlife, including the rare Durham argus butterfly. The path will take you from Seaham's smart new marina, along the cliffs (with views of Whitby on a good day), past smugglers' caves to the dunes of Crimdon where little terns return from Africa every year to breed on the beach.

⑥ Take the dog for a romp

The Northumberland coast is designated as an Area of Outstanding Natural Beauty and few appreciate this as much as our four-legged friends. The sight of dogs running and playing on the wide sandy beaches will gladden the heart of any pet lover. Dogs are permitted on all beaches in the county, except for the new stretch at Newbiggin-by-the-Sea.

Other National Trust beaches to walk the dog: Coleton Fishacre, Devon; Studland, Dorset; Chapel Cliff walk in Polperro, Cornwall.

Yorkshire and Lincolnshire

This is a coastline in two parts. The Yorkshire coast is all dramatic sandstone and chalk cliffs, deep valleys, boulder clay and large boulders deposited as glaciers retreated during the last Ice Age. Dramatic cliffs dip down to picturesque villages and harbours such as Staithes and Robin Hood's Bay, where a wealth of fossils captured in Lias sedimentary clay lie waiting to be discovered at the base of the cliffs. More evidence of this coastline's ancient past is found at the handsome and historic port of Whitby where the fossilized wood of the monkey puzzle tree, also known as jet, spawned a jewellery craze. The resorts of Filey and Scarborough have faded a little since their Victorian heyday but splendid hotels still overlook wide bays and the restless ocean.

Further south in Lincolnshire, the coastline flattens into endless stretches of sand lined with soft clay cliffs. These are easily eroded by the churning North Sea and damaging sea surges, creating a flat landscape that is slipping quietly into the sea. The long beaches and resorts of Skegness and Mablethorpe with their amusements and caravan parks have long been a popular holiday destination for Midlanders, not put off by the blustery conditions.

Previous pages: A view from the beach at Boggle Hole, North Yorkshire.

Left: Fossils collected at the disused Loftus Alum Works, North Yorkshire.

Yorkshire and Lincolnshire: dinosaurs and an encroaching sea

The coastal section of the 110-mile long Cleveland Way runs from Saltburn-by-the-Sea to Filey and takes walkers to the edge of the sea along cliff tops, dipping into picturesque villages as it goes. The first of these is Staithes, a sheltered harbour carved out during the last Ice Age, that once bustled with fishing boats and is now busy with visitors attracted by its painterly charm. The red-roofed houses and narrow alleys tumbling down towards the sea drew a group of artists (The Staithes Group, see feature below) who brought their version of Impressionism to Yorkshire. They painted the town *en plein air*, capturing its architecture, fishermen and nearby Runswick Bay, a collection of honey-coloured cottages huddled beneath a cliff overlooking a suitably scenic mile-long curve of sand.

Staithes also marks the beginning of the 'Dinosaur Coast', which runs south to the promontory of Filey Brigg. Coastal erosion of the sandstone cliffs constantly reveals its Jurassic past (layers of Lias sediment were laid down over milllennia, capturing marine animals as they did so), especially at Port Mulgrave (see page 58) where ammonites are frequently uncovered and where, in the 1990s, a fossil of a seagoing dinosaur was found.

Dinosaur footprints have also been found in the sandstone cliffs at Whitby, just one of its many curious attractions. Bram Stoker, hearing accounts of coffins washed ashore from the shipwrecked ship the *Demetrius*, set scenes from *Dracula* here, and every Halloween, enthusiasts assemble in the town for a weekend of vampire-inspired music and events, and climb the 199 steps to the atmospheric ruins of the Abbey.

'Coastal erosion of the sandstone cliffs constantly reveals its Jurassic past, especially at Port Mulgrave'

Right: Staithes

The picturesque village of Staithes is tucked in behind the headland of Cowbar Nab, seen here on the left.

Impressionism comes to Yorkshire: the Staithes Group

In 1894, inspired by the work of the French Impressionists, a group of artists clustered in the scenic village of Staithes on the Yorkshire coast. Their aim was to establish an artist colony, similar to those in St Ives and Newlyn, to follow the Impressionists' practices of painting socially realistic subjects (such as fishermen) *en plein air* (outdoors). Twenty to thirty artists, including Dame Laura Knight and her husband, fellow painter Harold Knight, responded to the call with many moving to Staithes, while others joined them for the summer months. The work of this group of artists, including Edward E Anderson, Thomas Barrett and Joseph R Bagshawe, can be seen at the Pannett Art Gallery in Whitby in the Staithes Room. The town still attracts artists drawn by its scenic opportunities, and their work can be seen at the annual Staithes Festival of Arts and Heritage held in September during which artists exhibit in cottages around the town.

From Whitby to chart the world: the voyages of Captain Cook (1728–1779)

A life-size statue of Captain James Cook stands on the West Cliff at Whitby, staring out to sea. The town is rightly proud of the explorer and navigator who moved there aged 17 to find work with a coal merchant, John Walker. Several years spent sailing between the Tyne and London gave him a taste for the sea and in 1755 he volunteered for service in the Royal Navy.

Quickly rising through the ranks and recognised for his navigational and cartographical skills, he was commissioned as commander of HMS *Endeavour*, which set sail to observe the transit of Venus from Tahiti in 1768. As part of the expedition Cook was ordered to search for the fabled southern continent. In so doing, he charted the coasts of New Zealand and eastern Australia. A second voyage sailed around the world from west to east, and included Antarctica and the first crossing of the Arctic Circle. His final exploration to search for the North West Passage ended with his death in a skirmish with natives on Hawaii. All three of the ships used for his first voyage were three-masted, broad-beamed sailing ships called collier-barks, known as 'cats', and were built at the Fishburn shipyard in Whitby.

The Walkers' home in Whitby where Cook lodged now houses the Cook Memorial Museum and is full of artefacts and information about the great explorer. Also find out more about the young Cook at the museum in his old school in Great Ayton, near the Trust-owned hill, Roseberry Topping. As a child, Cook often walked to the summit of Roseberry Topping which is said to have given him his taste for adventure.

Whitby was a prosperous port in the eighteenth century, its safe harbour providing the main refuge for mariners between the Humber and the Tyne. Trading in coal and alum was brisk, and the huge jawbones of a whale on the cliffs above the town are a reminder of its whaling history. As a result of its successful commerce, many fine houses and places of worship were built and the town still has a splendid air about it. Also on the cliff beside the whalebone, is a statue of Whitby's most famous resident: Captain James Cook whose first voyage of discovery on the *Endeavour* departed from the harbour (see feature, above).

A water cure and the arrival of the railway

The Cleveland Way continues to Robin Hood's Bay, 5 miles south of Whitby, another fishing village blessed with cobbled alleys and red-roofed cottages. Smuggling flourished here in the eighteenth century, as it did along much of the Yorkshire coast, and subterranean passageways are said to link many of the houses. These days the beach is popular with fossil hunters and rock poolers looking for a different kind of treasure. The cliffs and foreshore around the Bay include Lower Jurassic rocks of the Lias Group which yield many species of fossil ammonites and occasional marine reptiles.

Like many seaside resorts, Scarborough's fortunes benefited from the arrival of the railways in the nineteenth century. It had been established as a health-spa destination once its (unpleasantly coloured) spring water – with reputedly curative properties– was discovered in 1620. The train brought workers from industrial towns during Wakes Week for their annual holidays and smart hotels with white façades and grand foyers sprung up around the town's twin bays. The Grand Hotel earned accolades as the biggest brick building in Europe in 1867. These days, visitors come for its open-air theatre and annual festivals as well as more traditional seaside activities.

A mile south of Scarborough, the sandy sweep of Cayton Bay on the edge of the North Yorkshire National Park is popular with bird watchers and fossil hunters. The clay cliffs surrounding the bay are subject to frequent landslips, the most notable was in 2008 when three homes were lost at Knipe Point following heavy rain.

Left: Robin Hood's Bay

The village of the same name was reputed to be the busiest smuggling community on the Yorkshire coast in the eighteenth century.

'These days the beach is popular with fossil hunters and rock poolers'

Filey also built a reputation as a destination during the Victorian period, and the handsome terraces built at that time still overlook its 6 miles of sand. The northern end of the beach comes to a stop at Filey Brigg, a natural stone breakwater pointing out into the sea.

An elegant bridge and a fishing port

After the drama of 122m-high chalk Bempton Cliffs, laid down during the Cretaceous period, which chatter with sea birds nesting in the crevices from spring to mid-summer, and the high rolling plateau of Flamborough Head, the coast beyond Bridlington is something of an anticlimax. There are no more picturesque villages, coves and promontories. Instead, the sands of Holderness stretch in a featureless sweep ending at the 3.5-mile shingle spit of Spurn Head which curls into the Humber protectively gesturing towards Kingston-upon-Hull.

Hull is best approached by crossing the Humber Bridge, an elegant and airy single-span suspension bridge that has become a well-loved, and well-used landmark. Much of the original city was destroyed by bombing in the Second World War but it is still possible to trace its whaling and fishing past in the

Above: The Humber Bridge

This 2,220m single-span suspension bridge opened to traffic in 1981. Due to the shifting bed of the Humber, which affected the navigable channel, a suspension bridge with no need for support piers across the channel was considered the most appropriate design.

Right: Scarborough

View of Scarborough's historic Grand Hotel from the Esplanade overlooking South Bay.

Museum Quarter. The Deep, an aquarium shaped like a shark's fin designed by architect Sir Terry Farrell, is well worth a visit.

The southern shore of the Humber Estuary is characterised by industrial development created by the sea-fishing industry, now seriously in decline. The once large and important port of Grimsby has been hit particularly hard and the number of trawlers using it is now a fraction of what it once was. However, its fishing market is still the largest in the UK, although most of the fish sold is brought from other ports, principally from Iceland. The town's maritime past is relived in its National Fishing Heritage Centre, which has a trawler moored alongside manned by guides with tales to tell.

At low tide, the sea goes out for almost a mile at Cleethorpes, exposing a stretch of sand that has earned the town its place as a holiday destination. It also marks the start of the holiday coast with holiday camps and caravan parks peppering the shoreline towards Mablethorpe and Skegness.

The flatlands of Lincolnshire

During the night of 31 January 1953, a combination of a high spring tide and a windstorm over the North Sea caused a storm surge along the east coast of Britain. The stretch of coast between Mablethorpe and Skegness was overwhelmed by a flood that reached 2 miles inland and resulted in 43 fatalities. The sea's destructive potential has never been forgotten – it still eats hungrily into soft clay cliffs, occasionally causing caravan sites to crumble on to the sand. Most recently during the winter of 2013–14, storm surges from the North Sea combined with high winds, bringing severe flooding to several hundred homes along the east coast of England. Fortunately, vastly improved

infrastructure, forecasting and response times meant that damage was much reduced compared to that caused by the storm 60 years previously, but the results were still ferocious. These low-lying coasts are particularly vulnerable to increased risks of flooding and erosion as sea levels rise as a consequence of climate change.

Part of the resort of Mablethorpe was lost to the sea in the 1540s, and the town now has sea walls to protect its residents and holidaymakers. The town is well known for its fine sand and its amusements, and every September, its Bathing Beauties Festival asks artists to reimagine the Beach Hut. The colourful results and attendant activities have attracted a new generation of visitors.

The wind-swept nature of the coastline was sold as a positive in the famous 1925 railway poster by John Hassall of a jolly fisherman skipping along the sands above the declaration that 'Skegness is so bracing'. The unbroken 50-mile stretch of sands attracted holidaymakers, principally from the Midlands, not put off by potentially blustery conditions. It is also where Billy Butlin built his first holiday camp.

Three miles along the coast from Skegness, is Gibraltar Point, a National Nature Reserve, whose muddy seashore, saltmarsh and freshwater marsh, ponds and lagoons attract huge flocks of birds. Oystercatchers, dunlin and knots roost here after feeding on the mud flats of The Wash, the great U-shape bay of marshland, shingle, sand and reclaimed farmland that sweeps around from Lincolnshire into Norfolk.

A curious thing ... JET

Walk around Whitby and you will still see shops selling jewellery made from jet. Once in plentiful supply and found on the shoreline, Whitby jet is the fossilized wood of the Monkey Puzzle tree flattened by enormous pressure over 185 million years and is found in Jurassic rocks in the upper part of the Lias shales. Easy to carve and, once polished, with a lustrous finish, it has been made into jewellery since Roman times. It particularly came to prominence during the reign of Queen Victoria who wore it during her mourning for Prince Albert.

Explore National Trust places on the Yorkshire coast

The National Trust manages a string of fascinating properties along the coastal stretch of the Cleveland Way. These include:

Ravenscar

Perched on the cliffs between Scarborough and Whitby and surrounded by farmland and woodland, the small village of Ravenscar was once the site of a brickworks and eighteenth-century alum works; it is now a Scheduled Ancient Monument and well worth a visit. For more on alum, see page 59. At the beginning of the twentieth century, plans were made to turn the village into a holiday resort. Ambitions were high, roads and sewers were laid and some houses were built. But hopes of a destination to rival Scarborough were dashed by its distance to the nearest, rocky, beach, and the resort was never built.

Ravenscar is a good place to stop if you are walking the Cleveland Way or cycling along The Cinder Track – the old railway line between

Scarborough and Whitby will take you to the door of the visitor centre at the southern end of Robin Hood's Bay. Stop here to pick up information on the area, learn about local activities and have a cup of tea in the café. **North Yorkshire (01723 870423)**

The Old Coastguard Station, Robin Hood's Bay

Situated at the edge of Robin Hood's Bay village, the converted building now houses an exhibition about living, working and surviving 'at the edge' – where the land meets the sea. Interactive displays explain wind power, waves and other natural phenomena, and the rockpool tank is filled with creatures found in rockpools outside the centre, including blennies, winkles, sea anemones and prawns. Have a go at making waves and generating wind power with the hands-on wave, tide and wind machines, and find out what the National Trust rangers are doing to help protect and preserve this special place. Also keep an eye open for regular events at the visitor centre, including art exhibitions, talks, craft fairs and rockpool safaris. **Robin Hood's Bay, North Yorkshire (01723 870423)**

Holiday Cottage

On the second floor of the Old Coastguard Station, above the Trust's displays, is a one-bedroom holiday home. It has a sitting room with a dining area, an open-plan kitchen, a bathroom and, most importantly, uninterrupted views across the bay and out to sea. For more information see www.nationaltrustcottages.co.uk.

Left: The Old Coastguard Station

Located at the water's edge in the charming village of Robin Hood's Bay, this restored building is a National Trust visitor centre and holiday apartment.

Right: Ravenscar

The remains of the alum works at Ravenscar, at the southern end of Robin Hood's Bay, which are classified as a Scheduled Ancient Monument.

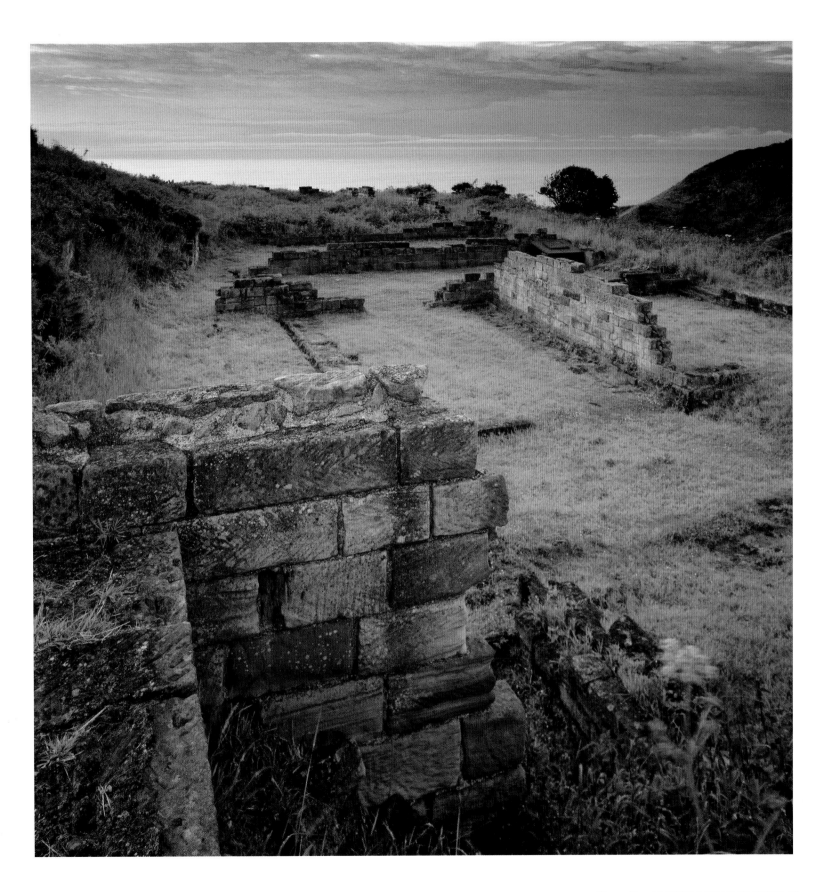

Fossils in the foreground of the disused Loftus Alum Works, which were in operation from the 1650s to the 1860s.

Port Mulgrave

Most visitors head to Port Mulgrave to hunt for fossils: the shales that comprise the coastal slopes make it one of the best locations to find ammonites in Yorkshire. The luckier collector may even find the fossilised remains of a reptile or the squid-like belemnite (for more information on fossils, see feature, page 182). The best fossils can be found after a new cliff fall but this brings its own dangers – tumbling rocks – so collectors must beware.

Many fossil hunters tap away at the rocks, oblivious to the settlement's bustling past: iron ore was extracted here in the mid-nineteenth century and used for shipbuilding on the Tyne. The old mine entrance is still visible above the high water mark as is the tunnel entrance which linked it by narrow-gauge rail to nearby Grinkle Park Mine and through which stone was transported. The harbour itself was destroyed by Royal Engineers during the Second World War to prevent it being used as an invasion site by Germans; consequently very little remains.

Look out for special bird boxes in the blackthorn bushes at Port Mulgrave. As there are few large trees in the area, National Trust volunteers have constructed 'sparrow terraces' to entice tree sparrows to nest. And it looks as though it is working: several pairs have used them to raise their young.

The Loftus Alum Quarries

Alum, little thought about these days, was once a vital ingredient for textile and tanning industries (see feature opposite). Between 1656 and 1863, this quarry complex was the most prolific on the Yorkshire coast and produced 900 tonnes of alum per year. Some remains of the works still survive, including two circular stone cisterns used for storing raw alum liquor, but the most noticeable reminder of this coastline's past is the way the cliff has been nibbled away. The upside of this quarrying is the geology and fossils that have been exposed as a result: two plesiosaurs, an ichthyosaurus and a pterosaur have been uncovered here. The site is designated a Site of Special Scientific Interest (SSSI) because of its geological importance. It is also a valuable place for wildlife as much of the quarry floor has turned to coastal dry heath, attracting invertebrates, reptiles and lichens.

Warsett Hill

It is worth the walk (see page 62) to reach this, the highest point between Saltburn and Skinningrove and to enjoy wrap-around views of the coast. This vantage point was exploited by Romans who built a signal station to defend the area against Anglo-Saxon attack. In 1892 a concrete building housing a gigantic fan was built here to draw air through the mine, allowing miners to work in the ironstone mines below. The fan was nearly 3m wide, had a diameter of 8m and rotated at a speed of 50rpm. The building, which is known as the Huntcliffe Guibal Fanhouse, remains intact and is something of a local landmark, although its brutish, concrete architecture divides opinion. It is a reminder of the importance of the ironstone industry, which not only provided employment for many of the communities but also shaped the local landscape.

Maister House, Hull

Although most of the building is tenanted, the entrance hall and staircase of this eighteenth-century merchant's house in Hull is open to the public. Rebuilt in 1743 after a fire, it is a survivor from Hull's international trading heyday. The National Trust has restored the house's exterior to its original Georgian appearance by removing Victorian bay windows and replacing stone steps and railings at the front entrance. The exterior is Palladian in style – quite plain and austere – but inside, an eighteenth-century wrought-iron balustrade by Robert Bakewell whirls giddily up the building. The stone staircase was constructed by owner Henry Maister after he lost his wife and child in a fire when a wooden staircase collapsed. It is surrounded by stucco panels, and on the wall above the stairs is a niche containing a statue of Ceres, goddess of harvest by Cheere; on the opposite wall is a plaque representing the philosopher John Locke. **160 High Street, Hull, East Yorkshire, HU1 1NL (01723 870423)**

Below: Maister House

Reflective of Hull's heyday as an important trading centre, this merchant's house is a vital part of the city's history.

Shore-spotter's Guide

1

The **common European adder** (*Vipera berus*) can be found on the coast near Ravenscar. Although venomous, it is not especially dangerous as it only becomes aggressive when disturbed. Bites can be painful but are rarely fatal (except for dogs). It feeds on small mammals, birds and amphibians and is found in a variety of habitats including chalky downland and coastal dunes.

2

National Trust rangers at Port Mulgrave have installed nest boxes to encourage the **tree sparrow** (*Passer montanus*). Built to replicate cavities in trees, they have already proved popular with the birds, which have suffered a nationwide population decline in recent years: an estimated 93 per cent between 1970 and 2008.

3

Blackthorn (*Prunus spinosa*) is common on cliffs and dunes along much of the UK's coast, and is plentiful near Port Mulgrave. The protection offered by this spiny plant makes it an ideal home for small birds such as dunnocks, yellowhammers, chaffinches and tree sparrows. The flowers are a great source of nectar for spring insects, such as hoverflies, mining bees and moths.

4

The large, noisy **herring gull** (*Larus argentatus*) is what most people think of as a 'seagull' and is often found on the coast and inland around rubbish tips. It has suffered a moderate decline over the past 25 years. The seabird colony at National Trust Cowbar Nab, near Staithes, is an important breeding ground for herring gulls which nest on the top of Cowbar Nab, rather than on its rocky ledges. Look out also for other seabirds, including kittiwakes, fulmars, razorbills, and even house martins, all of which breed on craggy Cowbar Nab at different times of the year.

5

From April to August, more than 200,000 birds flock to RSPB reserve Bempton Cliffs near Bridlington. One of the most visible of these is the **gannet** (*Morus bassanus*) which feeds by flying high then plunging into the sea to spear fish, hitting the water at more than 68mph: a spongy plate at the base of its bill reduces the impact. Gannets also colonise Bass Rock in the Firth of Forth, the Northern Isles and St Kilda in Scotland, and Grassholm in Wales. They arrive from January onwards and leave between August and October.

6

Gibraltar Point Nature Reserve on the Lincolnshire coast is a top birding and botanising site, consisting of sand dunes and salt marsh. Prominent and attractive duneland plants include sea rocket (*Cakile maritime*), prickly saltwort (*Salsola kali*), pyramidal orchid (*Anacamptis pyramidalis*), sea holly (*Eryngium maritimum*) and sea bindweed (*Calystegia soldanella*). The saltmarsh hazes purple with **sea lavender** (*Limonium vulgare*) in August.

Old Saltburn to Warsett Hill walk

MODERATE GRADE

Distance: 4.5 miles (7km)

Time: 1 hour 30 minutes

Starting in the Victorian seaside town of Saltburn-by-the-Sea, this walk has many interesting features. Though the area may seem like a natural landscape, when enjoying the coastal wildlife, man has had a significant impact here. During the late nineteenth century much of the area was mined for ironstone. Some fascinating remains from these industrial days can still be seen at Warsett Hill. For those who prefer man's more artistic creations, there are sculptures along the way, too. Before setting off for the walk, check out Saltburn's award-winning pier and cliff lift. The pier was opened in 1869 and was the first on Cleveland's coast. The cliff lift was added in 1884 and used an ingenious system of counter-balancing water tanks to transport visitors up and down the cliff.

Terrain

Paths and tracks occasionally muddy. Walking boots are recommended. Dogs are welcome, but please keep on leads, especially around grazing livestock.

Directions

1 Cross the road from the car park to the seafront. Turn right and follow the road.

2 Just after the Ship Inn, turn left at the National Trust sign. Climb the steps and follow the Cleveland Way for 2 miles (3.2km). In summer the grassland at Old Saltburn is a riot of colour as wild flowers bloom. Different species can be seen on the coastal slope where the grassland is free from man's influence. The cliffs at Huntcliff are home to breeding seabirds such as the kittiwakes and fulmars.

3 At the information panel about the Guibal Fanhouse (see Warsett Hill, page 59), bear right over the stile and cross the field diagonally to the railway crossing.

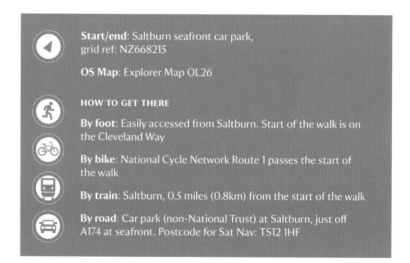

Start/end: Saltburn seafront car park, grid ref: NZ668215

OS Map: Explorer Map OL26

HOW TO GET THERE

By foot: Easily accessed from Saltburn. Start of the walk is on the Cleveland Way

By bike: National Cycle Network Route 1 passes the start of the walk

By train: Saltburn, 0.5 miles (0.8km) from the start of the walk

By road: Car park (non-National Trust) at Saltburn, just off A174 at seafront. Postcode for Sat Nav: TS12 1HF

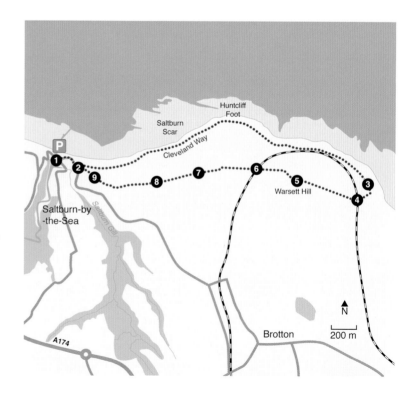

4 Carefully cross the stiles and railway. Cross two fields to the summit of Warsett Hill. At the summit, take a well-earned rest and enjoy the panoramic views of the coast and surrounding area.

5 Bear left at the triangulation pillar and cross the stile. Bear right following the fence down the hill. Where the path splits, bear left across the field to the railway crossing.

6 Carefully cross the stiles and railway. Head straight on, along the track.

7 At the intersection of paths by the cottage continue straight on.

Above: Saltburn Cliff Railway

The renowned Victorian cliff railway takes visitors down from the village of Old Saltburn to the beach and the pier beyond.

8 Where the track bends round to the left by the farm, continue straight on onto the path.

9 Bear left before the row of cottages following the cycle route 1 sign. At the road, retrace your steps to return to the car park.

Seaside things to do in Yorkshire and Lincolnshire

❶ Walk the Cleveland Way

The coastal tranche of the Cleveland Way National Trail stretches 50 miles from Saltburn-by-the-Sea to Filey. It takes in all the big-hitting sights of the Yorkshire shoreline, from fishing villages to soaring sea cliffs, with the region's industrial heritage and holy sites providing historic interest along the way. To walk the whole coast path takes four days (or nine, if you include the inland loop around the North York Moors), but the most popular short rambles lie between Whitby and Robin Hood's Bay. Quieter spots for hiking include the National Trust site of Ravenscar, or the hidden cove of Hayburn Wyke, with its pebble beach and waterfall.

❷ Go pond dipping

Walk the footpaths through Ravenscar, which lies on the coast between Scarborough and Whitby, and you will pass through open coastal farmland, woodland and freshwater ponds. Take a few moments to stop and look closely at the ponds: you might see damselflies, dragonflies, water boatmen, newts, frogs and toads. If you cautiously check the bushes and long grass nearby and you might even see an adder.

❸ Hunt for fossils at Port Mulgrave

This coastal village, 9 miles north-west of Whitby, began life in the nineteenth century as a centre for ironstone mining, but is most

Left: Hayburn Wyke

The waterfall at Hayburn Wyke, tumbling into a secluded cove between Scarborough and Whitby, falls directly onto the rocky beach.

'From April to August, around 200,000 feathered residents swirl across the rock faces.'

famous today for the fossilised treasures discovered in its shale slopes, including those of dinosaur bones. There are often loose fossils, such as ammonites, to be found among the pebbles on the beach – look for them after a storm when larger rocks get broken up and washed ashore. Other rich seams for Jurassic gems along this coastline include: Saltburn for devil's toenails (a type of extinct oyster), Robin Hood's Bay for ammonites and belemnites and Scalby Mills, near Scarborough, for fossilised plants. For more on fossil hunting and how to do it, see page 182.

④ Sail around Flamborough Head and Bempton Cliffs

If you're in the region during the breeding season, don't miss the annual seabird spectacular taking place at Flamborough and Bempton Cliffs. From April to August, around 200,000 feathered residents swirl across the rock faces – Bempton is the UK's largest mainland gannetry, and puffins, kittiwakes, guillemots and razorbills also nest here. You can catch the action from the cliff tops, but for a more interactive experience, take to the sea. The RSPB offers three-hour

guided Puffin and Gannet Cruises from Bridlington Harbour (usually one per weekend, May to July), while the Yorkshire Wildlife Trust runs 45-minute Living Seas Safaris (weekends, Easter to September) from the North Landing at Flamborough.

⑤ Ride Scarborough's miniature railway

For old-school seaside fun, head to Scarborough and ride a miniature steam train along the coast, courtesy of the North Bay Railway. Running since 1931, the shiny engines depart from Peasholm Park and offer glorious views of Scarborough's sandy North Bay during the stately, ¾-mile journey to Scalby Mills. There's a sea life centre by Scalby Mills station if you want to linger (especially if you've children on board), otherwise simply relax and take pleasure in the 20-minute trip back. Themed rides, such as Santa specials, are available according to season. For more information see www.nbr.org.uk.

⑥ See seals at Donna Nook

The grey seal colony at Donna Nook National Nature Reserve is one the UK's largest and, at pupping time (late October to December), visitors can have front-row access as hundreds of sea mammals haul themselves onto the beach to give birth near the sand dunes. A designated viewing area – separated from the seals by a double fence – gives a fantastically close look at the mothers and pups, and sparring males, and it's a great opportunity for (sensitive) photography. To avoid the crowds, which can be three-to-four deep at peak times, visit during the week. Further recommended Lincolnshire National Nature Reserves are Saltfleetby-Theddlethorpe Dunes and Gibraltar Point.

Left: The Cleveland Way

Waymarker at Ravenscar on the coastal section of the Cleveland Way National Trail.

Norfolk and Suffolk

The great curve of the East Anglian coast is constantly under attack from the North Sea. The relentless battering and sucking of the tides creates a dynamic yet precarious shoreline. The North Sea surge of 5 December 2013 was the worst recorded for 60 years with waves carving into the already fast-eroding cliffs, and washing away dunes and causing homes to fall into the sea. Improved defences and flood-warning systems minimised the effects, but the destruction and debris thrown up on beaches, including the area around Brancaster, Blakeney Freshes and Blakeney Point, was devastating.

Nowhere is the history of the sea's power to affect coastline more evident than at Dunwich, Suffolk. Once the medieval capital of East Anglia, the original town has been entirely enveloped by the sea over the centuries. Other towns and villages that were once on the coast have become engulfed by marshland and now find themselves inland. The shingle spits of Blakeney Point and Orford Ness constantly morph as longshore drift shunts and banks pebbles along their lengths. This shifting, windswept coast is the place to go to clear the head and stretch the legs. Expansive beaches never feel crowded, and the saltmarsh and dune systems provide perfect habitats for migrating birds – one of the UK's greatest nature spectacles – as they arrive from Siberia in winter.

Previous pages: Boats are beached at Blakeney Point at low tide, with storm clouds looming overhead.

Left: Bird's eggs on the shingle beach at Blakeney Point.

Norfolk and Suffolk: bird sanctuaries and seaside towns

The stretch of shoreline from Snettisham in north Norfolk to the pretty village of Stiffkey is a line of almost uninterrupted nature reserves. Birds flock to this stretch of coast: big tides push tens of thousands of wading birds from the mudflats of the Wash to their feeding grounds. In the winter, an early start with a pair of binoculars rewards birders with the sight of pink-footed geese flying in from their overnight roosts to feed. The National Nature Reserve at Blakeney, with its combination of saltmarsh, dunes and 4-mile-long sand and shingle spit, provides a unique and precious habitat for many of these birds, along with unusual plants, insects and seals (see page 85), as do the inter-tidal mud and sand flats at Brancaster (see page 74).

Saltmarsh and dunes all along the coast create a rich wildlife habitat which separates the sea from the mainland – to reach the shoreline often involves a walk or, as in the case of Wells-next-the-Sea, a 1-mile ride on the light railway.

Further along at Titchwell Marsh, marsh harriers fly over the reeds looking for prey, and avocets and terns flock to the lagoons. The saltmarsh of Scolt Head Island, which is jointly owned by the National Trust and Norfolk Wildlife Trust, is home to nesting colonies of terns (Sandwich, common, Arctic and little) and wintering wildfowl. Reach it by ferry from Burnham Overy Staithe.

In the nineteenth century, the 3rd Earl of Leicester planted pine trees behind the dunes at Holkham to provide a shelterbelt for farmland against wind-blown sand. Now well established, these trees give the Holkham Nature Reserve a distinctly European look and provide tree-climbing and den-building opportunities for children. The 12-mile long beach is reached through the trees via a boardwalk and remains unspoilt: there is plenty of room for everyone here, from naturists who have their own section of the beach, to bird spotters and families clustered behind windbreaks.

Above: Old Lifeboat House

The distinctive blue façade of the Old Lifeboat House at Blakeney Point, which was built in 1898 and is now an information centre.

Right: Blakeney Point

Aerial view over Blakeney National Nature Reserve. The shape of the sand and shingle spit is continually changing.

'Saltmarsh and dunes all along the coast create a rich wildlife habitat.'

Above: Aldeburgh

A row of colourful bay-fronted houses
on the seafront at Aldeburgh loom up
behind the steep-banked shingle beach.

Nearby, the beach at Wells-next-the-Sea has a row of colourful,
beautifully constructed beach huts. The town also boasts an excellent
fish and chip shop (French's) and genuine Dutch pancakes served
aboard the permanently moored *Albatros*, a North Sea Klipper.

A flock of holidaymakers

Further east, the twin resorts of Sheringham and Cromer both have
fine beaches protected by low cliffs. Cromer also has a pier that boasts

'... at high tide, sailors have been known to order a pint through its window.'

traditional, and these days unusual, end-of-the-pier entertainment in
the summer. Cley-next-the-Sea is separated from the sea by half a mile
of marshland – a draw for bearded tits, bitterns and common terns.

Great Yarmouth was once an important fishing port – it grew rich
on herring, with 1,000 drifters fishing from the town just before the
First World War. When the herring industry collapsed due to over-
fishing, the town was saved by the discovery of North Sea oil and it
became a centre for oil and gas exploration. It is also a popular resort
with fun seekers enjoying roller-coaster rides, piers, amusement
arcades and theatres that tumble noisily and colourfully along its
Golden Mile.

Lowestoft, Britain's most easterly point, also relied on herring
fishing for its livelihood until stocks ran out. These days it is better
known as being part of the Sunrise Coast, with its two piers, Blue
Flag beach and attractions pulling in the holidaymakers each summer.

A well-mannered pier and a house in the clouds

The Suffolk Coast Path starts at Lowestoft and runs for 50 miles to
Felixstowe. Along its route, it takes in two quintessential seaside
towns, Southwold and Aldeburgh. Southwold's quiet charms
include a well-mannered and delightful pier (check out artist and
inventor Hunkin's 'Under the Pier Show' for an alternative to the
usual amusement arcades, see page 89); a Blue Flag beach lined with
amusingly named beach huts; its own brewery, Adnam's; crabbing
championships, and fresh fish sold from wooden shacks. Little wonder
that during the summer it teems with daytrippers and weekenders.

Between the drowned city of Dunwich (see feature, page 78) and
Aldeburgh sits the curious holiday village of Thorpeness, created by
barrister and railway magnate Glencairn Stuart Ogilvie in the 1920s,
principally to entertain his friends. Designed in mock Jacobean and
Tudor Revival style, the village sits around an artificial lake and includes
tennis courts and a country club. The five-storey water tower was clad
in wood to resemble a cottage and this 'House in the Clouds' is a local

landmark. Since mains water was installed in the village and the water tank was no longer needed, it was converted into one of the coast's most eccentric holiday cottages.

Aldeburgh is well known for its music festival, which was established by resident and acclaimed composer, Benjamin Britten in 1948. Since 1967 it has been held a short distance inland at Snape Maltings, a converted Victorian barley shed, and still champions Britten's work alongside that of new composers and musicians. The town's long Georgian high street is lined with coffee shops, bookshops and generally a longish queue outside Aldeburgh Fish and Chips, whose evangelical customers can be seen scoffing their chips on the seawall.

The strangely beautiful and unsettling Orford Ness (see page 78) runs parallel with the shoreline, gesturing towards the busy docks of Felixstowe. Here shipping containers are offloaded from giant ships by cranes and piled up like a three-dimensional game of Tetris. Around the Ness on the River Orwell estuary is Pin Mill, a congregation of houseboats and moored yachts overlooked by the Butt and Oyster pub where, at high tide, sailors have been known to order a pint through its window from their boat's deck.

Above: Southwold

View of the town's famous pier and beach huts, looking out over the sandy beach and across the North Sea.

Explore National Trust places on the Norfolk coast

Blakeney National Nature Reserve

The best way to arrive at Blakeney Point, a sand and shingle spit stretching out into the sea from the heart of Blakeney National Reserve, is on a ferry from Morston Quay. Then you not only get a chance to see grey seals basking on sandbanks but you alight at the distinctive blue Lifeboat House, home to the Point's rangers and a visitor centre. (The Lifeboat House was badly damaged during the storm surge of 5 December 2013. It has subsequently been repaired.) From there you can explore the rare habitat and its inhabitants, which range from Sandwich terns to otters and yellow-horned poppies. The more energetic might opt to 'walk off' the point, a worthwhile though demanding tramp across 4 miles of shingle back to Morston.

The Trust bought Blakeney Point in 1912, and 218.5 hectares (540 acres) of Morston Marshes and Morston Quay in 1973. The area has proved popular with visitors, which has presented the challenge of safeguarding wildlife. For this reason, the western end of Blakeney Point is restricted access from April to mid-August to protect young birds nesting on the shingle, and from November to mid-January during seal-pupping season.

Nearby, Stiffkey Marshes, a vast expanse of saltmarshes, creeks and muddy basins, can be reached by foot on the Norfolk Coast Path on its way to Wells-next-the-Sea. It is the perfect place to see a wide range of wading birds and wintering fowl as well as sea lavender, which cloaks the marshes in late summer. **Morston Quay, Quay Road, Morston, Norfolk, NR25 7BH**

Brancaster Estate

At the heart of the Trust-owned estate is Brancaster Activity Centre, a residential base for outdoor activities, which include sailing, kayaking and orienteering (see also page 89). It is also the place to learn about sustainable building: the centre is housed in Dial House, a 400-year-old building that showcases the Trust's approach to sustainable

A curious thing … marram grass (*Ammophila arenaria*)

Marram grass is a common sight along the Norfolk and Suffolk coastline: you can see it at Blakeney Nature Reserve, where its clusters of spiky leaves punctuate the dune systems. Its fibrous roots form matting beneath the surface of the dunes, which stabilises them. Conservationists, aware of this, and its ability to withstand whatever the harsh coastal environment throws at it, plant it to help anchor the dunes, which in turn protect the surrounding landscape. But it must not be allowed to become too dominant as bare sand is a vitally important habitat.

renovation. All materials used were selected for low environmental impact: bricks were reclaimed, as were chalks and flints; timber was British hard- or softwood from sustainably managed forests; shredded paper made from natural plant fibres was used for insulation; photo voltaic/photo thermal panels generate electricity and heat, which is boosted by a ground source heat pump. The building took quite a knock during the storms of winter 2013/14, and the team there is looking at how it might be adapted to meet the challenges posed by sea-level rises.

Above: Stiffkey Marshes

Footbridge over a tidal creek at Stiffkey saltmarshes. The Norfolk Coast Path passes along its perimeter, where you can enjoy the birdlife and wonderful wide-open vistas.

Above: Sheringham Park

View of Sheringham Hall (which is not owned by the National Trust) across the parkland. The Regency Grade II listed building was designed by Humphry Repton and his son, John Adey Repton.

Elsewhere on the estate, Brancaster Staithes, a pretty fishing village famous for mussels, is a good place to start exploring the coastline, which takes in the generous, sandy Brancaster beach and the nature reserve Scolt Head Island (jointly owned by the National Trust and Natural England), reached by a ferry from Burnham Overy. **Brancaster Beach, Beach Road, Brancaster, Norfolk PE31 8BW**

Sheringham Park

The great landscape designer Humphry Repton described the parkland he designed around the hall at Sheringham as his 'favourite and darling child in Norfolk'. Considered to be the most complete and best-preserved example of his work, it was designed in 1812 for the then owners Abbot and Charlotte Upcher. The 405 hectares (1,000 acres) are a mixture of mature woodland, cliff-top walks and landscape park, and are packed with rhododendrons (at their best from May to early June), azaleas and many other species of tree and shrub. This

Left: Horsey Windpump

The restored drainage windpump has views over the Norfolk Broads and out towards the sea, which is just a mile away.

provides habitat for many wildlife species including one of the UK's smallest bird, the firecrest, admiral butterflies and the barbastelle bat. When visiting, take time to walk the 192 steps to the top of the Gazebo tower and be rewarded with views along the North Norfolk coast to Wells-next-the-Sea. Also drop by the wildlife pond to watch the dragonflies and go butterfly spotting in the Wildflower Meadow. **Upper Sheringham. Norfolk NR26 8TL.**

Heigham Holmes

Reaching the island of Heigham Holmes is an adventure in itself. Access is via a floating swing bridge over the River Thurne and is by prior written agreement only. Perhaps this is why it is relatively unknown and unspoilt. Situated in the Norfolk Broads, it is a 202-hectare (500-acre) wetland nature reserve. A lacework of dykes and pools knits together marshland, scrub and wet woodland, home to marsh harriers, barn owls, bittern and cranes and wading birds such as lapwing and redshank. A tenant farmer manages the site and is restoring the once-intensively managed farmland back to grassland and reinstating water levels to create wetland habitat. **Brancaster Beach, Beach Road, Brancaster, Norfolk, PE31 8BW**

Horsey Windpump

For panoramic views of the Norfolk coast, little beats a climb up the five-storeys of this Grade II-listed drainage windpump. A working mill until 1943, when it was struck by lightning, it is a well-loved landmark in Broads National Park. The mill is part of Horsey Estate managed by the Buxton family from whom the Trust acquired it in 1948. It suffered serious damage during the gales of 1987 but was repaired and re-opened in 1990. Take time to explore the surrounding landscape and village of Horsey: there is plenty of wildlife to be seen in the mere, reedbed and marshes. You might even spot a swallowtail butterfly in June; flowers have been planted especially to attract them. **Horsey, Great Yarmouth, Norfolk, NR29 4EF**

Holiday Cottage

Next to the windpump and 20 minutes from the sea, Horsey Barns are converted eighteenth-century barns that can sleep 3 to 6. Three different properties of varying sizes face each other around a courtyard, and all have been decorated and furnished in keeping with the style of the building. Timber beams and solid wooden doors all feel reassuringly traditional, and deep sofas will ease limbs tired from tramping the coastal path. For more information see www. nationaltrustcottages.co.uk.

Explore National Trust places on the Suffolk coast

Dunwich Heath and Beach

Late summer sees the 86.6 hectares (214 acres) of Dunwich Heath burst into a patchwork of purple and yellow as mounds of heather and coconut-scented gorse come into full bloom. Stretching right to the edge of the cliff top, this coastal lowland heath is a rare survivor: adjacent heathland has been used for agriculture or housing. As well as three varieties of heather, the Heath also has woods and open grassland and a sandy beach. Bought by the Trust in 1968 with the help of a donation from the Heinz company as part of Enterprise Neptune, it is rich in wildlife including the UK's largest population of Dartford warblers, nightjars, woodlark and the curious ant-lion. A good way to explore is to go in search of geocaches hidden around the heath. Pick up information at the Coastguard Cottages (which also has a café). **Dunwich, Saxmundham, Suffolk, IP17 3DJ**

Orford Ness National Nature Reserve

This vegetated shingle spit running parallel with the Suffolk coast, is one of only three major shingle landforms in Britain, and is a rare and

Dunwich: Suffolk's drowned town

As you travel along the Suffolk coast, it's easy to regard Dunwich as just one of a number of attractive villages. Walk into the local museum, though, and you will discover that all is not as it seems. From the sixth to eleventh centuries, Dunwich was an important trade centre and one of England's largest towns. A naval base and busy port, its population was half the size of London; it had a population of 3,000 and it held two parliamentary seats. Things drastically changed after a storm surge in 1286 swept much of the town into the sea, and successive storms and the encroaching sea eventually swallowed up the rest: there are accounts from 1540 of the sea reaching the marketplace. All Saints church, once the most impressive in Suffolk, was the last of the town's eight churches to crumble into the sea: by 1930 all that remained was a masonry stump. The legend of this drowned city is a powerful one – locals still swear that at certain tides you can hear church bells chiming beneath the waves. It also speaks volumes about the dynamism of our coast, and what we can expect from climate change in the future.

strange place. Formed by longshore drift and shaped by the constantly changing agents of erosion and deposition, it is made up of a complex sequence of shingle ridges and valleys deposited over centuries. The geomorphology records the daily effects of waves as well as tides and seasonal storms from prehistoric times up to the present day.

Left: Coastguard Cottages

The cottages overlook the National Trust's area of heathland conservation and Minsmere beach. The area is a great spot for birdwatchers.

Right: Dunwich Heath

The coastal lowland heath stretches right to the edge of the cliff top.

'... a mobile and transient habitat that is also threatened by rising sea levels and coastal erosion.'

This fragile, shifting bar of pebbles, dunes, reed and saltmarsh and brackish lagoons is populated by wildlife able to make its home in a mobile and transient habitat that is also threatened by rising sea levels and coastal erosion. Specialised and important flora communities have sprung up here: sea pea, for example, grows along the drift line and mats of sea campion and branched and brittle lichen grow on the shingle heath.

The National Trust ensures that the number of people and vehicles visiting the area is carefully managed so that nesting birds and the fragile shingle habitat are undisturbed. As a result, birds including avocets, oystercatchers and redshank are frequent visitors, and animals such as brown hares and Chinese water deer have settled here.

Barn owls also nest in a number of the unusual and mysterious buildings from Orford Ness's military past. These buildings, which stud the shingle with their strange silhouettes, date from 1913–87 when Orford Ness was used as a military test site. The first aircraft arrived in 1915 (part of the spit was levelled to create an airfield) and pioneering work on parachutes, aerial photography and bomb and machine-gun sights began. The most significant experiments at Orford Ness took place between 1935 and 1937 when top-secret research and development of an aerial defence system were carried out, later known as radar. The work done here is said to have played a vital role in the Battle of Britain.

During the 1950s, at the height of the Cold War, Orford Ness became one of only a few sites in the world where purpose-built facilities were created to test components of nuclear weapons. The Atomic Weapons Research Establishment (AWRE), based here, did much developmental work on the atomic bomb in test labs known locally as the 'pagodas' due to their distinctive shape. AWRE ceased work at Orford Ness in 1971, and from the 1970s until the last service personnel left the site in 1987, the spit was used by RAF Explosive Ordnance Disposal to destroy munitions.

The National Trust took ownership in 1993, recognising the importance of the fragile coastal vegetated shingle and the wildlife it supports. Some areas are still off limits and manned by military contractors. Look out for the former D-Day landing craft used to transfer supplies.

Catch the National Trust ferry to Orford Ness from Orford Quay (see www.nationaltrust.org.uk for times) and then explore this amazing place. Follow the waymarked trails to make the most of your time here and to see wildlife and look around buildings that have access. The unstable structures of pagodas on the AWRE site can only be safely explored on a guided tour.

Left: Orford Ness Lighthouse

The lighthouse at Orford Ness National Nature Reserve was completed in 1792 and decommissioned in June 2014. It stands in an exposed and precarious position at the edge of the shingle beach.

Right: Old Police Tower

The shingle bar is studded with derelict and mysterious buildings dating from its past as a top-secret military testing site.

On a wing and a prayer

The spectacle of seabirds massing on the British coast rivals the rain forest, says naturalist **Mark Cocker**. So it's more important than ever that we work to reverse their declining numbers.

It is often claimed that Britain is an important country for wildlife. If the idea has genuine substance, then it is in large measure because of its magnificent seabirds and especially the sheer numbers that breed in these islands.

Their nesting colonies, threaded like gems in a chain along our coasts, represent 45 per cent of Europe's entire seabird population. The massive gannetry on St Kilda, for example, is the largest on earth. The manx shearwaters in Rum – those goblin-voiced wanderers of the Atlantic Ocean that dig their nest burrows into these Hebridean hills in summer – represent a third of the world population in this one small island alone. In total, 90 per cent of the entire species breeds in Britain or Ireland. Lesser known but equally impressive are the great skuas or bonxies, to give them their name in the Shetland Isles, where their colonies hold almost two-thirds of the world total. Equally notable is Britain's stake in the planet's populations of shags (50 per cent) and razorbills (20 per cent).

The right kinds of coast

The reason these islands are so important for seabirds is the sheer length of our coastline (19,491 miles according to some estimates) and the fact that it includes the right kinds of coast – places of sheer rock close to nutrient-rich waters where seabirds can feed and breed in relative safety from any land-based predators.

Classic examples of these busy bird-cities are the soaring crags at the RSPB's Bempton Cliffs in Yorkshire or the National Trust's own reserve in the Farne Islands (see page 30). At this last site, which comprises an archipelago of 20 small islands off the Northumbrian shore, the sheer isolation works in conjunction with a very varied coastal topography to provide sanctuary for at least 60,000 nesting seabirds. The Farnes' vertical Dolerite cliffs, relentlessly eroded by wave and weather, have numerous ledges across the rock face where seabirds can perch and nest in safety. The classic occupant is the common guillemot, of which 25,000 pairs breed in the islands.

As they cluster together on their narrow nest-ledges the guillemots – looking rather like strangely pied milk bottles lined up in rows – are hugely engaging birds. However, for pure charisma they are undoubtedly outdone by another of the Farnes' resident auks, the Atlantic puffins, of which there are almost 40,000 pairs. Unlike their cousins, these parrot-beaked seabirds nest in underground burrows that they excavate in the lower-lying turf-covered sites on the Farnes. Day-tripping visitors are allowed to wander among these characterful little birds as they sun themselves by the nest chambers or fill the air with their comical sighing calls. It is hardly surprising that puffin colonies are considered the most engaging and touching spectacles in all British nature.

The decline of the kittiwake

A species we might not now automatically include in the seabird category belongs to a family that is seldom regarded among our most treasure wildlife. It is a type of gull called the black-legged kittiwake. Yet this beautiful bird has as much right to be considered a genuine maritime species as it should have claims on the nation's affection. It is the one member of its family that nests almost exclusively at rockier cliff sites such as those in the Farne Islands.

At one time this country held about a third of all kittiwakes in Europe and one-twelfth of the world's total. Yet the species' fortunes in Britain reflect

> '**It is hardly surprising that puffin colonies are considered the most engaging and touching spectacles in all British nature.**'

a larger, more pervasive issue affecting seabird numbers: the kittiwake is in decline. Its recent history in the Farne Islands typifies the wider picture. Today there are still enough kittiwakes to envelop parts of the islands with their strange repeated laughing calls. Yet this joyous cacophony is much less than it was. The species has declined by 25 per cent in a quarter of a century (approximately 4,200 pairs today).

We are still not absolutely certain what is causing the losses – possibly the hydra-headed effects of climate change along with the perennial problem of over-fishing in the North Sea – but these seabird declines are now as troubling as they are presently irreversible. If we really wish to appreciate what is at stake in the fluctuating fortunes of these birds then a good place to start would be St Kilda.

An unforgettable place

This archipelago lies almost 40 miles west of the Outer Hebrides and boasts not only a double designation as a World Heritage Site, but it also holds the highest sea cliffs in Britain. From the topmost granite ramparts of Conachair, this tumbling cliff falls away for more than 400m to the Atlantic waters below.

The geological drama of St Kilda undoubtedly imprints itself on the visitor's memory but it is the unceasing sounds, smells and ever-shifting movements of its seabirds that are truly unforgettable. Its million-strong population includes huge numbers of puffins, fulmars and especially gannets.

At a distance, the monolith of black granite called Stac Lee that rises sheer out of the Atlantic foam, seems to posses a vast triangular summit dusted with gleaming white. As the boat inches closer a visitor slowly realises that the areas of pale comprise 15,000 tiny pointillist dots and eventually each speck resolves into an incubating gannet on its guano-splashed nest.

The neighbouring island of Dun is equally impressive. It is ungrazed by any livestock so that its slopes are thickly carpeted in green turf. Against the jagged black rock the vegetation looks as lush as any English meadow, but the whole substrate is honeycombed with a vast warren of seabird burrows. Their occupants, mainly puffins, move continuously back and forth from these nest chambers.

At any one moment the visitor can pan from Dun to the adjacent sea surface and take in a panorama involving tens of thousands of birds. En masse and at such distances they resemble a boiling swarm of insects. Eventually it dawns on any eye-witness that from these cliffs and slopes emerges a raw ceaseless upwelling of life that resists comprehension, defies any sense of visual architecture and is as exhilarating as any sight in British nature. It is the northern hemisphere's equivalent of a rainforest – a place sublimely wild and free and precious beyond any human measure.

Mark Cocker is an author and naturalist based in Norfolk. His publications include Birds Britannica *(with Richard Mabey),* Crow Country, *and* Birds and People *(with photographer David Tipling), which was published in 2013.*

Shore-spotter's Guide

1

The distinctive black and white **avocet** (*Recurvirostra avosetta*), with its long, upturned beak, almost became extinct in the nineteenth century due to a combination of marshland drainage, over-shooting and the collection of its feathers for fishing flies. 'They are unmistakeable and breeding in good numbers on Orford Ness,' says Ranger, Dave Fincher. Its return in the 1940s and subsequent increase in numbers has earned this bird its place as the symbol of the RSPB.

2

'There are tremendous drifts of the mat-forming **sea campion** (*Silene uniflora*) on the vegetated shingle on Orford Ness in June and July,' says Dave Fincher. Look out for its whitish-pink petals surrounding an inflated calyx which resembles a bladder.

3

The lemon-coloured petals of **yellow horned-poppy** (*Glaucium flavum*) last for only one day. 'Look out for them along the track edges and on the shingle bank at Blakeney Point,' says Ranger, Ajay Tegala. 'It gets its name from its long seed pods.'

4

'We have lots of **brown hares** (*Lepus europaeus*) on the Ness,' says Dave Fincher. 'Get here early in the year (we open at Easter) and catch the first boat to see them.' Blakeney Point also has a healthy population, which can often be seen in the dunes. 'Rabbits died out on the Point in the 1990s,' says Ajay Tegala, 'after which time the hare population shot up and has remained healthy ever since.' When disturbed, it can be seen bounding across fields using its powerful hind legs to propel it forwards, often in a zigzag pattern. It is most visible in early spring when the breeding season encourages fighting or 'boxing'.

5

'Listen for the distinctive call of the **Sandwich tern** (*Sterna sandvicensis*),' says Ajay Tegala. 'You will hear one before you see one: it has a distinctive cry that has been compared to an unoiled cartwheel.' Over a third of the UK's Sandwich tern population (often around 4,000 pairs) nest on Blakeney Point, from April to August. Little, common and a few pairs of Arctic terns also nest on there.

6

Grey seals (*Halichoerus grypus*) have their pups in November and December, which are born in the dunes. 'They must shed their white fur before they can swim,' says Ajay, 'so for the first couple of weeks they feed on their mother's milk. The best way to see Blakeney Point's seals is on one of the local seal boat trips leaving from Morston Quay, but they can also be seen swimming in the sea if you walk along the spit.'

As recommended by National Trust Rangers
Dave Fincher *(Orford Ness, Suffolk) and*
Ajay Tegala *(Blakeney Point, Norfolk)*

Blakeney to Stiffkey walk

BEGINNER GRADE

Distance: 4 miles (7km)

Time: 1 hour 30 minutes

Enjoy Norfolk's vast open landscape and big skies on this lovely walk along the Coast Path beside pristine saltmarsh. Remember to bring your binoculars, as there are lots of wildlife-spotting opportunities across the marshes and scrub.

Terrain

Mostly level ground, but there are some uneven natural surfaces, which may become muddy after wet weather. Some steps between Blakeney and Morston and at Stiffkey Freshes; suitable for sturdier types of pushchairs. Dogs are welcome, but please keep them under close control along points 2 to 5. Leads recommended along roadside sections. Also welcome on Coasthopper bus, and ferries.

Directions

1 From the bus stop, head towards Blakeney village and turn right down the High Street. At the end you'll come out onto Blakeney Quay. This was once a busy commercial port, dealing in the export of corn and wool from the surrounding Norfolk countryside.

2 Turn left and follow the line of mooring posts. Join the Norfolk Coast Path that runs between the houses and the saltmarsh. Head away from the village, keeping the saltmarsh on your right and fields and houses on your left. In winter, the saltmarsh becomes home to many species of migratory wildfowl. See large flocks of dark Brent geese grazing on the marshes, and short-eared owls and hen harriers skimming over the saltmarsh. In summer, listen out for waders such as the noisy redshank, once known as the watcher of the marshes, which breeds on the higher, grassy areas of saltmarsh. Look for rare, salt-loving plants such as samphire, which colonises the open mud, and the silvery sea purslane which borders the creeks. Also, look out for the sea lavender in July and August.

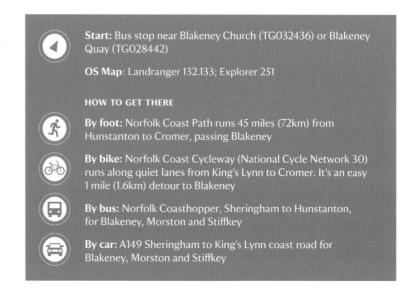

Start: Bus stop near Blakeney Church (TG032436) or Blakeney Quay (TG028442)

OS Map: Landranger 132.133; Explorer 251

HOW TO GET THERE

By foot: Norfolk Coast Path runs 45 miles (72km) from Hunstanton to Cromer, passing Blakeney

By bike: Norfolk Coast Cycleway (National Cycle Network 30) runs along quiet lanes from King's Lynn to Cromer. It's an easy 1 mile (1.6km) detour to Blakeney

By bus: Norfolk Coasthopper, Sheringham to Hunstanton, for Blakeney, Morston and Stiffkey

By car: A149 Sheringham to King's Lynn coast road for Blakeney, Morston and Stiffkey

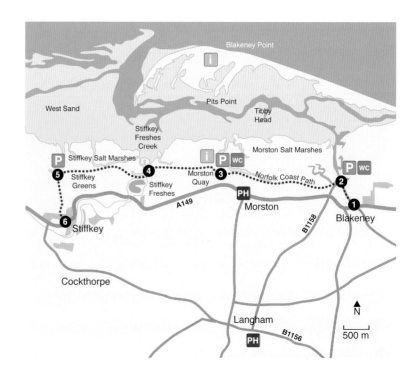

③ At Morston Quay, head past the National Trust Information Centre along a track to its left and pick up the Coast Path again (to the right of the building with 1922 on it). Continue walking beside the saltmarsh, but if you begin to cross a bridge onto the saltmarsh, you've gone too far north – head back to the information centre and turn right. Several local families run ferries from Morston Quay out to the shingle spit of Blakeney Point (see page 71).

④ Stay on the Coast Path, passing Stiffkey Freshes Creek on your right and Stiffkey Freshes on your left. Stiffkey Freshes is an area of freshwater marsh formed behind the sea defence. It's a good place to look out for birds such as the ringed plover, oystercatcher or dunlin. The creek is used by local mussel fisherman to access the harbour.

⑤ Continue on the path, passing Stiffkey Greens, until you reach Stiffkey Greenway car park. Either return the way you came or take the Norfolk Coasthopper bus back to Blakeney.

Top: Morston Quay
Boats moored peacefully on the tidal creeks and mudflats at Moreston Quay, Blakeney National Nature Reserve.

Above: Observation point
Boats in front of the National Trust Information Centre with its observation tower at Morston Quay.

Seaside things to do in Norfolk and Suffolk

❶ Photograph an eerie place

The Cold War architecture of Orford Ness (see page 81) makes an atmospheric subject for photography. The 'pagodas' – formerly used as laboratories by the Atomic Weapons Research Establishment (AWRE) – are not usually open to the public, but you can gain access on special tours during the summer months. Should natural, rather than military, history be your thing, bird-ringing and moth-netting mornings also take place regularly from May to October, and there is an abundance of wildlife and wild plants to see and photograph that have adapted to this hostile environment. Look for the yellow horned-poppy, sea pea and saltmarsh plants that survive immersion in salt water. Hares abound (and bound) in the spring, Chinese water deer love the wet marshes and marsh harriers glide above the wet pasture looking for prey.

❷ Go swimming and snorkelling

As the sea off the Norfolk coast is warmer and more benign than many places around Britain, it lends itself well to wild swimming – and snorkelling. If you're a confident swimmer, and you have a mask, you needn't go more than 50m off Sheringham to see the distinctive chalk reef, teeming with rockpool species, such as crabs, cuttlefish and gobies. In Stiffkey there's a natural swimming pool at Freshes Creek, which remains full even at low tide. Suffolk's Walberswick has a sandy beach that offers easy bathing; likewise gently eroding Covehithe and the shingle strand at Dunwich, where you can warm up at the NT Coastguard Tearoom afterwards. For your own safety at the coast, always check tide times and never swim unaccompanied.

Right: Family fun

Children learning to kayak during a 'Family Fun Week' at the Brancaster Millennium Activity Centre.

Left: 'Pagodas'

Two pagodas sit hunched on the shingle at Orford Ness. The buildings were used for the research and development of Britain's atomic bomb.

❸ Get the kids raft-building at Brancaster

The National Trust's Brancaster Millennium Activity Centre was founded in a former village pub at the end of the 1990s, and focuses primarily on providing residential outdoor learning opportunities for schoolchildren. During the school holidays, however, there is the chance to join in 'Family Fun Weeks' when kids aged 8 upwards can try out coastal pursuits such as raft-building, kayaking, sailing and orienteering. On a National Trust break here, adults are free to do their own thing or join in the activities (all food, equipment and accommodation is provided). For more information see www. nationaltrust.org.uk/brancaster-activity-centre.

❹ See birds from the Norfolk Coast Path

The Norfolk Coast Path, between Hunstanton and Cromer, packs in a huge variety of landscape into its 47 miles – from sand dunes and shingle beaches to fishing ports and saltmarshes. While exploring its length, through Brancaster, Blakeney and Cley, it's possible to see many of the bird species famously associated with this coastline. Look out for oystercatchers, terns and clouds of pink-footed geese in winter. (Always watch from a distance and keep dogs under control during the breeding and wintering seasons – see www.norfolkcoastaonborg.uk for guidance.) Beyond the scenery and wildlife, another added bonus is the level terrain, making many sections of the path accessible for buggy and wheelchair users. And the fantastic Coasthopper bus service returns many a weary walker back to the start of a linear route. For maps and information, see www.nationaltrail.co.uk.

❺ Experience the 'Under the Pier Show'

Want to whack a banker? Or rent a dog for a walk through Southwold? Then make tracks to Southwold Pier's 'Under the Pier Show' to sample a collection of eccentric, and occasionally hilarious, slot machines, hand-built by inventor and artist Tim Hunkin. Hunkin's past work includes Channel 4 series *The Secret Life of Machines*, and his irreverent humour comes across in games such as 'Alien Probe', 'meet a real alien', or the 'Auto Frisk', complete with automated rubber hands.

❻ Go for a run in a park

Running through a beautiful parkland, heath and woodland and looking out over coastal views, certainly beats the treadmill at the gym. Parkrun organises weekly 5km runs in parks throughout the country including at Sheringham Park (see feature below). They take place every Saturday at 9am (the café opens at 8.45am) and all abilities are welcome (as are dogs on leads).

Other National Trust places with coastal parkruns: The Leas, Durham Coast.

How running at Sheringham helped recovery

'I'd visited Sheringham Park for years, but one morning I turned up to find people in running gear everywhere. Curious, I found out that Sheringham hosted a weekly parkrun.

'When I got home I talked to my 15-year-old son David about it. He was recovering from a liver transplant and wanted to rebuild his fitness: we talked each other into going. The first week was a struggle – we walked most of it and at one point I didn't think we'd finish, but the other runners were so encouraging. We came last, but it was a big achievement, and each week after that got easier.

'I go to parkrun nearly every week now. I like feeling a part of something, surrounded by beautiful countryside and coastal views, doing something that's good for you, and sharing it with other people. I can't overstate how important completing that first parkrun was to us. David has recently finished a sprint triathlon and is now volunteering at Sheringham Park.' *Janet A, visitor*

Essex and Kent

The arrival of the railways in the 1850s brought carriages full of Londoners to the Essex resorts of Southend-on-Sea and Clacton-on-Sea. An hour's journey rewarded them with a day of seaside fun on the towns' piers and proms – a tradition that continues. But the 350 miles of Essex coastline offers more than funfairs and candyfloss. Relatively unvisited and unpopulated, it is the place to go for a touch of wilderness and isolation. Its estuaries with their muddy banks and creeks make ideal habitats for birds such as Brent geese whose guttural calls make a haunting soundtrack to walks along sea walls and shingle beaches. And the county's maritime history, built around the docks at Harwich and the Cinque Port of Brightlingsea, lives on with annual Thames barge and smack races, yacht clubs and the revival of boat building.

Kent has been associated more with its hop gardens, orchards and farms – the Garden of England – than with its coastline. This is starting to change as more people visit the area, drawn by the regeneration of its seaside towns such as Margate and Folkestone, and new attractions such as the Turner Contemporary gallery. Once there, visitors enjoy sandy beaches lined with white cliffs and studded with rock stacks, and a national symbol – the White Cliffs of Dover.

Previous pages: The White Cliffs of Dover, Kent, in the early morning light.

Left: Saltmarsh vegetation at the wetlands of Copt Hall in Essex.

Essex: boats, creeks and a bed full of oysters

The Essex coastline starts with the business-like bustle of freight and passenger ships at Harwich as they arrive from or depart for the Hook of Holland and Denmark. The town's position at the confluence of the Orwell and Stour rivers has facilitated a history of seafaring and adventure: this was where the *Mayflower* left for America in 1620 (calling in at Plymouth on the way due to bad weather), and Raleigh, Drake and Nelson all set sail from the adjacent port of Parkeston.

Passengers from paddle steamers used to disembark at the pier at Walton-on-the-Naze (built in 1875 and the second longest in England after Southend) to enjoy a visit to the town's sandy beaches and grassy recreational areas. These days most arrive by car, but the 26m octagonal tower that overlooks the town, which was originally built as a navigational aid, still remains: today it is a café and gallery.

Unlike its neighbour Clacton-on-Sea, which is lively with the sound of amusement arcades and holidaymakers, Frinton-on-Sea maintains an air of restrained pleasures. Developed as an elegant resort with wide tree-lined boulevards in the 1890s by Sir Richard Cooker, it keeps a lid on anything it considers 'vulgar': the seafront is free from attractions, and the town's first pub opened in 2000.

The River Colne has brought maritime trade to the city of Colchester since Roman times (Colchester was the first major Roman settlement in Britain). It still sees much nautical action: Brightlingsea at its mouth is a major yachting centre and home to the Colne Smack Preservation Society which runs annual races, and Wivenhoe has a history of boat building which dates back to Elizabethan times.

The river is also a rich source of oysters: Colchester is famed for them and they have been cultivated in the lower reaches of the Colne since Roman times. All along the estuary, Colchester natives can be sampled in oyster shacks and restaurants (when in season). One of the most popular places to do this is The Company Shed on Mersea Island but be prepared to queue and also keep an eye on tide times: the island's causeway, The Strood, becomes flooded at high tide, often stranding the unaware.

Lonely shores and pleasure seekers

Mersea Island is one of three islands situated within the Blackwater Estuary, the largest estuary in Essex: the other islands are Osea and Northey (see page 102). The National Trust is working with Essex Wildlife Trust to conserve special places within the 1,031 hectares (2,548 acres) of the estuary. Habitats here are varied and include mudflats, salt and grazing marsh, intertidal mudflats and one of the largest reedbeds

Right: Blackwater Estuary

Thames barges in the shallow waters of the Blackwater Estuary with a view of Northey Island behind.

The Battle of Maldon

In AD 978 when Aethelred the Unready succeeded as King of England, Viking fleets were starting to raid the east coast from Southampton. By the 990s these raids had turned into sustained invasions and were a significant threat: Vikings demanded pillage or tribute, an effective way of acquiring wealth and securing political power.

In 991, 93 Viking ships attacked Folkestone, Sandwich and Ipswich before coming to Maldon. Byrhtnoth held the Earldom of Essex, but could not defeat the invaders and was killed in combat during a battle, which most probably took place on the Blackwater Estuary where Northey's causeway links to the mainland. The battle was recorded in an Anglo-Saxon poem and as such Northey Island and surroundings are the oldest recorded battlefield in Britain.

'All along the estuary, Colchester natives can be sampled in oyster shacks'

Opposite: Northey Island

Northey is a magical world of marshes, an island that can be reached by a causeway at low tide.

Left: Southend Pier

The pier is the longest in the world, and extends over a mile into the Thames Estuary. You can choose to walk to the end or take the train.

in Essex. This allows for a large number of birds, including over-wintering waterfowl (4,000 Brent geese feed here in winter, along with teal and shelduck), and invertebrate species to flourish.

To reach St Peter's Chapel, at Bradwell on the Dengie Peninsula (bounded on one side by the Blackwater River), you have to walk the last half-mile. This mini-pilgrimage feels appropriate – the tiny church, built in AD 654, is one of the oldest and most atmospheric places of worship in the UK and deserves a little reverence. As does the surrounding lonely shoreline and saltmarsh whose muddy

'This offshore track runs for 5 miles parallel to the shore, to Foulness Island.'

tussocks are alive with wading birds and whose beaches are composed, in part, of yellow cockleshells. A walk along the sea wall around the peninsula's perimeter takes you to the pretty town of Burnham-on-Crouch, once a centre of the cockle, whelk and oyster trade, and now famed for its sailing activities centred around the prestigious Royal Corinthian Yacht Club.

In his book *The Old Ways*, Robert Macfarlane describes the Broomway as 'the unearthliest path I have ever walked'. This offshore track runs for 5 miles parallel to the shore, to Foulness Island. Marked by wooden poles or 'brooms' it is only uncovered at low tide and can be treacherous: 66 fatalities are buried in Foulness churchyard.

The Broomway couldn't be more different than nearby Southend-on-Sea, a town dedicated to pleasure and thrill seeking, particularly for London's Eastenders, who have visited here since the beginning of the nineteenth century. Nearby Leigh-on-Sea offers quieter pleasures including a sailing club and cockle sheds selling tubs of seafood.

Kent: where the Thames enters the sea

Because of its situation, facing the container port of Tilbury, Gravesend has always been the centre of a great deal of activity on the river – the headquarters of the Port of London Authority's Thames Navigation Service is based here. Watch the ships enter the Thames Gateway – as this part of the river is called – from Gordon Promenade, a lofty spot in the town centre.

Nearby Chatham is seeped in maritime history. Attractions include its Historic Dockyard houses, a Cold War submarine, a Victorian naval sloop, and a ropery where visitors can watch rope being fabricated. The Isle of Sheppey, reached from the mainland by crossing the Kingsferry Bridge, is not packed with visitor attractions, but avocets, marsh harriers and teal are often spotted at its RSPB reserve at Elmley Marshes.

Further east along the coast past Faversham, the seaside town of Whitstable has been known for its oysters since Roman times, and evidence of this is everywhere, from the weather-boarded fishermen's cottages (some now converted into oyster restaurants) and black-tarred boats to its annual oyster festival, and nickname 'The Pearl of Kent'.

An island that isn't an island
The Isle of Thanet, a promontory bulging out into the North Sea, was once an actual island separated from the mainland by a mile-wide stretch of water. Over the centuries, this area has silted up and

Red Sands Forts
Looking like aliens resting before continuing their long walk across the sea, the Red Sands Forts in the Thames Estuary have an otherworldly quality that piques the interest of all who see them. Sited 12 miles from Herne Bay, they were designed by civil engineer Guy Mansell in 1943 to provide anti-aircraft fire during the Second World War. The group was one of three sets that were towed down the river and lowered on to the seabed by hand winch. Originally inhabited by 265 men, the structures are now deserted: following occupation by pirate radio stations, the Admiralty removed access ladders. A conservation project, Project Redsand, is raising money to restore the Forts and wants to reinstate access. Until that time, chartered boats, including a Thames barge, take curious visitors out to see them at close hand.

now Thanet is an island in name and spirit only. Unlike the rest of the Kent shoreline, it has sandy beaches and seven sheltered bays running in a continuous stretch. The prettiest and most photographed of these is Botany Bay, where chalk stacks become marooned in the sand at low tide and the cliffs yield ammonites to fossil hunters.

The sandy shoreline is the main reason why three resorts sprung up along Thanet's edge. The first of these, Margate, has attracted

'Whitstable has been known for its oysters since Roman times, and evidence of this is everywhere.'

Londoners for over 200 years with its curl of sandy beach and sunny aspect. Now, after a slump in its fortunes caused by the package-holiday exodus, visitors are returning. Its fairground, Dreamland, which had fallen into serious disrepair, is being reborn as a museum of fairground attractions; a new art gallery, the Turner Contemporary, has opened to great success; and the Old Town has been enlivened with the introduction of new independent shops and cafés, restaurants and an influx of artists.

Broadstairs is a gentler and more sedate resort. It boasts Georgian and Regency houses, a scenic situation and the former occupancy of Charles Dickens who stayed here every summer from 1837 until

the late 1850s. The town celebrates the life of its famous author every year during a week-long festival, which sees residents dressed up as their favourite Dickens character. The town of Ramsgate with its sweep of elegant nineteenth-century terraces overlooks the harbour, which jangles with rigging from yachts and pleasure boats moored there. The annual regatta, Ramsgate Week, considers itself to be the friendly version of Cowes.

Treacherous sands and an otherworldly place

Hidden beneath the sea for most of the time and lying in the middle of a confluence of major shipping lanes, it is not surprising that the Goodwin Sands has earned its nickname 'the Ship Swallower'. More than 2,000 ships have been wrecked here, victims of this 12-mile-long, 5-mile-wide sandbank, which is constantly shifting. Situated 6 miles off the coast at Deal, the Sands also, more cheerfully, was the venue for an annual cricket match that took place at low tide until 2003.

' ... the Goodwin Sands
has earned its nickname
the Ship Swallower '

Above: South Foreland Lighthouse

This Victorian lighthouse on South Foreland in St Margaret's Bay was built to warn ships of their approach to the Goodwin Sands.

Margate and J M W Turner

More than 100 of Turner's works, including some of his most famous seascapes, were inspired by his visits to the East Kent coast. He was a frequent visitor to Margate especially, and sketched here from the age of 21. From the 1820s onwards, he became a regular visitor, drawn by the sea, the quality of the light, the Thanet skies, which he described as 'the loveliest in all Europe', and by his ardour for his landlady Mrs Booth, with whom he had a relationship. His legacy lives on in the Turner Contemporary gallery, which opened on Margate's seafront in 2011, and which shows his work alongside contemporary artists. www.turnercontemporary.org

What's so special about … chalk downland?

Chalk downland, or calcareous grassland, used to cover large parts of Europe but today only fragments remain, mainly in France and England, and most noticeably on the tops of the White Cliffs. A combination of shallow soils and exposure to wind and rain make it difficult for large plants to become established on chalk downland. Instead, small clumps of a variety of plants grow together in proliferation. The grass is kept short and fertile by allowing two herds of Exmoor ponies and small flocks of Hebridean sheep to graze the cliff tops. Managed by the National Trust, they help to encourage biodiversity and rich varieties of species as well as control growth of scrub brush. The Hebridean sheep browse coarse vegetation and happily eat docks, thistle flowers and nettles.

Chalk is a soft, white, finely grained, pure limestone, formed in shallow seas over millions of years from the hard parts of minute marine invertebrates. When the invertebrates died, their remains sank to the bottom of the ocean and gradually became compressed to form chalk.

Because Deal has a shingle beach, it didn't see an influx of holidaymakers during Victorian times: they were drawn to the sandy shores of Broadstairs and Margate instead. As a result, the seafront is much as it was in the eighteenth century: a row of fishermen's cottages and small houses that extend back into its conservation area. In its heyday, it was a busy harbour with boats anchoring in its sheltered, deep waters. Nowadays many of the fishermen's cottages are holiday homes.

The proximity of this stretch of the coastline to France becomes apparent as mobile phones switch providers to French services from the beach at St Margaret's Bay. This is the starting point for Channel swimmers who dive into the sea and swim the 21 miles to the Continent. It is also where Noel Coward leased a holiday home and entertained Katharine Hepburn and Spencer Tracy.

Most people don't stop as they travel through Dover to catch a ferry to France (it has been England's main cross-Channel port for 2,000 years) but by doing so they miss out on the town's unexpected attractions. Its medieval castle, built by Henry II, is the largest castle in Europe and presides magnificently over the town and any potential invaders; a short walk along the cliff top will take you to the White Cliffs and South Foreland lighthouse (see pages 104–105), and the seafront has been refreshed with sculptural ramps based on wave forms by landscape architects Tonkin Liu.

One way to reach Folkestone from Dover is to walk the North Downs Way along the chalk cliff tops. It's a pleasant way to arrive at the town and to reach its Creative Quarter. The town doesn't have much of a seafront, but what it does have is cliff-top gardens lined with elegant white-stucco terraces. Known as The Leas, they run for a mile towards Sandgate, which is noted for its Napoleonic military officers' houses, now converted to private homes, and can be reached by a water-powered lift built in 1815.

The coast of Kent comes to a halt at one of the largest expanses of shingle in Europe: the windswept, otherworldly promontory of Dungeness. A National Nature Reserve (NNR) and Site of Special Scientific Interests (SSSI), it hosts a remarkable variety of wildlife. Feeling like a frontier community, it is a landscape of shifting shingle banks, low-growing plants, nautical detritus and lonely buildings. Artists and photographers are drawn here – most famously the filmmaker Derek Jarman who made his home and garden on the shingle – as are anglers, bird watchers and architects who have erected homes in the shadow of Dungeness A and B nuclear power station.

Below: Dungeness

Disused railway track and derelict shed on the otherworldly promontory of Dungeness.

Explore National Trust places on the Essex coast

Copt Hall Marshes

The flatlands of coastal Essex have a uniquely wistful atmosphere and nowhere more so than the shoreline and islands around the Blackwater Estuary. Copt Hall Marshes lie north of the Salcott Channel, and its saltmarsh and wet grassland habitat not only make it a place worth visiting but provide a haven for birds: lapwings, barn owls, kestrels and marsh harriers wheel overhead, silhouetted against an often-watery sky. The National Trust has a tenanted working farm here which endeavours to balance crop production and access with coastal nature conservation. Farming is carried out with wildlife in mind: hedgerows are well managed and wet grassland maintained for wading birds and wildfowl. Visitors to the marshes can watch the birds from hides and walk along the centuries-old sea wall, which was built to claim land to graze sheep. Rising sea levels are now having an impact on the shoreline and the National Trust is managing the challenges and opportunities this presents.

Northey Island

Reached only by a causeway at low tide (unless you arrive by boat), Northey Island is one of the three tidal islands in the Blackwater Estuary. Unoccupied, except for holidaymakers staying in its one rental property and its caretaker, it is a wild and lonely spot. The island, at the heart of the new Marine Conservation Zone designation, is the perfect place to escape to for a few days and watch the many birds that are drawn here by the mudflats, rich with invertebrates: Brent geese flock here in their thousands in winter, and redshank, plover, godwit and

'The flatlands of coastal Essex have a uniquely wistful atmosphere.'

Northey: an island without a buffer

On 6 December 2013 a high astronomical spring tide surged over Northey's sea wall at several locations and inundated most of the island: it rose to 20cm below the house's door sills, and if the wind had been easterly, would have been 30cm higher.

A natural sea defence in the form of intertidal saltmarsh surrounds the north-eastern and western sides of the island, at its widest extent providing almost 1km of protection, but the north-west of the island has lost its natural saltmarsh buffer. The south side of the island has some protection from a highly successful coastal realignment project undertaken at Northey in 1991 – the first of its kind in the UK.

With predictions for rising sea levels, increased frequency of storm events and astronomical surge tides such as those we have witnessed during the winter of 2013/14, the flood defences of Northey Island and its main assets need to be addressed.

Above: Copt Hall Marshes

There is a network of paths through the marshes for a brisk stroll with a dog at heel.

avocet also make regular appearances. Access is by advance permit only, see www.nationaltrust.org.uk/northey-island/ for details.

Every year, usually in June, the National Trust runs 'Castaway', a camping weekend on the island. It is a good opportunity to surround yourself with nature and to get a close-up look at the island's wildlife. There are also stalls, a beer tent, hot food and live music to enjoy. (See page 110). Note that no dogs are allowed on the island because of the sensitivity of the bird population. **Maldon, Essex, CM9**

A curious thing … Maldon salt

The Blackwater Estuary in Essex is surrounded by saltmarshes and has been an important salt-making area for more than a thousand years: 45 salt pans are listed in the locality in the Domesday Book of 1086. Sea salt has been produced commercially in Maldon by the family-run Maldon Crystal Salt Company since 1882. The process captures the abundant salt produced by the spring tides, which is evaporated to form crystals, then dried to create the flaky sea salt much favoured by chefs and restaurateurs.

Explore National Trust places on the Kent coast

South Foreland Lighthouse

The proximity of the treacherous Goodwin Sands, which proved the undoing of so many boats sailing through the Strait of Dover, has meant that some form of lighthouse has existed on South Foreland since 1643. The current one was built in 1843 on the site of two earlier lighthouses. Seamen would line up the beams from the Upper and Lower lighthouses, to enable them to safely sail past the southern tip of the Sands.

Keeping the lighthouse at South Foreland on Langdon Cliffs was considered a plumb job: unlike many other lighthouses situated far out at sea, it was land-based, enabling keepers to live with their families. This may have been why the Knott family remained lighthouse keepers here for five successive generations. These days their memory lives on in Mrs Knott's tea room (where leaf tea is served in bone china cups) and in a Trust-run holiday cottage, both of which were part of the Knotts' former home.

South Foreland played an important part in the development of electricity for lighthouses: during the 1840s and early 1850s, the first successful experiments with direct-current limelight and alternating current were carried out here by Trinity House. Another important innovation took place on Christmas Eve 1898, when Guglielmo Marconi set up an experimental link between South Foreland and the East Goodwin lightship 12 miles away. His first message was Christmas greetings to relations. In 1899 he exchanged wireless messages across the Channel between South Foreland and Wimereux near Boulogne in France.

Left: White Cliffs

Visitors climb a ladder to investigate the Langdon Lights, one of three searchlight batteries set into the cliffs during the Second World War to illuminate ships as they entered the bay.

The arrival of automation in 1969 meant that lighthouse keepers were no longer needed, and by 1989 modern navigational aids rendered South Foreland Lighthouse redundant; it was decommissioned in 1988. The National Trust has managed the property since 1989 and it has been open to the public since 1990. A climb to its top rewards visitors with views across the English Channel to France and a chance to see the original clockwork mechanism that made the light flash. **The Front, St Margaret's Bay, Dover, Kent, CT15 6HP**

 ## Holiday Cottage

For panoramic views and a remote setting, little beats staying in a lighthouse. East Cottage was built in 1843 as part of improvements to Upper Lighthouse and was once quarters for the principal lighthouse keeper. Imagine what life was like for the Knott family who lived here and enjoyed the unusually spacious rooms and inside toilet. Now fully modernised, it has its own private courtyard and access to the lighthouse grounds after hours. It also boasts unrivalled sunrises over the Channel, viewed from the comfort of the lounge and kitchen. For more information see www.nationaltrustcottages.co.uk

The White Cliffs of Dover

The 110m high, startlingly white cliffs, where the North Downs run into the English Channel, are more than just a spectacular place to visit: they are a national symbol. This is where British armed forces returned to following evacuation from Dunkirk in 1940, and where Churchill subsequently constructed gun batteries to repel enemy forces. Representing home-coming and defiance, they famously helped boost a nation's flagging morale in Dame Vera Lynn's wartime hit '(There'll be Bluebirds Over) The White Cliffs of Dover'.

In sunlight, the cliffs are a brilliant white. Romans, looking out from the shores of Gaul, may have called the mysterious island across the water Albion from *alba*, Latin for white, as a result. Caesar's first impression was of a wild island with giant natural fortifications and he noted this in his *Commentarii De Bello Gallico*, the first eye-witness account of Britain that survives in literature.

Remains of wartime defences can still be seen along the cliffs, but these days visitors come to walk the 2 miles to the South Foreland Lighthouse, and enjoy the distant views of France, wild flowers including the pyramidal orchid, and abundant wildlife such as the chalkhill blue butterfly.

And if you have ever wondered why the cliffs stay white, it's because they are allowed to erode naturally: the White Cliffs retreat about 5-10cm per year. If they were protected from erosion, plants would colonise the surface and they would become The Green Slopes of Dover. **Langdon Cliffs, Upper Road, Dover, Kent, CT16 1HJ**

The National Trust's White Cliffs of Dover Campaign

In 2012 the National Trust launched a campaign to raise £1.2 million to acquire a 0.8-mile stretch of the White Cliffs. This acquisition was the missing link that would unite the section between the Visitor Centre and the South Foreland Lighthouse. It was important to the National Trust that access to the White Cliffs was guaranteed and that ecological conservation was implemented. The campaign quickly drew attention and was supported by names such as Dame Judi Dench, Ben Ainslie, Dan Snow, Paul O'Grady and Rick Stein. Philosopher Julian Baggini spent a week at the South Foreland Lighthouse in August 2012, considering the White Cliffs' importance in the national psyche. His conclusions were published in a pamphlet 'A Home on the Rock'. 'The White Cliffs of Dover are among the symbols which are formative of Britain's national identity,' he wrote. 'If they stand for us, then what we see in them we will also see in ourselves. And so we should make sure we are happy with what we see in the chalk.'

The campaign was successful and the target was quickly met due to the generosity of 16,000 people and organisations. Since then staff and volunteers have been building on the nature conservation work already in place and the plan is to open one of the Second World War gun batteries, Fan Bay Deep Shelter, which is on the newly acquired land. The White Cliffs is now a truly public space we can all visit, and where we can lie among wild flowers and stare out to sea.

'Remains of wartime defences can still be seen along the cliffs'

Shore-spotter's Guide

1

'Although the **harbour porpoise** (*Phocoena phocoena*) is a shy creature, it can be easy to spot as it usually stays near the surface of the sea, coming up about every 25 seconds to breathe' says Ranger, Robert Sonnen. 'Use binoculars to spot one from the White Cliffs as they swim about searching for fish. They have a blunt, rounded head and greyish bodies and are about 1.5m long.'

2

'You should see **Adonis blue** butterflies (*Lysandra bellargus*) on the White Cliffs of Dover flying over short, grazed turf, during June and again in August and September. The male butterfly has brilliant, azure-blue wings but the female is brown. Both sexes have white fringes to the wings which are intersected with black lines. Its numbers are increasing after a serious decline. Grazing by Exmoor ponies has increased the population here greatly.'

3

'Many different wild flowers can be seen on the White Cliffs including **common knapweed** (*Centaurea nigra*), which is a valuable source of nectar and a favourite flower of butterflies. A cross between a cornflower and a thistle with a large purple flower head, it grows to 1m high and flowers from June to September on dry grasslands and cliffs where the soil is lime rich. The scarce Nottingham Catchfly (*Silene nutans*) occurs commonly along the bare cliffs. It looks like a small white campion but only opens its flowers in the evening and is actually a type of pink.'

4

'Related to the albatross, the **fulmar** (*Fulmarus glacialis*) is mostly seen offshore and feeds in flocks out at sea. It looks similar to a gull with grey upper parts and white underparts and you can see them with binoculars on cliff faces where they breed and ride the updraughts.'

5

'The population of **kittiwakes** (*Rissa tridactyla*) is in decline, perhaps through a shortage of its food – sand eels. However, a small number breed on the White Cliffs. Look out for a medium-sized gull with a small yellow bill and a dark eye. It has a grey back and is white underneath.'

6

'**Oxtongue broomrape** (*Orobanche picridis*) is a rare, parasitical plant that grows on the roots of other plants such as clover or legumes. It has no proper leaves, only fleshy pointed scales on the stems. Look out for it on ledges at the edge of the White Cliffs; it has a creamy/yellow flower spike and grows to about 50cm tall from June to September.'

As recommended by National Trust Countryside Ranger
Robert Sonnen *(White Cliffs and Winchelsea)*

White Cliffs of Dover walk

MODERATE GRADE

Distance: 4 miles (6.4km)

Time: 1 hour 20 minutess

Discover the spectacular coast and countryside of south-east Kent and stroll along the famous White Cliffs of Dover. Walking from Langdon Cliffs to South Foreland Lighthouse, you'll see great numbers of butterflies and wild flowers. Summer is also a fabulous time to encounter the cliff-side antics of kittiwakes, fulmars and peregrines.

Terrain

Naturally uneven and undulating surfaces with some steep slopes. Height gain of 107m (350ft). Do not approach the cliff edge as it can crumble at any time, and take special care when the ground is wet, as the grass and exposed chalk can become very slippery. Please keep dogs under close control at all times due to stock grazing.

Directions

① From Gateway to the White Cliffs Visitor Centre, head east to the Coast Path with the sea on your right. The cliffs are being eroded by 5–10cm every year, although winter storms can cause several tonnes to fall. Here you can also see the remains of the Convict and Military Prison above the Port of Dover. Exmoor ponies graze the grass at Langdon Cliffs, helping to keep it short and prevent scrub invading and smothering the wild flowers. Look out for the yellow flowers of wild cabbage, from which our garden varieties were bred. Spring and summer bring the colourful blooms of greater knapweed, horseshoe vetch and oxtongue broomrape (a parasitic plant living on the hawkweed oxtongue). In spring, look out for the rare early spider orchid, only found on the south coast.

② As you continue along the path, take in the magnificent views of the French coast from the rim of Langdon Hole. On a clear day you can see 21 miles (33.8km) across the Channel. The chalk downland habitat along the cliff tops is a SSSI and an AONB due to the array of flora and insect life which thrives here. Above Fan Bay look out for pyramidal and fragrant orchids in June. This area is well known

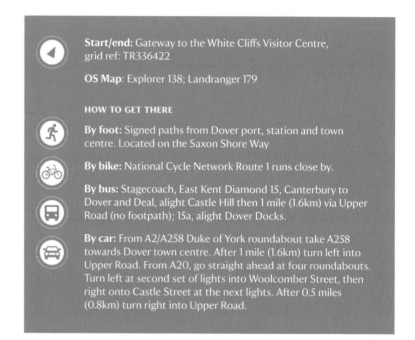

Start/end: Gateway to the White Cliffs Visitor Centre, grid ref: TR336422

OS Map: Explorer 138; Landranger 179

HOW TO GET THERE

By foot: Signed paths from Dover port, station and town centre. Located on the Saxon Shore Way

By bike: National Cycle Network Route 1 runs close by.

By bus: Stagecoach, East Kent Diamond 15, Canterbury to Dover and Deal, alight Castle Hill then 1 mile (1.6km) via Upper Road (no footpath); 15a, alight Dover Docks.

By car: From A2/A258 Duke of York roundabout take A258 towards Dover town centre. After 1 mile (1.6km) turn left into Upper Road. From A20, go straight ahead at four roundabouts. Turn left at second set of lights into Woolcomber Street, then right onto Castle Street at the next lights. After 0.5 miles (0.8km) turn right into Upper Road.

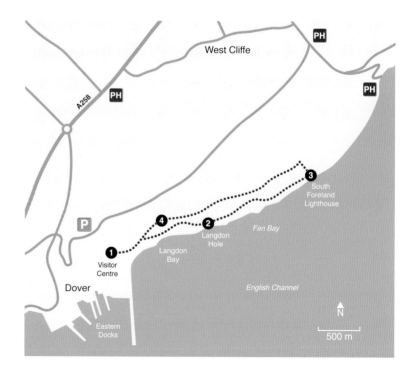

for butterflies, especially the small, Adonis and chalkhill blues. As the name suggests, the chalkhill blue is commonly found in chalk grassland habitats where it can find its favourite plant, the horseshoe vetch. Red admiral, painted lady and clouded yellow can be seen in large numbers during migration when some come to the UK from Europe or Africa. July is the month to spot several rare moths such as the day-flying straw belle. Also look out for Britain's largest fly, the endangered hornet robberfly, ermine moth caterpillars over-wintering in hawthorn bushes, and a recent colonist, the wasp spider.

③ Continue on to South Foreland Lighthouse (see page 104). Watch out for kittiwakes in summer, breeding on tiny ledges on the precipitous cliffs. They can be very noisy birds. Also listen out for the melodies of skylark and meadow pipit filling the air. As well as kittiwake, fulmar live here in summer and you may see a peregrine falcon swooping from the cliff walls where they breed. They hunt pigeons, small birds and rodents to feed their fledglings. Some areas of scrub have been left to grow as they provide shelter for warblers such as the whitethroat, and for colourful seed eaters, linnet and yellowhammer.

'... you'll see great numbers of butterflies and wild flowers'

Top: SS *Falcon*

The wreck of the Steam Ship *Falcon* can be seen from the cliffs overlooking Langdon Bay, where she beached in 1926 after a fire on board. It can be reached by descending a steep path.

Above: Chalk grassland

Walking along the cliff top with a view of the Port of Dover in the distance.

④ Return to Gateway to the White Cliffs Visitor Centre, following a surfaced path just inland, this time keeping the sea on your left. The remains of a Roman lighthouse (Pharos) can be seen within the grounds of Dover Castle, near the church.

Seaside things to do in Essex and Kent

1 Camp on Northey Island

Once a year, the National Trust offers a real-life 'Castaway' experience on Northey Island in the Blackwater Estuary, far removed from the distractions of modern life. For a small fee, campers can spend two nights on the remote wildlife haven – accessible only by boat or causeway at low tide – and join in a weekend of outdoor fun. Hear talks and demonstrations about the area's natural history, or get stuck into raft-building and racing on one of the creeks. In the children's tent, little ones can set up a snail race or learn how to make a grass trumpet. The Trust lays on a barbecue all weekend, plus a bar and live music in the evenings – a perfect accompaniment to watching the sun go down over the water. See www.nationaltrust.org.uk/northey-island for dates and more details.

2 Fly a kite at South Foreland Lighthouse

The cliff-top lawn at South Foreland Lighthouse becomes a wide-open play space on sunny days, and with a stiff sea breeze blustering in from the Channel, it's ideal for kite-flying. No need to bring your own kite – simply borrow one from the Trust for free (just ask at visitor reception). Start by standing with your back to the wind, and pull and release the line to gain height, then watch it loop the loop. See www.nationaltrust.org.uk/south-foreland-lighthouse for opening times.

Other coastal National Trust places good for kite-flying: Bembridge and Culver Downs, Isle of Wight; Brancaster Beach, Norfolk.

3 Go butterfly-spotting on the White Cliffs

Though it's tempting just to look up and out to sea when exploring the White Cliffs, the chalk grassland at boot level also rewards closer examination on account of its vibrant ecosystem. There's an astonishing number of butterfly species here year-round – from the rare Adonis blue to the silver-spotted skipper. Pick up a copy of the Trust's butterfly identification sheet and see how many you can tick off during a walk along this iconic frontier. A good route to follow

Right: South Foreland Lighthouse

A family enjoys flying a kite on the lawn outside the distinctive white lighthouse.

leads from the NT Visitor Centre to South Foreland Lighthouse (a 4-mile round trip). Listen for the ululations of skylarks en route, and check out the wreck of the SS *Falcon*, beached on the shore below since 1926.

❹ Spend a day in the marshes

Old Hall Marshes, the RSPB nature reserve near Maldon, Essex, is situated on land created 400 years ago when banks were built to hold back the sea. Cattle and sheep have grazed on the marshland created as a result, and it is now also the winter home of dark-bellied Brent geese: the RSPB originally bought the land to create a refuge for them. Late autumn and winter is a good time to visit: alongside the Brent geese are other waterfowl also in residence for the season. In the spring, bitterns breed in the reed beds, and marsh harriers, pochard and bearded tits have also made this unusual habitat their home. Also look out for thousands of anthills which stud the marsh.

❺ Learn stand-up paddle boarding at Joss Bay

For a faster way to get up and ride waves than conventional surfing, have a go at stand-up paddle boarding. Owing to the larger size of the board and the added stability of the paddle, 90 per cent of beginners are able to stand upright by the end of their first lesson, and this sheltered rural cove – the South East's top surfing beach – is a great place to learn. Local surf schools will point you in the right direction.

❻ Take a Thames barge down the Blackwater Estuary

When in Maldon, embark upon a little time travel by sailing down the Blackwater Estuary on a Thames barge. These flat-bottomed, red-sailed craft were widely used from the nineteenth to mid-twentieth century for transporting cargo (see feature, below), and at Cooks Yard in Maldon several restored vessels are still in active service for day trips. It's a leisurely way to explore the wild, meditative landscape of the Essex coast and to catch sight of some stellar species, such as oystercatchers and curlews. In spring and autumn, birdwatching boat trips are led by the Essex Wildlife Trust to Osea Island and Brightlingsea. For details, contact 01621 857567 (www.topsail.co.uk).

Below: Maldon

Thames barges at Maldon's Hythe Quay, which is home to the largest collection of these flat-bottomed barges with their rust-red sails.

Thames sailing barges

During the late nineteenth century, the red sails of barges sailing between London and the estuaries of Essex were a common sight. These flat-bottomed, wooden-hulled boats were designed to navigate through shallow waters and narrow rivers, and were perfect for transporting cargo in bulk. Cargo included stones and brick to London for house building and hay and straw for horses from the farms of Suffolk, Essex and Kent. The community of agricultural workers, shipwrights and sailmakers that grew up around the barges was lost when railways and road links meant that this means of transport became redundant. Fortunately conservationists and enthusiasts have kept the wind in these red sails by restoring old vessels and racing them in annual 'Matches' from Pin Mill, Maldon and Southend-on-Sea, and barges can also be chartered for excursions along the coast.

A perfect place to watch the races is from the seventeenth-century Butt and Oyster pub in the hamlet of Pin Mill on the banks of the River Orwell. The river comes right up to the walls of the pub and pints have been known to be passed through its windows directly to (non-competing!) sailors. While you are there, walk along the riverbank to look at the houseboats, and to relive moments from Arthur Ransome's *Swallows and Amazons*, which was set here, before heading off to the National Trust-owned forest Cliff Plantation for a signposted woodland walk.

East and West Sussex

The South Downs come to an abrupt halt at the East Sussex coast, the chalk cliffs dropping giddily to the sea as they roll along the shore in the great undulations of the Seven Sisters. These chalk cliffs were severely battered by the storms of the winter of 2013/14, and are receding at a rapid rate, and at Birling Gap, The National Trust had to take down buildings in anticipation of cliff falls. But it's not all chalk cliffs on this stretch of coastline: there is the meandering Cuckmere Estuary to explore, the great sand dunes at Camber and the unspoilt sand-dune spit of East Head. These natural landscapes are a welcome interlude on a coastline that is lined with resorts and attractions including Brighton and the more sedate Eastbourne.

The shoreline of West Sussex is one of two halves. From Shoreham to Bognor, the coast is all about traditional holiday-making, and hotels, caravan parks and holiday camps line the shore in a continuous strip. From the county's most westerly point, Selsey Bill onwards, everything changes as buildings give way to untouched beaches and the glorious expanse of Chichester Harbour with its bobbing boats, estuarine wildlife and picturesque villages.

Previous pages: A magnificent view of part of the Seven Sisters range across Birling Gap in East Sussex.

Left: Exploring the beach at Birling Gap, which is an ideal spot to go rockpooling.

East Sussex: where the Downs meet the sea

The coastline of East Sussex starts with a surprise: the immense sandy beach at Camber. Not only is it an anomaly amid the shingle shorelines of the rest of the county, but it is hidden from view behind a bank of sand dunes. Its 7 miles of beach that expand to half a mile in width at low tide are revealed in a panoramic sweep as visitors clamber from the road over the dunes. These towering dunes, which have formed over the last 350 years, are still growing – the current estimate is $7,500m^3$ a year – and provide a rich habitat for wild flowers including sea spurge and sea buckthorn and a natural sea defence.

There is plenty of room for everyone on Camber Sands. Kite boarders and windsurfers share the space with horse riders cantering through the surf. Dogs run free in designated zones as sandcastles are built, picnics are enjoyed and barbecues fired up.

At the mouth of the River Rother, Rye Harbour, 2 miles from the town of Rye is a small collection of weatherboard buildings, a café and pub. It is also a 465-hectare (1,149-acre) nature reserve where birds, including colonies of little, common and Sandwich terns can be watched from hides around shingle pits and drainage ditches in the reclaimed saltmarsh.

The sea once flowed right up to the medieval town of Rye but it is now 2 miles inland, although it is surrounded by water on three sides: the rivers Rother and Tillingham and the Royal Military Canal to the south. Rye was an 'Antient Town' which supported the Confederation of Cinque Ports (see feature, below) and the resulting commerce led to fine buildings being built within protective medieval walls and warehouses on the waterfront. The town also drew writers including Henry James, who lived here in National Trust-owned Lamb House (see page 126), and E F Benson who was mayor of the town and set his 'Mapp and Lucia' books in 'Tilling', which has more than a passing resemblance to Rye.

'The sea once flowed right up to the medieval town of Rye.'

Right: Historic Rye

Fishing boats on the River Rother, with Rye perched above, one of the best-preserved medieval towns in England.

A curious thing ... The Confederation of Cinque Ports

During the fifteenth century, five ports along the south-east coast, the area most vulnerable to invasion from the Continent due to its proximity, were contracted by the Crown to provide a fleet when required. (These were the days before England had a navy.) In return, they enjoyed certain privileges including exemption from various taxes. These towns – Hastings, Dover, Hythe, New Romney and Sandwich – were called The Confederation of Cinque Ports (from the French for five).

As one of our oldest fishing ports, Hastings has the largest beach-launched fishing fleet in Britain. In the distance is the East Cliff funicular railway.

Winchelsea, another 'Antient Town' was, until 1287, an important trading post situated on a shingle spit. In that year, a great storm engulfed it and the town was rebuilt a mile inland. Over the years, a build-up of shingle marooned Winchelsea and it is now a scenic and tranquil spot worth visiting for its views and its handsome church, St Thomas the Martyr, where comedian Spike Milligan is buried.

A fishing fleet and a touch of modernism

Britain's largest beach-based fishing fleet operates from Hastings and gives the town much of its character. Fresh fish, all caught in local waters, is sold from stalls on the Stade (the beach) and tall black net huts cluster around the boats and the Jerwood Gallery, an exhibition space showing British and contemporary art which opened in 2012. The Old Town is packed with antique shops, independent retailers and cafés, and is lively with shoppers. The town's pier by Eugenius

Birch (see feature, page 137) had been abandoned to fall into the sea following storm damage in 1990 and a devastating fire in 2010, but has had a change in fortune following a successful fundraising appeal by residents to restore it.

The neighbouring town of St Leonards-on-Sea was designed by architect James Burton and his son Decimus in the early nineteenth century, and much of its original layout, including Mercatoria (the market area) and Lavatoria Square (the laundry area)

remain. Marine Court on the seafront is a handsome Art Deco building (once the tallest block of flats in the UK) built to resemble an ocean liner and, together with seafront apartments, it houses galleries, shops and a café.

An even more impressive 1930s building can be found at Bexhill-on-Sea, a mile or so from St Leonards. The De La Warr Pavilion, designed by architects Erich Mendelsohn and Serge Chermayeff, was built in 1935 in the International Style with clean lines, plenty of glass and wonderful curves. It fell into some disrepair during the 1970s and 1980s but following £8 million funding, it re-opened in 2004 as a contemporary arts centre.

Where the downs meet the sea

The South Downs roll down to the Channel, ending dramatically with the sheer white cliffs of Beachy Head. Translated as 'beautiful headland' from the Norman French *beau chef*, the cliffs at 162m are the highest series in England and rise from the sea like the maw of a whale. A walk along the top delivers views along the coast as far as Dungeness to the east and the Isle of Wight to the west. The classic view of the Seven Sisters rolling along towards Beachy Head, on the other hand, is from the resort of Seaford. Two rivers cut through the Downs, the Ouse and the Cuckmere. The Ouse flows through Lewes and emerges at the busy ferry port of Newhaven. The Cuckmere flows through the Seven Sisters Country Park to Cuckmere Haven.

The cliff path is also a good place to survey the white stucco hotels and palm trees on the long seafront at Eastbourne. The resort has a quieter pace than nearby Brighton with a two-deck promenade lush with tropical planting, an ornate pier complete with camera obscura (damaged by fire in July 2014), and a handsome bandstand topped with a glazed ceramic roof. The town grew fashionable in the middle of the nineteenth century when it was developed by the 7th Duke of Devonshire and architect Henry Currey, who designed a street plan based on European models. The seafront with its series of grand Victorian hotels has changed little since then. A recent addition is the new Towner Gallery designed by Rick Mather Architects which opened in 2005 and shows contemporary art alongside work from its permanent collections.

Arguably, Brighton became the first seaside resort in Britain when a Doctor Russell published a book advocating sea bathing

Above: Beachy Head
The chalk headland lies immediately east of the Seven Sisters. Belle Tout Lighthouse stands in a striking location at the bottom of the cliff.

at Brighthelmstone (as Brighton was then called). (Other resorts including Scarborough and Weymouth also make this claim.) Taking the waters, including bathing in and drinking sea water, was fashionable at the time and became more so when the Prince of Wales (later Prince Regent and George IV) visited Brighton in 1783 to find a cure for his swollen neck. He was so taken by the town that he moved there, building the Royal Pavilion in which to live and lavishly entertain his guests. His spirit of fine living and appreciation of the arts lives on in the resort, which still has a bohemian air.

West Sussex: holiday camps and a harbour

Resorts line the 17-mile stretch of coastline of West Sussex from Shoreham-by-Sea to Bognor Regis – Worthing itself has 5 miles of seafront. Each town in the conurbation has its own particular attractions: Shoreham has a natural harbour formed by the River Adur which runs parallel to the shore; Worthing has a fine pier and promenade; Littlehampton has attracted a new crowd since the opening of the architecturally interesting East Beach Café, designed by Thomas Heatherwick; and Bognor Regis is home to one of Billy Butlin's original holiday camps which opened in 1960.

The shoreline changes at Pagham Harbour, where housing and hotels give way to tidal mudflats and creeks, part of a 405-hectare (1,000-acre) nature reserve. Rich in marine life, species including the lagoon sand shrimp and starlet sea anemone thrive here.

The sandy Blue Flag beach at West Wittering is similarly undeveloped. Untouched by commerce (there are no amusement arcades, chips shops or caravan parks here), and reached down a narrow lane from the village, all there is to see are gently shelving sands at the foot of a pebble bank, sun-warmed tidal pools, a row of beach huts and groups of people enjoying it all. This is largely due to the efforts of local residents who bought the beach and surrounding grassland to keep it exactly as it is.

Nearby, National Trust-owned sand-dune spit, East Head (see page 128), is a rare patch of wilderness – one of the last surviving areas of natural coastline in West Sussex – and the place to head for solitude,

Opposite: West Wittering

The dunes and wide, sandy beach at East Head, West Wittering, on the eastern side of Chichester Harbour.

Right: Bognor Regis

A classic seaside scene – striped deckchairs on the shingle beach at Bognor Regis.

'This estuarine habitat attracts large populations of wildfowl'

wildlife spotting or simply to walk, sunbathe and swim. A Site of Special Scientific Interest (SSSI), it is one of the fastest evolving spits in the UK and a fragile yet dynamic habitat. The shingle, sandy beach and dunes that graduate into saltmarsh are rich with wildlife and a rare example of an unspoilt shoreline on the south coast.

The tidal inlets and creeks of Chichester Harbour, which weedle their way into West Sussex's fertile farming land, are rich with saltmarsh and intertidal mudflats. This estuarine habitat attracts large populations of wildfowl who feed on a rich diet of plants and invertebrates. Brent geese flock here in the winter, with numbers reaching 9,000 birds. It is also a popular spot for yachtsmen and sailors: 17 yacht clubs are based here, and basins and boatyards, jetties, quays and moorings abound. The pretty creekside villages of Bosham and Itchenor with their flint,

brick and tile-hung cottages overlook the harbour with the water reaching the doorsteps of some houses when the tide is especially high. The National Trust owns Bosham Meadow, which has spectacular views across the harbour and the yachts moored up there.

Martello Towers

You don't have to go far along the south-east coast to come across a Martello Tower. These squat, sandcastle-like fortresses were built in 1805–12 to defend the coastline from potential invasion by Napoleon's troops. Based on the design of a fort at Mortella in Corsica (hence their name), they were built of brick (4m thick on the seaward side) were about 9m high and had a cannon on the roof. The invasion never happened and the towers didn't see action, although some were used as observation posts in 1940. Originally 103 towers were built, 74 of which were sited along the Kent and Sussex coastline from Folkestone to Seaford. Forty-five towers remain, some of which have been converted into homes or, as in the case of the one at Seaford, into a museum.

Opposite: East Head

Wooden piles driven into the beach at East Head, West Wittering.

Left: Bosham Meadow

Bosham is a quayside village in Chichester Harbour. The Meadow has stunning views across the harbour.

Explore National Trust places in East Sussex

Birling Gap and the Seven Sisters

The Seven Sisters, a series of chalk cliffs that roller coaster along East Sussex between Eastbourne and Seaford, form one of the longest stretches of undeveloped coastline on the south coast. The South Downs Way runs along their edge, passing the decommissioned Belle Tout Lighthouse (now a B&B) at Beachy Head. A good place to start exploring them is at Birling Gap, east of the last peak, where the National Trust has a café and shop on the edge of a cliff with a 9m drop, and where the beach below can be accessed via a set of steps. The latest addition is the visitor centre 'Life on the Edge', which has interactive displays about coastal erosion, wildlife in the South Downs National Park, shipwrecks and leisure. **Birling Gap, East Dean, near Eastbourne, East Sussex BN20 OAB**

Adapting to change at Birling Gap

Managing a stretch of coastline like this means always being at the mercy of the elements. This proved especially to be the case during the winter storms of 2013/14, which saw 5–7m of cliff lost along this stretch of coastline following a wet winter and tidal surge. The pace of erosion – seven year's worth in two months – was breathtaking: the National Trust had not expected such levels of damage for another decade.

Eye witness account … *Adrian Harrison, Head Ranger, South Downs East, on the storms of 2013/14*

'Birling Gap feels raw in winter and there are often relentless winds hitting this stretch of coast. The storms that rolled in one after the other during the winter of 2013/14 pounded heavily at the cliff. With each approaching storm came nervous anticipation, and the securing of buildings and loose objects outside. We waited the storm out inside buildings that have stood through over 100 years of storms and, through rattling windows, watched the massive seas crash against the cliffs, foam and sea spray billow up from the beach, airborne stones crack car windows, and visitors watching it all in awe.

'As winds eased, we emerged to assess the impact on the buildings and cliff, with the biggest falls happening within a few hours. Seeing the huge waves crashing high up the Seven Sisters and the grey swollen sea rolling in reminded us of the power of nature. The storms brought unexpected change and sadness at the loss of historic buildings and cliff-top gardens, but it is these natural processes that makes this site so stunning.'

Peter Nixon, the National Trust's Director of Land, Landscape and Nature, believes that traditional flood defences can make the situation worse and advises against trying to 'engineer our way out'. 'A false sense of security in artificial defences can lead you to a catastrophic collapse, as opposed to a managed impact,' he says. 'You can't hold the line everywhere. It's physically impossible and it's not good for society.'

In the case of Birling Gap, this meant taking down the sun lounge of the café, the ice-cream kiosk and the safety boathouse before they became dangerous. Anticipating accelerated erosion, the National Trust had already constructed cliff-top fences and beach steps, which were designed to be moved back as the cliffs eroded. There is a long-term plan to create a new building further back from the cliffs. Adrian Harrison, head ranger, South Downs East, says, 'The long-term prospects for the Birling Gap is that the cliffs are going to

Right: Birling Gap

A sweeping view along the coast at Birling Gap, part of the Seven Sisters range, looking west.

continue to erode. We need to look at and take down parts of the buildings as they get too close to the edge.'

'The White Cliffs here are beautiful because of erosion,' says Phil Dyke, the National Trust's Coast and Marine Adviser. 'If there was no erosion there would be green slopes running down to the sea. The National Trust manages 742 miles of coastline. We are now putting into place plans that we thought we had the luxury of another 5–10 years to develop. With Birling Gap, we are looking 30–40 years into the future and thinking about what coastline we need to acquire to assure that, as the cliffs retreat, we can continue to provide the benefits of public access and nature conservation.'

Cuckmere Valley

A walk along the Cuckmere river as it meanders in loops from Alfriston to the sea at Cuckmere Haven, rewards with spectacular views of the Seven Sisters. Along the way, past oxbow lakes and chalk hills, you will cross species-rich chalk grassland lush with wild flowers in the spring, butterflies in summer, and wildfowl in the winter. Other habitats including water meadow, shingle beach, chalk cliffs and rock pools by the sea's edge, guarantee a rich ecosystem with many opportunities for wildlife spotting from aquatic birds, to butterflies to sheep and cattle grazing on the grassland.

High and Over Hill, a dramatic river cliff carved by the river into the soft chalk, is a good place for picnics and kite flying, and has wonderful views of the surrounding landscape. A white horse was cut into its soft chalk on the steep scarp in 1886 and has become a local landmark. Drop into National Trust-managed Frog Firle Farm near Alfriston, for a chance to see calves in spring and autumn. The farm also holds open days in the summer with games, farm crafts, expert-led walks and cream teas in the barn, which was built in the 1800s. The Cuckmere river carved through the soft chalk and was an important 'gap' used by eighteenth-century smugglers. A straight channel was dug in 1847, making a new course for the river and the meanders were cut off. The meanders are slowly silting up and will eventually disappear so, that like the old saltmarsh creeks on the eastern side of the river, we will only see them marked out by a change in the colour of the grass. Perhaps one day the river and its meanders will be re-united. **East Sussex, BN26 5TT (01323 423 197)**

Lamb House, Rye

Built in 1722 by the Lamb family, Lamb House has welcomed some illustrious figures, including King George I who sheltered here during a storm in 1726. It is best known, however, as the home of writer Henry James, who bought it in 1899. He wrote the novels *The Wings of the Dove*, *The Ambassadors* and *The Golden Bowl* here, and entertained peers such as H G Wells, Joseph Conrad and Rudyard Kipling. The house also played a part in the books of another resident, E F Benson,

Below: Cuckmere Valley

View of meandering waterways in the flat grassy plain on Chyngton Farm, on the west bank of the Cuckmere Estuary.

whose 'Mapp and Lucia' books are set in 'Tilling' a town that closely resemble Rye. Mapp lived in 'Mallards', which is Lamb House to all intents and purposes. **West Street, Rye, East Sussex, TN31 7ES**

Blackcap, Devil's Dyke, Ditchling Beacon, Saddlescombe Farm and Newtimber Hill

This cluster of National Trust sites on the South Downs is heaven for hikers, and includes some of the highest points in East Sussex – Ditchling Beacon, for instance, is 248m above sea level and from its chalk ridge you can survey the south coast, weald and surrounding hills. A similarly jaw-dropping panorama can be seen from Blackcap, near Lewes, while Devil's Dyke – Britain's longest, deepest and widest dry valley – has an outlook that Constable described as 'the grandest view in the world'. At Newtimber Hill, there is ancient woodland to explore – see if you can spot the thousand-year-old lime tree – plus the Trust's working Saddlescombe Farm – see online for special open days. Revive your limbs after all that climbing at the Hiker's Rest Café. **Blackcap: Lewes, BN7 (01323 423923); Devil's Dyke, near Poynings, BN45 (01273 857712); Ditchling Beacon: Westmeston, BN6 (01323 423923); Saddlescombe Farm: Saddlescombe Road, Brighton, BN45 7DE (01273 857712)**

Left: Lamb House

The red-bricked Georgian house is in the old town of Rye.

Below: Devil's Dyke

Panoramic view down the dry valley of Devil's Dyke.

Explore National Trust places in West Sussex

East Head

Approached from the western end of West Wittering beach car park near Chichester Harbour, this sand dune spit is a Site of Special Scientific Interest (SSSI) and has been managed by the National Trust since 1966. Approximately 1,000m long and 400m wide and joined to the mainland by a strip known as The Hinge, it is one of the fastest evolving spits in the UK and a fragile yet dynamic habitat. Plants such

Making time and space for change at the coast by Phil Dyke

'In the future there may be a place for sea defences but the National Trust is clear that these structures are only appropriate as a mechanism to enable us to buy time. Our challenge is to develop long-term and sustainable approaches to managing the coast in the future. In some places this may involve breaching seawalls on reclaimed land. It will also involve unpicking failed, failing and counterproductive sea defences, but more generally it will be about adapting to what comes our way. Working with natural processes and being adaptable means that some of the decisions we face will be difficult and on occasion controversial. We have to effectively communicate the long-term benefits of this approach.

'A key issue for the National Trust is the need to think long term. Thinking in 20-, 50- and 100-year timeframes needs to become the norm, to replace our current practice of thinking in short five-year planning and political cycles. Our Coastal Management Principles and Coastal Adaptation Strategies help staff at our coastal sites to put this thinking into practice. Our 'Shifting Shores' documents illustrate how the National Trust is approaching the conservation of buildings, the management of visitor infrastructure and the creation of opportunities for wildlife, and ensuring we understand the significance of archaeological features as they are exposed.'

as yellow-horned poppy and sea holly grow on the vegetated shingle, having adapted to the windswept environment that lacks both soil and moisture. Landward of the dunes is saltmarsh which wildfowl such as sanderling, redshank and oystercatchers have made their home. A rare patch of wilderness lying close to the popular beach of West Wittering, it is a place to escape, preferably with a dog at the heel (they are allowed on the beach). Perfect for picnics, flinging a Frisbee, and watersports such as sailing and surfing, it is very easy to while away a day on the beach and dunes. The National Trust's Dune Bug campervan is parked up on the beach and has information on all its activities. **Coast Guard Lane, Chichester, West Sussex PO20 8AT (01243 814 730)**

Above: East Head

Low tide reveals creeks in the saltmarsh of the coastal spit. This is a dynamic environment.

Right: Sand dunes

The vast dune landscape at East Head. Sea holly and sea bindweed grow through the sand and bring vibrant colour in the summertime.

'... it is a place to escape, preferably with a dog at the heel'

Shore-spotter's Guide

1

The Cuckmere Valley is a fantastic place for wildlife, with its juxtaposition of brackish ditches, full or rare plants such as **flowering rush** (*Butomus umbellatus*) and insects, including scarce dragonflies, and the steep chalk grassland slopes of High and Over, where the scarce silver-spotted skipper butterfly abounds during August.

2

A common sight along this part of the coast, but especially at Birling Gap, **gorse** (*Ulex europaeus*) is an important shrub that provides shelter and food for many insects and birds. A spiny, evergreen bush with bright yellow flowers, it can be invasive if not kept in check. Its flowers also smell strongly of coconut.

1

2

3

Originating from North Africa and southern Europe The **clouded yellow butterfly** (*Colias croceus*) is a regular summer visitor to the UK. It favours short turf habitats including downland slopes like those around Birling Gap. It has greenish yellow underwings with two silver-white spots; its upper wings are gold with dark edges. It is a strong and powerful flyer, but only arrives on our shores during hot summers.

4

Sand-dune habitats like those at East Head suit **sea holly** (*Eryngium maritimum*), a strictly coastal plant that is in leaf all year. It gets its name from its spiky leaves, which cover the whole plant. Its burr-shaped spiky, metallic-blue flowers (from June to September) make it easily recognisable.

3

4

5

The small, dumpy, short-legged wading bird, **ringed plover** (*Charadrius hiaticula*), can be seen on the beach at East Head. It is brownish grey above and white below with orange legs and an orange bill tipped with black.

6

The **whimbrel** (*Numenius phaeopus*), a large wading bird, stops off in the UK during its migration to Africa in spring and autumn. Sometimes it uses Rye Harbour as a staging post in its migration. Brownish above and whitish below, it has long legs and a long bill that curves near the tip.

Butterfly world

The UK coastline is rich with butterflies and insects, many of which have travelled far to enjoy its rich habitats. And, what's more, the numbers look likely to increase, says **Matthew Oates**.

In hot weather, our coasts are truly alive with butterflies, many of them visiting flowers in nearby gardens, or frequenting garden plants such as red valerian which have become naturalised on cliffs or dunes. Sea cliffs, combes and dunes are some of the best habitats for butterflies in the UK with many of the richest places on land owned by the National Trust, acquired through Enterprise Neptune. At least 40 species of butterfly are seen annually along our coasts, more than two-thirds of our butterfly fauna. Only eight of our species are not capable of breeding along or very close to some part of the coastal fringe. Being a coastal butterfly is, however, a high-risk strategy, for populations in exposed places can be blasted away by summer storms.

Curiously, none of our butterflies can be classified as being truly coastal species. The nearest we have is the Glanville fritillary, which breeds along the eroding cliffs of the Isle of Wight and on some of the nearby chalk downs and meadows, and the Lulworth skipper which is restricted to calcareous grasslands on or close to the Dorset coast, particularly on Purbeck. The Glanville fritillary breeds on a common wayside and meadowland weed, ribwort plantain, but requires the extra heat that the Island's crumbling soft cliffs provide. Most of its colonies are on National Trust land. The Lulworth skipper's caterpillars feed on tor grass, a rough grass that occurs commonly on many downs. We do not really understand why it is restricted only to Dorset. Unlike the moths, there are no butterfly specialists of saltmarsh habitats, and none that is wholly restricted to sand dunes.

A variety of species and some oddities

A number of our butterflies do best along the coast, really because of the extent and quality of habitat there. Good examples are the grayling, though it also occurs on sandy heaths and on Carboniferous Limestone hills inland, and the wall brown, which has inexplicably retreated to the coast in recent decades, having been a common wayside and grassland insect inland. The gatekeeper is also commonest in sheltered coastal places. The dark-green fritillary is frequently found along our sea cliffs, and in sea combes and sand dunes, though it also occurs in a variety of other habitats almost throughout the UK. Also, colonies of the small pearl-bordered fritillary occur in sea combes along our south-western coasts, often producing a second brood, during August, in these hot places.

The coast holds some oddities, most notably the wood white, a rare and delicate butterfly of sheltered grassland habitats, which is found somewhat incongruously along the South Devon undercliff between Sidmouth and Lyme Regis. A similar species, Real's wood white, occurs in sea combes and on dunes in Northern Ireland. It is common in the fore dunes of Murlough Dunes, County Down. Also, colonies of the silver-studded blue are found in sand dunes on the coasts of Cornwall and Pembrokeshire, and in coastal limestone grassland on Purbeck and on the Great Orme, Conwy.

Insects and migrants

The bigger picture is that our coastline provides some of the richest habitats for insects generally, many of them highly specialised creatures. Away from the seaweed-and-sand-hopper zone, there are insects that inhabit saltmarsh, sand dunes, coastal heaths, sea combes and, especially, crumbling cliff faces. The latter are called soft-rock cliff specialists. Some of them love hot bare sand or clay, others cliff-side mud or fresh water seeping down the cliff face. There's even a daddy-longlegs that lives under sea-cliff waterfalls. These weird and wonderful creatures – beetles, flies, moths and bees or wasps in the main – require warmth, even deep heat, which bare cliff

'These weird and wonderful creatures – beetles, flies, moths and bees or wasps in the main – require warmth, even deep heat, which bare cliff slopes provide.'

Left: Painted lady

Painted lady butterflies feeding on red valerian at Trelissick Garden in Cornwall.

slopes provide. They are restricted to the coast simply because of their need for extreme heat. For some, our south coast forms the northern limited of their European range.

The coast is also where the migrant insects arrive – butterflies, dragonflies, hoverflies, ladybirds and a large number of moths. The bulk of these arrive along the south coast, but not necessarily only from France. Some of our migrant insects arrive on the east coast, emanating from Holland and Scandinavia. This is where our Queen of Spain fritillaries and Camberwell beauties originate. The extreme South West – Cornwall, Devon and Pembrokeshire – is another favoured migration route, particularly for red admiral, painted lady and clouded yellow. The Scilly Isles are a particularly good landfall site, accounting for most modern-era records of the monarch butterfly, a rare vagrant from North America. The coast of Kent and East Sussex is a favoured landfall area, especially for large and small whites, though in 2013 it saw a significant influx of long-tailed blues, a very rare migrant, which established a number of short-lived colonies there.

From far-flung places

These migrant insects, including the butterflies, are either long- or short-haul migrants, or in some cases both. The painted lady is an amazing long-haul migrant. Scientific research found that the massive immigration that occurred in 2009 emanated from the northern edge of the Sahara Desert, and that a return migration occurred – at high-altitude level. Better still, monarch butterflies are occasionally disturbed off their migration routes and carried across the Atlantic by storms. We also receive a number of long-haul migrant moths, from the Mediterranean in the main but also from as far afield as south-east Europe, north Africa and north America. The large white and small white are good examples of short-haul migrants, and the large tortoiseshell is probably an occasional short-haul migrant.

Certainly, the south coast is the front-line trench for new colonisation from the Continent. If climate change provides warmer summers and milder winters, we can expect migrant butterflies such as the long-tailed blue and clouded yellow to become genuine or quasi residents along our south coast, the large tortoiseshell to re-colonise places like the Isle of Wight, the Queen of Spain fritillary to establish itself on our east-coast sand dunes, and the continental race of the swallowtail to invade and conquer much of the warmer, sunnier parts of southern England. Butterflies, after all, push limits, and are forever seeking new places to live.

Matthew Oates is the National Trust's National Specialist on Nature and Wildlife. He has written a number of books about butterflies including Butterflies *(National Trust).*

Birling Gap and the Seven Sisters walk

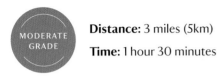

MODERATE GRADE

Distance: 3 miles (5km)

Time: 1 hour 30 minutes

This circular walk allows you to enjoy great views over the Downs and coast. By following old drovers' and smuggling routes to the sea from this small downland village you may also feel a sense of the landscape's long history.

Terrain

Mostly grazed farmland on chalk grassland, well-drained soil so not too muddy, some gravel track and Tarmac road. There are some gates but no stiles and four short steep sections on the whole route. Dogs are welcome on leads.

Directions

① From the Tiger Inn walk straight across the green opposite the pub, on to the small road and turn right. You will see to your right on the flint wall of a house a blue plaque, 'Sherlock Holmes retired here 1903–1917'. Follow the road as it goes round to the right and, after a few metres take a left up the small track towards a field. Here you pass a National Trust sign for Farrer Hall, on your left a former scout hut that was used as a school classroom during the Second World War.

② Go through the gate and follow the footpath straight up through the field (named Hobbes Eares). Near the top of this field is a short, steep section but after this the terrain is fairly flat and dry. From the vantage point of this hill you get a great view of East Dean – Belle Tout Lighthouse is in the distance to the east. (You'll have different views towards this landmark for most of the walk.) You may see several interesting breeds of sheep from the Seven Sisters Sheep Centre as this is one of their grazing areas. In summer, it's covered in downland flowers such as yellow rattle.

③ At the top you reach Friston church. Go through the kissing gate leading into the churchyard. Walk straight along the path to the gate with an arch over it; called a tapsel gate with its interesting opening mechanism. The village pond is in front of you and to your right is the

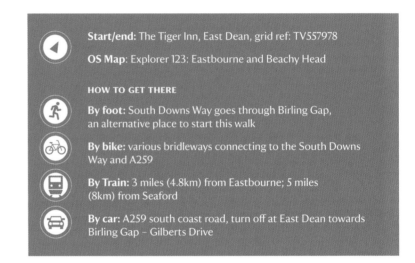

Start/end: The Tiger Inn, East Dean, grid ref: TV557978

OS Map: Explorer 123: Eastbourne and Beachy Head

HOW TO GET THERE

By foot: South Downs Way goes through Birling Gap, an alternative place to start this walk

By bike: various bridleways connecting to the South Downs Way and A259

By Train: 3 miles (4.8km) from Eastbourne; 5 miles (8km) from Seaford

By car: A259 south coast road, turn off at East Dean towards Birling Gap – Gilberts Drive

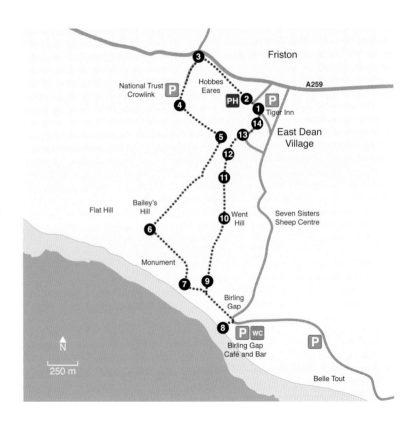

A259 coast road. Turn left up the Tarmac lane between three houses along the narrow road.

4 You'll soon come to the welcome sign for National Trust Crowlink car park. Go through the walkers' gate to the left of the cattle grid. Follow the fence line on your left, with the water trough on your right.

5 Follow the fence line and as it turns right you're facing south towards the sea. Be aware of rabbit holes on this section. You'll spot the red barn roof and then a line of windswept trees as you pass several gates on your left. As you reach the corner of the field you're now quite near the sea on Bailey's Hill, the second of the Seven Sisters. If you look at the direction the wind has shaped the trees here they all point away from the prevailing south-westerly winds. A few trees like this amongst the flower-rich chalk grassland provide valuable shelter to wildlife and stock that are out in all weathers.

6 Go through the kissing gate in front of you, with thorny gorse bushes around it, then go left downhill to the east. You'll spot the Belle Tout Lighthouse in the distance in front of you. Walk downhill past the gorse – near the bottom of the valley look back to your right where the monument is overlooking the sea. Carry on east, up the next hill, called Went Hill. It's rather steep but take this opportunity for a breather as you look for flowers such as the purple violets in spring, pink common century in summer and lilac field scabious in late summer/autumn.

7 The brow of the next hill is Went Hill, keep going east and take the right path to join the South Downs Way, which runs parallel to the cliff. Take care not to go near to the cliff edge. As you keep walking, Birling Gap hamlet will come into view in the valley. You'll shortly reach a gate with a signpost and map of Crowlink, showing you in more detail the land you have walked over.

8 At the next gate, take the right path downhill under cover of pine trees and the private road down to Birling Gap. At the bottom of the track to your right are steps leading to the café and bar. Take some time to go to the top of the steps by the beach at Birling Gap for a fantastic view of the Seven Sisters, or go down to the beach from the nearby steps to get a close-up view of the white chalk.

9 The return journey is shorter and will give you more views over towards Belle Tout. Go back up the private road, but instead of taking the gate on the left go straight up to the top of the track past the last house (Seven Sisters cottage) to another gate through Crowlink.

10 Following the hedgerow on your right, go through the next gate ahead of you and continue straight ahead along the track until you come to the red barn you saw earlier. Go straight past, keeping the barn on your right. Don't take the track leading left to the derelict stone barn, instead follow on to the field-boundary edge with trees until you spot a waymark post with a pink arrow on your right.

11 Take the small path on your right leading down through some trees – you'll have a view of the village below. The path is quite steep and can be slippery with leaves so take care.

12 After leaving the trees go through the gate and along the path to the next gate – you'll see a clay-tiled roof and other houses. Follow the flint wall through the final gate which leads on to a small road.

13 Beware of traffic as you walk down the lane, bear left to return to East Dean village. You'll pass a house on your left which has a plaque to commemorate all the families in East Dean who looked after children evacuated from cities in the Second World War.

14 You should now see the Tiger Inn again where you started the walk.

Seaside things to do in East and West Sussex

1 Go canoeing at Cuckmere Valley and East Head

The meanders of the Cuckmere river in East Sussex are shallow and calm, providing optimum conditions for novice canoeists in the summertime. And for the more experienced, the tidal sections leading out to sea offer a greater challenge. In West Sussex, the waters and saltmarshes surrounding East Head are also popular with paddlers. If you're after a *Swallows and Amazons*-style adventure, aim for the sheltered parts of Chichester Harbour (owing to strong currents, always check tide information). Before heading out, the Trust recommends making sure you are properly equipped and can swim at least 50m. For further guidelines, see pages 18-19. See also www.gocanoeing.org.uk.

2 Enjoy family fun at Birling Gap

The awe-inspiring landscape of the Seven Sisters is more than just a photo opportunity, it's a fantastic spot for families to enjoy the coast, hands-on. Head down the steps to the beach from Birling Gap car park, and see what creatures you can find in the rock pools (or join in one of the regular National Trust Rockpool Rambles).

Fossick around in recent chalk falls and you might uncover fossilised plants – or even dinosaur bones. In August, the Trust lays on weekly events at the site, from kite-making to walking the smugglers' trail. For more information see www.nationaltrust.org.uk/birling-gap-and-the-seven-sisters.

3 Try trail running in the South Downs

An exhilarating 13km cliff run cuts through the roller coaster terrain of the South Downs, taking in Beachy Head, Birling Gap and the Seven Sisters, with spellbinding Channel views nearly all the way. Long-distance races take place annually along the South Downs Way (see www.endurancelife.com). A quieter, more easy-going 7km trail on the West Sussex side of the Downs, close to Cissbury Ring, starts at Steyning Clock Tower and finishes at Findon High Street (see www.nationaltrust.org.uk for details). Needless to say, the same tracks can be enjoyed by walkers at a more leisurely pace.

4 Watch hang gliders at Devil's Dyke

The precipitous valley of Devil's Dyke is, perhaps unsurprisingly, one of Europe's best sites for paragliding and hang gliding. When the wind is from the north, you'll see the aerial daredevils taking flight (or contact local operators, if you fancy having a go yourself). Watch the 'hangies' soar, then have a hot drink at the pub/restaurant nearby. Further activities available here include mountain biking (use the network of bridleways for a thrilling ride); hiking (see www.nationaltrust.org.uk/devils-dyke) and kite-flying.

5 Follow the 'string of pearls' art trail

The 'string of pearls' refers to a chain of recently established cultural attractions stretching around the south-east coast, which have

Left: Family fun

A family enjoys playing in the sea at Birling Gap.

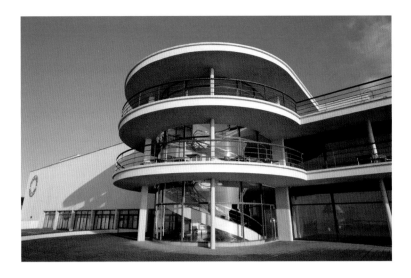

brought new visitors and indeed new life to the region's seaside towns. Three of these can be found on the Sussex shoreline. Working east to west, the first is the white concrete Towner Gallery in Eastbourne. Built by Rick Mather Architects and opened in 2009, it is best known for its nineteenth- and twentieth-century British artworks. Next is the De La Warr Pavilion in Bexhill-on-Sea – a slice of Grade I-listed, 1930s Modernism, operating as a centre for contemporary arts since 2005. The final link is Pallant House Gallery in Chichester. This Queen Anne townhouse was augmented by a cutting-edge new wing in 2006, and houses British Library architect Sir Colin St John Wilson's collection of modern art.

6 Soak up seaside history in Brighton

Delve into the history of seaside tourism on a walking tour of Brighton, which first became fashionable as a resort to 'take the waters' in the 1750s. Start at the Royal Pavilion, built in 1787-1823 for the Prince Regent, later George IV, as a pleasure dome for the Royal Family (until Queen Victoria sold it in 1850). Then make for the seafront to see the grand Victorian hotels and sole surviving pier from this period. Although the Chain Pier was lost in 1896, its replacement, Brighton Pier, still thrives, with rides and arcades attracting three million visitors a year. Next, stroll towards Hove for a closer look at the spectral remains of Eugenius Birch's West Pier (see feature, right), half-sunk out to sea (and check out the progress of the new i360 viewing tower at its foot). Finally, return via the prom to Brighton Pier and go for a nostalgic ride on Volk's Electric Railway (open Easter to end September). Dating back to 1883, it is the oldest of its kind in the world.

Left: De La Warr

The Art Deco façade of De La Warr Pavilion at Bexhill-on-Sea, one of the 'string of pearls' art trail.

Above: Brighton sea front

View of the ornate ironwork of Brighton Pier and the Aquarium Station for Volks Electric Railway that runs along the promenade.

The pier genius: Eugenius Birch (1818–1884)

Eastbourne Pier, with its ornate ironwork, minarets and camera obscura is one of the finest on the British coast. Despite the fire of 2014, which destroyed a third of it, much of its glory remains. It was built in 1872 by Eugenius Birch, the foremost Victoria pier engineer. Before turning his hand to piers, Birch was the engineer of the Calcutta-Delhi railway, Exmouth Docks, Ilfracombe Harbour and West Surrey waterworks. He used what he had learned as a civil engineer and from his time in India, to create 14 piers, many of which are inspired by the Orient. His most revolutionary idea was to replace wooden piles with cast-iron screw piles that could be fitted directly into the ground. This gave the piers greater flexibility and strength. West Pier in Brighton, with its dome and arcaded pavilion, was his most famous pier before it was consumed by fire in 1917. More cheerfully, his pier at Hastings is undergoing a process of renovation following a successful campaign by local residents.

Birch's 14 piers: Aberystwyth Royal Pier; Birnbeck Pier, Weston-super-Mare; Bournemouth Pier; Brighton Pier; Deal Pier; Eastbourne Pier; Hastings Pier; Hornsea Pier; Lytham Pier; Margate Pier; North Pier, Blackpool; Plymouth Pier; Scarborough Pier; West Pier, Brighton.

Hampshire and
The Isle of Wight

With attractions including the New Forest and the cathedral town of Winchester drawing visitors, Hampshire's coastline is often overlooked, which is a shame as its marshy harbours, inlets and low-lying islands have much to offer. Yachtsmen, however, know all about its sheltered waters, which are good for mooring and for dinghy sailing, and savvy walkers take to the 60-mile long Solent Way that follows the coastline from Emsworth Harbour to Milford-on-Sea.

Proximity to Europe has meant that Hampshire's coast has played an important role in the defence of the country, and evidence of this maritime past is all around, from the hull of the Mary Rose preserved at Portsmouth Historic Docks, to Nelson's shipwright's cottage at Buckler's Hard. But this is also a commercial coastline with the docks of Southampton constantly busy with cruise liners coming and going, and oil refineries punctuating the shoreline.

The diamond-shaped Isle of Wight is separated from the Hampshire coast by a sea channel, the Solent. For such a small island it has a surprising diversity of coastline, from the chalk stacks, the Needles, to saltmarsh, tidal creeks and swathes of sandy beaches.

Previous pages: The tumbling sandstone cliffs and golden sands of Compton Bay, Isle of Wight.

Left: Yachts competing in the Round the Island Yacht Race off the Isle of Wight, having just rounded the Needles.

Hampshire: bustling harbours and historic dockyards

It's not surprising that Emsworth Harbour is peppered with yachts and sailing craft: it sits beside sheltered Chichester Harbour and overlooks Hayling Island with its inlets and sandy beaches. Once known as a smugglers' haunt, and for its oysters (which declined after a pollution scare), Emsworth is now a popular destination for sailors (there are two main sailing clubs) and for ramblers enjoying a stroll beside its two tidal millponds to the sea.

Hayling Island sits in the middle of Chichester Harbour and its 4 miles of sandy beaches fringed with grassy dunes on the south shore attract plenty of day trippers alongside sailors and watersports enthusiasts during the summer months. Shaped like an inverted T, it is reached by a two-lane road bridge that can get congested at the height of the season. The east and west of the island are predominantly marshland and attract all manner of wildlife, best appreciated by walking the old railway line from West Town along the west shore.

It is easy to forget that the busy commercial port of Portsmouth is located on an island, Portsea Island, albeit one only separated from the mainland by a small channel, Portsbridge Creek, which is crossed by three major roads including the M275. The surrounding water and the Solent can be seen from the top of Spinnaker Tower, a 170m viewing tower on the seafront, shaped like a yacht's headsail (see pages 165). Stand on the transparent Sky Walk if the vertiginous drop below your feet doesn't faze you, or head outdoors to the Sky Deck for blowy, wraparound views.

The city was established as a naval dockyard during the reign of Henry VII and there is still a flavour of the original town in the streets of Old Portsmouth. Its naval history is preserved in Portsmouth Historic Dockyard where Nelson's flagship, HMS *Victory* and the warship HMS *Warrior* are preserved, as is the hull of the Henry VIII's warship the *Mary Rose*, which sank in the Solent during a sea battle against the French. It is now on display in a new museum alongside thousands of artefacts raised with her from the seabed in 1982.

It is said that Henry VIII witnessed the loss of the *Mary Rose* from near his (newly completed) castle at Southsea. Built in 1544 to defend Portsmouth Harbour, it has been strengthened over the centuries and is still pretty intact. Portchester Castle occupies a commanding position at the northern end of Portsmouth Harbour and was an important structure during the Middle Ages when Portchester was a significant port.

Left: HMS *Warrior*

One of four historic ships in Portsmouth Historic Dockyard, which include the *Mary Rose*, HMS *Victory* and the Second World War submarine, *Alliance*.

Left: Buckler's Hard

Georgian terraced cottages line the single street of this shipbuilding village that leads down to the River Beaulieu.

Southsea also has two piers and a long shingle beach and offers boat trips around Portsmouth Harbour. On the other side of the harbour and linked via pedestrian ferry, Gosport is home to the Royal Navy Submarine Museum which has four submarines (including *Holland I*, the UK's first) to look around.

Cruise ships and shipbuilding

Southampton is a city defined by its coastal setting. It sits at the head of Southampton Water, a deep-water estuary fed by two rivers, the Test and Itchen, which eventually flow into the Solent. No surprise, then, that it has been a major port since Roman times. The Pilgrim Fathers set sail across the Atlantic from Southampton in 1620, and it was William the Conqueror's port for ships coming across from Normandy. These days, its 6 miles of quay and docks mainly service ferries and cruise ships, including some of the world's largest cruise liners.

The city's maritime history is told in the SeaCity Museum where visitors will also learn that 500 Southampton households lost someone in the *Titanic* disaster – many local people worked as crew on board the ship. The annual Southampton Boat Show attracts sailors, watersport enthusiasts and super yachts and marks the end of a week of sea-themed events.

There is more maritime history along the coast at Buckler's Hard, a village with an important shipbuilding history now restored to its eighteenth-century appearance. Two rows of cottages, including a re-creation of a shipwright's cottage, lead down to the River Beaulieu and the yacht harbour. Its location, on the banks of a deep, sheltered river with a gently sloping beach and near woodland, made it ideal for building ships including several which fought in Nelson's fleet at Trafalgar.

Shipbuilding also thrived at Lymington, and the handsome Georgian buildings that line the cobbled streets reflect the town's commercial success. Nowadays it is geared more towards sailing, with two marinas and two sailing clubs catering for its yachting community.

'The Pilgrim Fathers set sail across the Atlantic from Southampton in 1620.'

Isle of Wight: across the lively strait of the Solent

For a small island, the Isle of Wight has a surprisingly large number of different terrains. This is down to its unique and fascinating geology: it is made up of many layers of sedimentary rock of the Cretaceous and Paleogene ages, deposited over many millions of years under water. The layers consist of fine-grained minerals, sands and fossils forming rocks such as mudstones, shales, sandstones and limestones. Some of these layers are poorly consolidated and are easily eroded by the seas; others are hard like the chalk limestone, which forms the high downland that runs across the island from the Needles to Culver Cliff.

The oldest rocks (126–110 million years ago) are the multicoloured mudstones and sandstones laid down when the English Channel and much of southern England formed part of the valley of a large river. This landscape was home to dinosaurs, including the Iguanodon, the Neovenator and the Pterosaur. Fossilised bones and footprints of these creatures have been found on the island. About 7,000 years ago, sea levels rose as ice sheets melted and the island became separated from the mainland.

The National Trust manages almost 17 miles of the coastline of the Isle of Wight out of 56.5 miles in total, much of it saved through the Neptune Coastline Campaign. Their variety reflects the diversity of the island's landscape and geology, which ranges from sheer chalk cliffs, to grassy downland, rolling fields, saltmarsh and tidal creeks, all vital habitats for wildlife. The most recent Neptune acquisition is Sudmoor and Roughlands, which link Brook Chine with Mottistone Estate on the south-west coast. Newtown, the island's only National Nature Reserve, is alive with birds, insects and rare plants. Management of these sites is often focused on returning them to an earlier state by careful management. The grassland near the Needles, for instance, is cropped by Trust-introduced Hebridean sheep, which keep growth of young ash trees at bay and allow rare plants such as the early gentian to establish.

The Isle of Wight Coastal Path is 67 miles in length, and is broken into sections of manageable walks, all of which are clearly signposted. The island also holds two annual walking festivals in May and October with more than 70 walks to choose from. The majority of National Trust coastal sites have unrestricted access, apart from where this could disturb wildlife.

Below: Exploring the beach

The Isle of Wight has miles of award-winning beaches from seaside resorts to quiet stretches of open sands.

' ... footprints of these creatures have been found on the island.'

The southern half of the island: resorts, long beaches and coastal erosion

In a clockwise direction from the most eastern point of the lozenge-shaped island, National Trust-owned Culver Down (see page 150) stops at the sea's edge with a 91m drop: the white chalk of Culver Cliff. This is a perfect habitat for nesting sea birds – peregrines and ravens can be spotted by the vigilant. From here and adjoining Bembridge Down, there are splendid views of Bembridge Harbour and the long sandy beach at Sandown Bay.

Two resorts, Sandown and Shanklin, sit on the bay and both are popular with holidaymakers, who appreciate not only the generous stretch of beach but the pier at Sandown, and the amusements at both. The sheltered, south-facing beach at Ventnor, another resort further along the coast, is reached by a precipitous road which zigzags down steep slopes into the town. In its Victorian heyday, winter visitors were attracted by Ventnor's reputation as the warmest place in the country, and tall, elegant hotels with double-decker verandahs were built to maximise the sun. Guests included Russian novelist Ivan Turgenev, Karl Marx, who convalesced here, Mahatma Ghandi, who

Right: Compton Bay

Waves lapping the sandy shoreline at Compton Bay, a good hunting ground for dinosaur fossils.

Palmerston's Follies

As you cross the Solent to the Isle of Wight on the ferry, you may spot four isolated, granite structures rising from the sea. These are not rocky islands but massive fortresses built in the 1860s on the orders of Prime Minister Lord Palmerston as part of a nationwide coastal defence system against the French navy. By the time the forts were completed, the threat of invasion had passed and, although they were rearmed later, they were never used for the purpose they were intended, hence their nickname 'Palmerston Follies'.

The four sea forts are:

1. **No Man's Land Fort** was built to protect Portsmouth and cost the princely sum of £462,500 in 1867–80. It is now owned by Clarenco (which also owns Spitbank Fort and Horse Sand Fort) and plans are afoot to turn it into a hotel.

2. **Spitbank Fort** was finished in 1878 and is smaller than Horse Sand Fort and No Man's Land Fort: it is 49m in diameter. It was declared surplus to requirements by the Ministry of Defence in 1982 and is now a luxury spa hotel with nine bedroom suites.

3. **St Helen's Fort** was built in 1867–80 to protect the St Helen's anchorage. It is now in private ownership. Every year a causeway is revealed by the lowest tide (usually occurring in the first half of August) and a walk takes place from Bembridge on the Isle of Wight to the fort.

4. **Horse Sand Fort** is, with No Man's Land Fort, one of the largest: it is 73m in diameter. Built between 1865 and 1880, it has two floors and a basement and was built on large concrete blocks with an outer skin of granite. Owned by Clarenco, there are plans to turn it into a museum.

stayed in Shelton's Vegetarian Hotel, and Alice and Edward Elgar, who honeymooned here. Many of these hotels still exist and lend the resort an air of elegance that its neighbours lack. Nearby, Ventnor Botanic Gardens also makes the most of the subtropical microclimate with many tropical plants flourishing. A footpath from the gardens leads to Steephill Cove, a delightful collection of cafés and B&Bs clustered around a sand beach.

Beyond St Catherine's Point, the most southerly point of the island (see page 153), Blackgang Chine sits at the start of a great sweep of beach that runs along the southern edge to the Needles. Due to its topography, the Isle of Wight has many chines – steep-sided river valleys that flow into the sea.

The longest stretch of road on the Isle of Wight is the A3055, also known as the Military Road, which connects the village of Chale with Freshwater Bay. Originally built in 1860 to link different forts and barracks, it runs alongside the predominantly shingle Brighstone Bay to the sandier Compton Bay (see page 153). This south-eastern

' ... the Needles are the island's most distinctive landmark.'

coastline of the island is subject to landslips driven by hydrology as water drains to the coast, with many properties obliterated over the years, including the Military Road itself, which has been rebuilt and relocated several times.

The northern half of the island: plenty of yachts and a queen's retreat

The three 30.5m chalk pinnacles that constitute the Needles (see page 154) are the island's most distinctive landmark and make a satisfying end to a walk along Tennyson Down (page 154). Those preferring a more sedentary (though just as spectacular) way to reach them, should

Left: Cowes

Royal Yacht Squadron starting cannons at Cowes Castle. There are 22 miniature bronze cannon in total, taken from George IV's children's yacht *Royal Adelaide*, which are fired to start the yacht races.

Opposite: Ventnor Downs

View of the Downs from the north-west side of Bonchurch Down in the direction of St Martin's and Shanklin Downs.

'Cowes is one of the world's greatest yachting centres hosting numerous regattas.'

try the chairlift from Alum Bay. The bay is named after the alum that was mined there (see page 59 for more about alum), and is famous for its many different coloured sands: white quartz, red iron oxide, yellow limonite and other minerals can all be seen on the beach and in the surrounding cliffs.

Every year, hundreds of gaff-rigged boats sail into Yarmouth Harbour for the Old Gaffers Festival, a three-day programme of races. Yarmouth, a little town with a pebble beach, is a natural harbour at the mouth of the River Yar and attracts boats all year including the ferry that crosses The Solent to Lymington.

The National Trust owns and manages the village of Newtown and the nature reserve that encompasses the estuary of the Newtown river and 4 miles of shoreline. The 324-hectare (800-acre) reserve has five types of habitat: saltmarsh, shingle, sand, the sea bed within the estuary, woodland and pasture, 300 species of plants and 180 species of bird (see page 158).

Split by the River Medina, the town of Cowes is one of the world's greatest yachting centres, hosting numerous regattas during Cowes Week every August, and its Royal Yacht Squadron is ranked as one of the world's most prestigious yacht clubs. The town first became fashionable in the 1890s when Edward, Prince of Wales raced yachts here. These days, Cowes Week is still part of the social 'season' and the more egalitarian annual Round the Island Race in June attracts a wide range of sailing abilities from amateur to Olympic class.

Wanting a country retreat for herself and her family, Queen Victoria asked Thomas Cubitt to build Osborne House on the outskirts of Cowes in 1845–51 to designs by her husband Prince Albert. She came to regard this Italianate house as her 'little paradise' and spent many happy times with her family there. The house remains much as the Queen left it and, due to a bequest by Edward VII in 1902, is

open to the public, who can look around Victoria's state and private apartments and even visit her private beach.

The expansive sands of Ryde, the Isle of Wight's largest town, are revealed at low tide extending for almost a mile out to sea. The town's pier was built in 1814 to breach the distance between the town and visitors arriving on boats, who previously had to trudge across the wet sand. A railway track was built to run alongside the pier and still connects travellers on the pier head with the esplanade and the eastern side of the island, and to the Wightlink catamaran service which sails between Ryde and Portsmouth.

National Trust-owned Bembridge Windmill (see page 150) overlooks Bembridge Harbour at the most easterly point of the island. The harbour, which is semi-enclosed by spits of land, provides good anchorage for pleasure craft, fishing boats and houseboats.

Above: Old Gun Battery

Tunnel leading to the parade ground and gun emplacements at the Needles Old Battery, a Victorian fort built in 1862.

Right: Osborne House

A visit to this 'little paradise' offers an intimate glimpse into Queen Victoria's family life, with access to the nursery and Victoria and Albert's private apartments.

Explore National Trust places on the Isle of Wight coast

St Helens Duver

'Duver' is an Isle of Wight dialect term for a sand dune, and the largest surviving one on the island is at St Helens. The National Trust manages this stabilised dune system which covers 15 hectares (37 acres) and has built up over hundreds of years. It provides a habitat for 250 species of flowering plants including sea campion, thrift and sea buckthorn.

The limestone ledges at St Helens are one of the best places in southern England to go rockpooling when the tide is out. Crevices provide shelter for whelks, limpets and periwinkles, sea anemones live in the pools, and sea squirts cling to the rocks. Look closely and you may also see small fish such as blennies and gobies among the seaweed and perhaps even a seahorse. Further out below the sea, are large beds of eelgrass – an important shelter for marine creatures and food for over-wintering Brent geese. Birdwatchers also come to St Helens Duver to see flocks of geese, little egret and waders overwintering in the lagoon. The open grassland and dunes are perfect spots for a picnic (the car park is close by) and for dog walking. **St Helens Duver, St Helens, Isle of Wight**

Bembridge and Culver Downs

This promontory, situated north of Sandown, is part of the same chalk ridge that forms the Needles and the cliffs of Tennyson Down in the west. From the downland cliff tops, there are fine views over Sandown Bay and the Solent and of miles of beach. There are good, level walking paths along its top, which is also a good observation point from which to view seabirds nesting in the cliffs below.

A massive granite obelisk, the Yarborough Monument, is the predominant feature in the area. It was built in memory of Charles Anderson-Pelham, the 2nd Baron Yarborough (1781–1846), who through circumstances of birth and marriage, became a large landowner on the Isle of Wight and was one of the founding

> '**The limestone ledges at St Helens are one of the best places in southern England to go rockpooling**'

members of the Royal Yacht Squadron. Also look out for Bembridge Fort, which was built in the 1860s and is owned by the Trust. It is in poor condition and is only accessed by pre-booked guided tour. **Culver Down, Bembridge, Isle of Wight**

Ventnor Downs

Rising above Ventnor to 241m, St Boniface Down is the island's highest point. Many of the south-facing slopes of the downs have been colonised by the holm oak, an evergreen tree introduced to the area by plant-hunting Victorians from the Mediterranean. The holm oak has proved to be invasive, causing butterfly and insect populations to dwindle. Rather than resort to herbicides, in 1993 the National Trust introduced Old English goats which graze on Bonchurch Down and Coombe Bottom, and are doing a fine job of stripping bark and chomping on new growth. Flower-rich turf has since established and the numbers of butterflies, such as the Adonis blue, which rely on these chalk-loving plants has increased. The hope is that they will continue to keep the spread of the holm oak at bay.

Right: Bembridge Windmill

This is the only surviving windmill on the Isle of Wight. Built around 1700, it still has most of its original machinery intact.

An early radar station was established at Ventnor in 1937 as part of the Chain Home radar network and warned of approaching German aircraft and later of V-weapons as they crossed the Channel. The station played an important part in the Battle of Britain and was bombed by Ju-87 Stuka dive bombers in 1940. During the Cold War, there was an underground nuclear operations room hidden underneath a bungalow. A few Second World War brick structures remain near the car park at Ventnor Down. **Ventnor Downs, Wroxall, Isle of Wight, PO38**

St Catherine's Down and Knowles Farm

St Catherine's Lighthouse on the southern tip of the Isle of Wight is a reminder of the dangers of the coast. In 1836, the *Clarendon* (with a cargo of rum, coconuts and turtles) was shipwrecked here with the loss of 23 lives. The lighthouse was built in response to the tragedy and began operation in 1840. It was fully automated in 1997.

On the mainland behind the lighthouse, Knowles Farm has a different place in history. It was where Guglielmo Marconi, the inventor of radio,

set up an experimental radio station in 1900. From here he made contact with his radio station at Lizard Point in Cornwall, 196 miles away, the furthest distance radio waves had ever travelled. (See also Chapter Nine.)

St Catherine's Down is an uplifting place to walk: there are views right across the island and to wooded Wydcombe valley with its ancient paths below. St Catherine's Oratory, known colloquially as the Pepperpot because of its shape, is a good starting point. Overlooking Chale Bay, it is all that remains of a fourteenth-century oratory that fell into disrepair following the dissolution of the monasteries in the sixteenth century. **Blackgang, Isle of Wight, PO38**

Compton Bay and Downs

Compton Bay is a 2-mile stretch of contrasting dark and golden sand that runs along the west coast of the Isle of Wight. Popular with surfers, windsurfers and kite surfers, it is also the place to head with a picnic, a windbreak and a bucket and spade. There is a basic toilet block and an ice-cream van in the Hanover Point car

Opposite: Compton Bay

The golden sandstone of Compton Bay eventually gives way to the white cliffs at Freshwater Bay, seen here in the distance.

Left: St Catherine's Point

A yacht sails past St Catherine's Lighthouse. The first light at St Catherine's was set up in about 1323 by one Walter de Godyton.

park but apart from that, the beach is as it has been for centuries. Many millions of years ago, though, this area was a series of muddy lagoons and was frequented by dinosaurs. They left their footprints in the mud, and their bones became fossilised over millions of years. You may find a small piece of fossilised dinosaur skeleton (it has a honeycomb structure), a piece of fossilised wood, oyster shell or ammonite if you're lucky. To see a dinosaur footprint, head to Hanover Point at low tide.

Just inland of the coast is the massive whaleback of the chalk ridge – East Afton, Compton and Brook Downs – one of the richest tracts of chalk downland in the UK, full of rare plants and butterflies including the Glanville fritillary, the Adonis blue and chalkhill blue. Brown argus and grayling can also be spotted. Since the 1940s, Brook, Tennyson and Compton Downs have been grazed by a free-ranging herd of Galloway cattle, run by National Trust tenant farmers at Compton Farm. **Compton, Isle of Wight, PO30 4HB**

The Needles Headland and Tennyson Down

Tennyson Down, named after the popular Victorian poet (see feature, below), is one of the most popular places to walk on the island. It's easy to see why Tennyson loved walking here: it is a high, wide-open, chalk grassland with views of the white cliffs and the wild sea all around. Since the 1920s, fewer grazing animals on the headland meant that ash trees grew unchecked on the north side and the number of species of flowers and butterflies diminished. The Tennyson Trail traverses the top of the downland ridge and is probably the best area of downland on the Isle of Wight for flowers and butterflies. Much of the downland has been without tree cover from the end of the Ice Age, 10,000 years ago, due to its exposed position. For more on chalk grassland, see page 101. **Tennyson Down, Totland Bay, Isle of Wight, PO39**

Right: Tennyson Down

Paragliders soar above Freshwater Cliffs at Tennyson Down.

Alfred, Lord Tennyson and the Isle of Wight

You can see why the Victorian poet Alfred, Lord Tennyson was attracted to Farringford House near Freshwater on the southern tip of the Isle of Wight. He was looking for a decent-sized house to bring his wife Emily and son Hallam that was far from the bustle of London. The family moved into the house in 1854. Emily loved its views of the sea and Tennyson its proximity to the downs, where he walked for four hours a day, composing poems in his head.

In his day, Tennyson was as famous as Queen Victoria and Gladstone and for a while Farringford offered him the privacy he required. After the success of poems such as 'The Charge of the Light Brigade' and 'The Lady of Shalott', however, the public began to congregate outside his home hoping for a glimpse of the great poet. To escape their attention, Tennyson built a bridge over the land as an escape route to the downs. A monument to Tennyson was erected after his death in 1897, and stands on the highest point of the downs where he walked.

The Needles Old Battery and New Battery

A walk along Tennyson Down will lead you to one of the Trust's most unusual properties: the Old and New Battery. Situated at the westernmost tip of the island, perched over the Needles and surrounded by the sea, the Old Battery was built in 1861–3 as one of Lord Palmerston's Forts, later to be known as his Follies (see also feature, page 145) to protect Portsmouth from invasion by the French. A spooky underground tunnel leads to a searchlight emplacement with the closest views of the Needles you will get from dry land. Talking of the Needles, note that there is a gap between the first and second stacks, which was where a fourth stack, called Lot's Wife because it resembled a pillar of salt, stood. This collapsed during a storm in 1764. On the furthermost stack you will see the Needles Lighthouse, which was built by Trinity House in 1859. A platform was dynamited from the chalk to create a water tank, coal store and cellars: a considerable feat of engineering. The lighthouse was manned until 1994 when it became fully automated.

Subsidence and worry about the cliffs crumbling, led to the building of the New Battery, higher up the cliff, in 1895. This was later used as a research centre to test space rockets from the 1950s to the 1970s.

'A spooky underground tunnel leads to a searchlight emplacement.'

Both batteries were manned during the two World Wars to defend the Isle of Wight against air attacks and to fire on German torpedo boats. **West High Down, Alum Bay, Isle of Wight**

 ## Holiday Cottage

Sitting high on the Needles headland, this row of single-storey former coastguards cottages has expansive views and is surrounded by 150 hectares (370 acres) of National Trust-owned open downland. Perfect, then, as a base to explore the island and to set off on foot for uplifting walks. 'Pomone', is slightly smaller than 'Irex' and 'Varvassi', but all offer open fires and comfortably furnished rooms. There is shared grassland outside the terrace with picnic benches to enjoy the spectacular views. For more information see www.nationaltrustcottages.co.uk.

Left: Needles Old Battery

Searchlight emplacement inside the battery provides dramatic views overlooking the Needles.

What's so special about … sea stacks?

The Needles – a row of chalk pinnacles that rise out of the sea off the western end of the Isle of Wight – are fine examples of sea stacks. Sea stacks are typically formed in horizontally bedded sedimentary rocks by hydraulic action: the force of the sea crashing against the rock. This starts to open up small cracks on the headland. The cracks get deeper, eroding into small caves. Eventually the cave wears through the headland and forms an arch. Further erosion causes the arch to collapse, leaving a pillar of hard rock standing away from the coast – the stack. The Needles and their Purbeck companions, Old Harry Rocks, form part of what was once a continuous chalk ridge running from Lulworth to the Isle of Wight until breached by the sea at the end of the last Ice Age.

Other sea stacks: Old Harry Rocks, Dorset; Sugarloaf Rock, Isle of Man; Botany Bay, Broadstairs, Kent; South Stack Cliffs, Anglesey, Wales; Rathlin Island, Northern Island.

'The lucky and patient can see black-tailed godwits and osprey'

Newtown National Nature Reserve

Situated on the north coast of the island, between Yarmouth and Cowes, Newtown is the only National Nature Reserve on the Isle of Wight. It is a rare and special place with many different habitats to explore, from the saltmarsh and wetlands surrounding the harbour to the ancient woods further inland. Unsurprisingly, it teems with wildlife. The lucky and patient can see black-tailed godwits and osprey from one of its three hides, and rare butterflies and red squirrels are frequently spotted.

Newtown has an interesting past: until 80 years ago, salt was produced here by the evaporation of seawater. In the seventeenth century, there were 14 saltpans along the coastline producing salt largely for preservation of food until mined salt and other means of preservation made the production of salt in this way redundant. To find out more about the history of the area, visit Newtown Old Town Hall, a seventeenth-century building adjoining the nature reserve.

The Town Hall has an intriguing history in itself: it was given to the National Trust by the mysterious Ferguson Gang, a group of masked young women who used fictitious names such Bill Stickers and Sister Agatha. With the aim of preserving examples of 'traditional England', a masked 'Ferguson' made a radio appeal which persuaded 600 people to join the National Trust and raised £900 in donations. They successfully bought two buildings: Shalford Mill near Guildford and Newtown Old Town Hall.

Town Lane, Newtown, Isle of Wight

Where sheep safely graze

A walk on National Trust land on the Isle of Wight may bring you face to face with a surprising eco-tool: the Hebridean Sheep. With dark brown or black wool and at least one set of horns, it is not easy to miss. These small, hardy, self-sufficient creatures were introduced by the Trust in the early 1990s to control unwanted scrub. Unlike other breeds of sheep, the Hebridean thrives on vegetation with poor energy values and leaves flowers such as orchids or cowslips alone. This makes it a vital asset in the restoration and maintenance of chalk grassland. Look out for them on St Helens Common, Bembridge Windmill, Culver Down and Ventnor Downs and at Freshwater Bay.

Right: Newtown Town Hall

This seventeenth-century town hall without a town has a fascinating history and is the only remaining evidence of Newtown's former importance, where elections were held for Members of Parliament.

A day in the life of ... *Sean Adams, West Wight Ranger*

'It's 5.30am on a crisp autumnal morning as I arrive at Newtown. First light enables me to check the Trust's flock of Hebridean sheep as they peacefully graze the small meadows of the reserve.

'I spot three red squirrels then head back home for a quick breakfast before a 4-mile run to my yard. What a commute! Down the coast road and west toward a view framed by the chalk cliffs of Tennyson Down – my destination for the day.

'Our team of six staff and volunteers tackle chalk grassland restoration in a most exposed location. We work fast to keep warm in the keen wind, reversing 100 years of neglect. The ash and thorn scrub is quick to clear. As I stop to refuel my chainsaw, the view catches my breath. This incredible island lays out before me to the east, the Solent to the north, and south the moody English Channel.

'The day draws to a close, our trailers and trucks bursting with firewood, split and ready to sell. A small part of a long-term vision has been achieved today. Hedge laying at Newtown tomorrow. Is it any wonder that I can't wait to get up in the morning?'

Shore-spotter's Guide

1

Once widespread in Southern England the **Glanville fritillary** butterfly (*Melitaea cinxia*) is now only found on the south-west coast of the Isle of Wight. Its perfect habitat is gradually eroding – warm, south-facing cliffs with only the first stages of colonisation by plants, which it finds at Compton Bay. On the nearby downland ridge, it often breeds amongst the cut or burnt gorse. It is a medium-sized butterfly with orange and black and white chequered patterns on its wings, and is a strong flyer.

2

Ninety per cent of the rare, endemic species **early gentian** (*Gentianella anglica*) is found on the Isle of Wight. Its trumpet-shaped purple flowers are found on open grassy places with light warm soil, such as Tennyson Down. It flowers earlier than others members of the gentian family, in May–June, hence its name.

3

The **shag** (*Phalacrocorax aristotelis*) looks similar to the cormorant but is smaller with dark glossy green plumage in the breeding season and a prominent crest on its head. It breeds on sea cliffs including Culver Down on the Isle of Wight, where it can be seen diving to the sea bottom for food.

'It flowers earlier than other members of the gentian family'

The large wading bird **black-tailed godwit** (*Limosa limosa*) arrives at Newtown Nature Reserve from Iceland in the winter. Its winter plumage is black and white strips on its wings: in summer it has an orangey-brown chest and belly, which is more greyish-brown in winter.

The most common seaweed on British shores is **bladder wrack** (*Fucus vesiculosus*) and it can be found in quantity at St Helens Duver, Isle of Wight. A good source of iodine, its fronds have a prominent mid rib and almost spherical bladders which usually come in pairs.

The chalk grassland whalebacks of Tennyson Down and Afton, Compton and Brook Downs are some of the loveliest downs in the UK. Flowers abound, including unusual species such as **saw-wort** (*Serratula tinctoria*), and these downs are alive with butterflies, notably huge populations of the lovely Adonis blue (*Polyommatus bellargus*) and chalkhill blue (*P. coridon*).

Tennyson Down, Isle of Wight walk

EXPERT GRADE

Distance: 7 miles (11km)

Time: 2 hours, 30 minutes to 3 hours

An invigorating downland walk with a splendid view of the iconic Needles and the chance to visit a nineteenth-century fort, a Cold War rocket test site and a monument to a Victorian poet laureate. **Note:** This figure-of-eight walk can be split into two shorter walks of 3 and 4 miles (4.5 and 7.5km).

Terrain

A figure-of-eight circuit built from 4-mile (7.5km) and 3-mile (4.5km) loops. Total ascent 450m (1450ft). Four stiles. This is an exposed headland and the winds can be ferocious. The chalk paths can be very slippery, and the path from the car park to the Tennyson Monument is steep. Do not go near the cliff edge. Dogs are welcome, but please keep them on a lead around wildlife and take any mess away with you.

Directions

① Facing the quarry, take the left-hand path out of the car park. After 45yd (40m) turn right and climb the steps by a wooden bench. The steep upward path continues through a gate to the top of the hill and the Tennyson Monument, which marks the highest point of the chalk cliffs of West Wight, 147m (482ft) above sea level.

② By the Tennyson Monument turn right and follow any of the cliff-top paths, aiming for the aerial mast visible on the skyline to the far west. Skirt the right boundary of the aerial building then head diagonally left and downwards to a concrete road, by the corner of the coastguard station. Cross over and follow the signs to the Needles viewpoint.

③ Return to the road, turn left and climb the steps on the left just beyond the coastguard station, just before the New Battery. Follow the path down to the Needles Old Battery, then the Tarmac road towards Alum Bay.

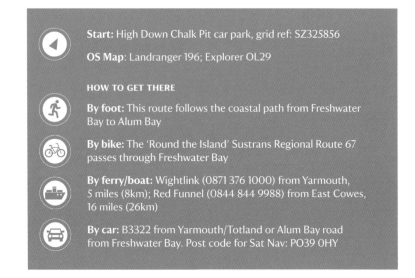

Start: High Down Chalk Pit car park, grid ref: SZ325856

OS Map: Landranger 196; Explorer OL29

HOW TO GET THERE

By foot: This route follows the coastal path from Freshwater Bay to Alum Bay

By bike: The 'Round the Island' Sustrans Regional Route 67 passes through Freshwater Bay

By ferry/boat: Wightlink (0871 376 1000) from Yarmouth, 5 miles (8km); Red Funnel (0844 844 9988) from East Cowes, 16 miles (26km)

By car: B3322 from Yarmouth/Totland or Alum Bay road from Freshwater Bay. Post code for Sat Nav: PO39 0HY

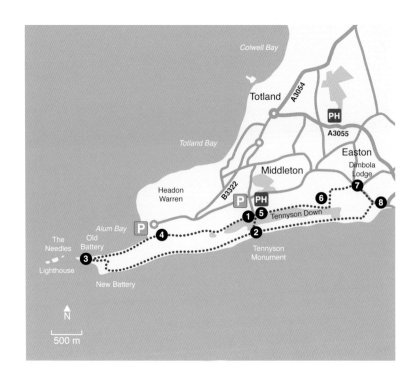

Left: The Needles

View of the Needles stacks and lighthouse from the Old Battery.

Below: Weathered sign

Sign to the rocket-testing site, which is situated in the Needles New Battery.

④ At the corner where the road bends sharply left towards Needles Park, go straight ahead and climb a few steps then cross the stile. Keep to the path along the lower boundary of the slope, with thefence on the left, passing the farm, until it starts to rise by a gate. Follow the track diagonally upwards to a beacon. Cross the stile and take the rutted path gently downhill on the left, returning to the car park after a gate. The north side of the downs is being restored to chalk grassland with gorse management and clearance of young trees. The turf is kept short by a large rabbit population and grazed by sheep and cattle.

⑤ For the longer walk, follow the outward track from the car park but go straight on instead of turning right to climb the hill. Pass through a gate and follow the path at the bottom edge of the trees, ignoring two footpaths on the left and a rising path branching right.

⑥ At a four-way junction by a marker post, turn 90 degrees left through a gate and down the bridleway. Turn right at the T-junction and go along the path, with the golf course and glimpses of Farringford on the left.

⑦ Turn right towards Freshwater Bay at the road, passing the thatched church of St Agnes.

⑧ Just after Dimbola Lodge, turn right through a gate into a field and go straight up the hill and through the gate on the skyline. Bear gently right and carry on uphill until the Tennyson Monument is reached. Turn right, head to the gap in the trees and retrace your steps down the steep path back to the car park.

Seaside things to do in Hampshire and the Isle of Wight

① Walk the Wight downs

With more paths per square metre than any other English county, it's no surprise that the Isle of Wight is deemed one of the UK's top spots for walking. Indeed, the May walking festival is the largest of its kind in the country. Exploring the island on foot gives unrivalled access to Wight's highest vantage points, cinematic views of the chalk downland and Solent, and an insight into its pivotal role in past conflicts, through the ring of batteries, beacons and forts encircling the coast. Among the Trust's self-guided trails, highlights include a route from Freshwater Bay to Tennyson Down, for the Needles and Tennyson Monument, plus butterfly- and bird-spotting walks on Compton Downs and Bembridge and Culver Downs. Or enjoy a fascinating historic ramble, encompassing wild scenery and island landmarks – among them a pillar built for a Tsar and a medieval oratory – at St Catherine's Down. For more on walking on the Isle of Wight see www.nationaltrust.org.uk/isleofwight.

② Surf and kitesurf around Compton Bay

Compton Bay to the south west is Wight's best-loved surfing beach for boarders of all abilities, thanks to the consistent swell (which can be 2–5ft in optimum conditions). There can't be many more scenic locations to learn, either, with the majestic backdrop of cliffs and downland, and views towards the Needles. It's a great patch for kite surfing, too, but to avoid conflict with swimmers and surfers, the Trust recommends heading for Brook Bay, to the east. Please note: there are no lifeguards operating regularly at Compton Bay.

Left: Isle of Wight Downs

Walking the downs at Ventnor. On the island there are self-guided trails, and guided walks by Trust volunteers, as well as a walking festival organised by the Isle of Wight Council that takes place in May.

③ Go geocaching on Bembridge and Culver Downs

If you're new to geocaching – a thrilling high-tech treasure hunt, using GPS – the Isle of Wight is a great place to start, as there are a number of caches on Trust land here, with several on Bembridge and Culver Downs. All you need to play is a handheld GPS device – and your wits. Download the coordinates of the caches (these are treasure boxes, squirrelled away) from opencaching.com or geocaching.com, or download a free geocaching app for Android or iPhone. When you've located the prize, write in the logbook (or, if you find a keepsake inside, swap it for something of yours) and replace it for another adventurer to find. For more on geocaching see www.nationaltrust.org.uk.

④ Play soldiers at the Needles Old Battery

Budding military historians can re-enact the duties of soldiers stationed at this Palmerston Fort during the two World Wars, through various interactive exhibits provided by the National Trust. Pick up one of the free discovery packs, and look out for ships in the Solent, or try on the protective gear servicemen used when handling gunpowder. Then find your way into the secret underground tunnel, and look for Major Mindup and his gunners, hidden around the Battery. An exhibition of cartoons by comic-book artist Geoff Campion helps to illustrate the wartime engagement of the site in a child-friendly way. For details of regular events see www.nationaltrust.org.uk/needles-old-battery-and-new-battery.

⑤ See Southampton's Superliners from the Hythe ferry

A ferry service has operated between Southampton and Hythe village since the Middle Ages, and today it's a fun way of joining in the port's watery rush hour and of eyeing the imposing ocean superliners, such as *Queen Mary 2* and *Queen Victoria*, at close range. Ferries depart half-hourly for the 25-minute round trip. If you're disembarking at Hythe, enjoy the 640m ride along the pier railway – the oldest working pier train in the world – before checking out the yachts in the marina.

Right: Spinnaker Tower

The tower first opened in 2005 and has become Portsmouth's most prominent landmark. The 350-degree view from the top affords views from West Wittering and Selsey Bill in the East to the New Forest to the West.

⑥ Zoom up Spinnaker Tower

This cloud-busting, sail-shaped viewing tower – a Millennium project first opened in Portsmouth Harbour in 2005 – soars up to 170m and gives visitors a 23-mile view of the south coast and surrounding countryside. There are three viewing decks (thankfully, accessed by high-speed lift), overlooking a 350-degree panorama, from Selsey Bill to the South Downs, with the Isle of Wight in between. Interactive touch screens allow you to zoom in on places of interest, and the glass-floored 'Sky Walk' at an altitude of 100m is not for the faint-hearted. Joint tickets can be purchased for the Tower and Portsmouth Historic Dockyard.

Dorset

Anyone wanting a beginner's guide to the Mesozoic era (around 250–65 million years ago), that time of geological upheaval and dinosaurs, should walk the Dorset coastline. Three-quarters of the shoreline makes up a large section of the 95 miles of the Jurassic Coast, a UNESCO World Heritage Site, whose rocks record 185 million years of Earth's history. This stretch of coastline – the result of millions of years of tectonic shift – comprises teetering stacks, top-heavy cliffs, chalk arches and lonely spits. Frequent landfalls bring fossils tumbling to the base of these unusual landforms, especially around the cliffs at Lyme Regis after stormy weather, where vigilant fossil hunters scoop them up.

The other quarter of the Dorset coast delivers traditional seaside fun in buckets and spades: the two natural harbours of Christchurch and Poole brim with boats and watersports enthusiasts, and between them Bournemouth with its sandy beaches and holiday entertainments pulls in punters by the coachload as well as conference business. For quieter attractions, the National Trust-owned Brownsea Island is a wildlife sanctuary and a safe haven for red squirrels – the perfect place to spend a day strolling and picnicking.

Dorset: beach huts and boats, and plenty of fossils

The headland of Hengistbury Head wraps its protective arm around Christchurch Harbour, creating a safe mooring for the 1,400 small boats within it. The Head packs a lot into its 2-mile length: this spit of land (known as Mudeford Spit) has a ridge of low hills, mud flats, sandy and pebbly beaches, woodland, meadow, and saltmarsh. No wonder then, that it is the most sought-after spot for beach huts in Britain, with some of its 300 privately owned huts fetching record-breaking prices. Declared a Local Nature Reserve in 1990, it is also popular with migratory birds, which stop off here in huge numbers.

Christchurch Harbour, at the confluence of the rivers Stour and Avon, is a particularly popular tourist destination, attracting 1.5 million visitors a year. Its proximity to densely populated areas combined with sandy beaches, three sailing clubs, and nature reserves, makes it a must for daytrippers or staycationers. Mudeford Quay, with its piles of lobster pots, weatherboard buildings, pub and string of beach huts is also the perfect place for a spot of crabbing. During the summer months, a ferry shuttles back and forth between Mudeford Quay and Mudeford Sandbank, dropping its passengers on the stretch of sand that adjoins Hengistbury Head at the mouth of the harbour.

A recent £12 million regeneration scheme has done much to improve the infrastructure of Boscombe/Bournemouth and has also increased its seaside attractions. Visitors have always come for its 7 miles of clean white sand and to swim in its safe waters. They have also appreciated the pleasures of its prom, theatres and abundant, well-maintained gardens. Now there is a new surf school on the beach and beach pods to hire designed by Gerardine and Wayne Hemingway.

Like many British seaside resorts, Bournemouth grew rapidly following the arrival of the railways in 1870 and with the fashion for sea bathing. Much of the existing architecture was built then: elegant villas, hotels and theatres, as were the public gardens that were built in the chines (ravines) running down to the sea.

Right: Beach hut

The huts on the stretch of sand at Hengistbury Head are much sought-after.

Below: Mudeford Quay

Lobster pots and fishing line piled up at the quay.

' … it is the most sought-after spot for beach huts in Britain'

Millionaires' Row and an adventure island

The quality of the beach on the Sandbanks Peninsula – fine golden sand that shelves safely away into the sea – and its location at the edge of Poole Harbour drew a moneyed crowd who started to build homes there in the twentieth century. (Prior to this the sandy spit was considered too precarious to build on and the only buildings were shacks.) As more expensive and exclusive properties were built, its reputation grew until it became the fourth most expensive place to live on the planet by area. It costs nothing, however, to walk along the beach and gawp at the mansions with their walls of glass and tiers of balconies that tower over the beach. A chain ferry will take you away from all this luxury to the simpler pleasures of Studland Beach (see page 187) on the other side of the mouth of Poole Harbour.

Poole Harbour is famed for being the largest natural harbour in the UK. Expansive, with safe, sheltered waters and with two main high tides and two mini high tides per day, it has all the credentials sought by yachtsmen and watersports enthusiasts. As a result, sailing clubs proliferate and its marina is packed with superyachts and lined with smart shops. The world-renowned superyacht company, Sunseeker, was founded in Poole and its headquarters are still there. The importance of sailing to the town is recognised in its Twin Sails Bridge, which opened in 2012 and has two triangular shaped leaves representing the sails of a yacht.

'… sailing clubs proliferate and its marina is packed with superyachts'

The town of Poole has an important maritime history: in the seventeenth and eighteenth centuries, boats sailed from here to cross the Atlantic to work the abundant Newfoundland fishing grounds. Poole was also one of the main departure points for the D-Day landings. As well as having the largest natural harbour, Poole also has the biggest arts centre in the UK, The Lighthouse Arts Centre, which was refurbished in 2002 at a cost of £8.5 million, and has a rolling programme of theatre, dance and music events.

At the heart of the harbour, Brownsea Island is reached by passenger ferry from Sandbanks or Poole Quay. Its 202 hectares (500 acres) of heath and woodland is owned by the National Trust and is open every day from Easter to September (see page 178).

National Trust-owned Studland Peninsula, which lies directly opposite Sandbanks, sweeps around to Old Harry Rocks (see page 178), which mark the eastern end of the Jurassic Coast. After the bustle and liveliness of Bournemouth and Poole, Studland feels open, windswept and exhilarating. The South West Coast Path runs along the nearby cliffs at Ballard Point before dropping down to the town of Swanage, a traditional family resort with a harbour and sandy beach. It was also a holiday destination and home for Enid Blyton who wrote several books here, some based at Corfe Castle (see page 188). The Coast

Above: Brownsea Island

The quayside buildings on Brownsea Island, seen from the ferry.

Opposite: Poole Harbour

The largest natural harbour in the UK is popular with sailors and watersports enthusiasts.

Path continues along the cliffs to St Aldhelm's Head with its remote and lovely thirteenth-century chapel on the southernmost point of the Isle of Purbeck (see page 196). The chapel is reputedly the first building in the world on which a radar signal was bounced back to a receiver. Purbeck limestone has shaped the landscape of sea cliffs topped with grassland and provides great opportunities for walkers, climbers and coasteerers.

An ancient landscape shaped by the sea

The wonders of the Jurassic Coast really start at Kimmeridge Bay whose cliff and foreshore contain a high proportion of Kimmeridge Clay, once the floor of an ocean during the Jurassic period. Important fossils continue to be found in the Clay but hammering is forbidden: fossils can only be collected from the beach (see page 182 for the National Trust's tips on fossil hunting). Between the layers of clay are limestone ledges that run out to sea, providing platforms from which to peer into rockpools and get close to the abundant marine life.

The almost circular Lulworth Cove was created almost 10,000 years ago by waves battering at joints in the limestone cliffs and breaking through to attack the softer clay behind. The shape of the cove deepened until the waves met the resistant chalk that forms the back wall. The resulting sheltered horseshoe-shaped bay is ideal for sunbathing, kayaking and snorkelling.

Waves also shaped Durdle Door, one of Dorset's best-loved landmarks. This natural limestone arch loops into the sea at the end of a chalk ridge and was formed by waves wearing away soft rock, leaving the harder stone behind. Eventually the arch will collapse leaving a stack similar to Old Harry Rocks (see page 178) but until then it will remain the subject of many photographs and postcards and the destination of countless coastal walks.

The Ministry of Defence owns more than 2,833 hectares (7,000 acres) of land between Lulworth and Wareham, which it uses as tank-training firing ranges. Walks through the ranges, taking in the ghost village of Tyneham – evacuated by order of Winston Churchill in 1943 and compulsory purchased by the MOD in 1948 – are permitted at weekends with visitors being advised to keep to footpaths: the threat of unexploded ordnance is a real one.

Right: Durdle Door

The natural limestone arch at the end of a chalk ridge is one of Dorset's best-loved landmarks.

The Jurassic Coast

Walk the 95 miles of the Jurassic Coast along the South West Coast Path (which runs its entire length) and you will step back in time. This stretch of coastline is an amazing guide to rocks through the ages, from the oldest at its western end to the progressively younger rocks that form cliffs further to the east. Starting from Orcombe Point near Exmouth in Devon to Old Harry Rocks in Dorset, this journey takes in the Triassic (250–200 million years old), the Jurassic (200–145 million years old) and the Cretaceous (145–65 million years old) periods, and displays many landforms including Golden Cap (see page 184) and Old Harry Rocks (see page 178), owned and cared for by the National Trust. Other notable landmarks include the natural arch Durdle Door and limestone folding at Lulworth Cove. Evidence of the area's extreme age is seen in well-preserved fossils that tumble from cliff faces after rock falls. For more on the Jurassic Coast see www.nationaltrust.org.uk/jurassiccoast.

Two unlikely neighbours

Despite being neighbours, Weymouth and Portland couldn't feel further apart. Weymouth is all Georgian seafront terraces, built to reflect the patronage of George III, and the sheltered harbour, whereas the Isle of Portland is more about quarries and angry seas lashing the rocky headland. Both places saw an upsurge in fortune during the 2012 Olympics Games and Paralympic Games: sailing events were held in Portland Harbour, and as a consequence surrounding roads and infrastructure were spruced up. The Weymouth and Portland National Sailing Academy in Portland Harbour, where the races were held, is the place to go to learn to sail or to relive memories of Olympic glories. The harbour is one of the largest man-made harbours in the world and was built in 1847 by prisoners awaiting deportation to Australia. It was a major navy port until 1992 but is now a successful commercial port.

Joining the Isle of Portland to the mainland is Chesil Beach, a 10-mile long tombolo (a spit joined to land at both ends), which spins thread-like into the sea, straight and pale. This remarkable shingle bank is 6,000 years old and is a place for gentle pleasures – picnics or sunbathing perhaps – rather than walking: it's a hard trudge across

'… many sailing ships have perished when swept on to its shore'

those pebbles. It is also a place of danger: many sailing ships have perished when swept on to its shore by south-westerlies whipping across from Lyme Bay, or have been sucked beneath the waves by its vicious undertow. During the storms of winter 2013/14, thousands of tonnes of shingle were shifted by wind and waves, hurtled against the sea wall at Chiswell and, in some cases, flung over it. The result was that the beach was reshaped – instead of sloping into the sea, it plunges steeply into the water.

The Isle of Portland is reached by driving along the A354, which runs along a causeway parallel with Chesil Beach and has wide-open sea on either side. The world-famous Portland stone is made of a white-grey limestone formed in the Tithonian stage of the Jurassic Period,

Left: Portland Bill

The lighthouse is one of three on the Isle of Portland – testament to the treacherous waters that surround it.

Left: Lulworth Cove
Landslips frequently reveal
fossils such as ammonites for
eagle-eyed hunters to claim.

from which the local houses are built: ranks of stern terraces look out towards Weymouth. Portland stone, quarried locally has the twin qualities of being weather-resistant and easy to carve, so is used extensively in monuments, statuary and architecture. It has made the area famous and can be seen in Buckingham Palace and St Paul's Cathedral and even Sydney Opera House.

At its southern tip is Portland Bill, whose three lighthouses are testament to the treachery of the waters that surround them. An ancient rock stack, Pom Pom Rock, near Portland Bill, once popular with climbers, was lost to the sea after severe battering during storms in January 2014. Ferocious pounding by waves and 70mph winds reduced the Jurassic stack to boulders.

A brackish tidal lagoon called The Fleet, tucked between Chesil Beach and the mainland, is home to wading birds, and a colony of mute swans at Abbotsbury who feed on the plentiful supplies of eel grass. This is the only nesting colony of mute swans in Britain and dates from the eleventh century when Benedictine monks reared the birds for meat. Their number rises to nearly 1,000 in winter. Abbotsbury itself is an impossibly pretty village with stone cottages, a fifteenth-century thatched tithe barn and a subtropical garden.

A town full of fossils

The handsome town of Bridport and its neighbour West Bay (Bridport's nearest harbour) made its fortune through ropemaking during the age of the sailing ship. Its proliferation of listed buildings, wide streets and lively cultural and foodie events, now attracts many second

homeowners and a regular stream of visitors. Nearby, the highest cliff in England, Golden Cap with its golden sandstone summit, is part of the National Trust's 81-hectare (200-acre) estate that takes in most of the coastline between Charmouth and Seaton (see page 184).

One of the most famous fossils found on the Jurassic Coast, an ichthyosaur (a prehistoric marine reptile like a porpoise), was discovered at Charmouth by a 12-year-old girl, Mary Anning, with her brother Joseph in 1811. Anning went on to find many other important fossils in the Lyme Regis area and her knowledge and finds played a key role in scientific research and the new scientific discipline of Palaeontology, although she was given little credit at the time.

Lyme Regis is the last coastal town in Dorset and sits on the border with Devon. With narrow streets winding past fossil shops and bow-windowed ancient inns to a harbour fronted by pastel-coloured Georgian buildings, it has a charm that attracts and inspires artists and writers. Most famously, Jane Austen had foolish Louise Musgrove falling on the steps of the Cobb (the harbour wall) in *Persuasion*, John Fowles (a resident) set *The French Lieutenant's Woman* here and artist James McNeill Whistler rented a studio in the town.

Landslips in the surrounding cliffs are frequent with each one exposing fossils in the Blue Lias clay (limestone and shale layers laid down in Triassic and early Jurassic times). In fact Black Ven to the east of the town is reputedly the largest landslip area in northern Europe. Fossil shops abound and the beaches are packed with eagle-eyed children looking for that special and often elusive ammonite.

Explore National Trust places on the Dorset coast

Old Harry Rocks and Ballard Down

The Purbeck Hills' most southerly point is Ballard Point, the headland of Ballard Down – rolling downland that overlooks Old Harry Rocks. Formed of chalk 66 million years ago, the hills cut across the Isle of Purbeck before reaching the sea. Old Harry Rocks, a stack and a stump at Handfast Point, are the sea-battered remains of the chalk ridge which surfaces again at the Needles on the Isle of Wight. Old Harry is the taller of the two stacks, and Old Harry's Wife, once a taller stack, is the stump reduced to its present state by the hydraulic action of the sea. The stacks are a popular landmark and a destination for walkers journeying from Studland Village. Hang gliders and parascenders can be seen flying overhead when conditions are favourable, and kayakers can follow an inshore trail to Old Harry from Middle Beach, Studland.

The National Trust welcomes controlled and responsible hang gliding on its land. For more on sea stacks, see page 157.

Other National Trust places to try hang gliding: Compton Down and Culver Down, Isle of Wight; Devil's Dyke, West Sussex; Cuckmere Valley, East Sussex.

Brownsea Island

Reached by passenger ferry, Brownsea Island, with its combination of woods, heathland, lagoons and rare wildlife, is the perfect place for a day of exploration and adventure. It makes sense that Robert Baden-Powell chose to hold the first Scout camp here in 1907, with 22 boys camping in the woods, practising woodcraft and other scouting skills in

Left: Sand lizard

This male, seen in the dunes at Studland, has turned a bright green colour as it's the mating season.

Right: Chalk pinnacles

The chalk stacks around Ballard Point are the battered remains of a chalk ridge that once ran to the Isle of Wight.

'The stacks are a popular landmark and a destination for walkers'

Wildlife spotting on Brownsea Island

Ranger John Lamming has lived and worked on Brownsea Island for over 30 years. He lists his wildlife highlights:

'It is difficult to choose as we have all the child-friendly wildlife – peacocks, sika deer, golden pheasant, rabbits, chickens, ducks and geese (and obviously the red squirrels). But then we have all the wildlife on the lagoon – which boasts internationally important numbers of black-tailed godwit, shelduck as well as oystercatcher, and nationally important numbers of avocet, redshank and dunlin. Oystercatchers are here throughout the season with their whistling call and bright beaks. Brownsea isn't awash with wild flowers so we chose the maritime pine as it provides food for our squirrels.' (For more on red squirrels, see page 188.)

1. **Oystercatchers** breed on the shores of Brownsea, and winter high-tide roosts on the lagoon can exceed 1,000 birds. One oystercatcher ringed on the island in 1960 was found 31 years later on the Isle of Wight.

2. There are thousand of pale **daisy anemones** buried in the soft sand around the shores of Brownsea. At low water, the tentacles retract into a gelatinous disc in the sediment, which, if touched, instantly dips below the surface to avoid being harmed.

3. **The sea slater** is a giant woodlouse-like crustacean that hides under pebbles and weed on the shore during the day, becoming active at night when it feeds on detritus.

4. Restricted in Britain to southern coastal regions, the **maritime pine** is also known as the **Bournemouth pine**. On Brownsea, the cones are eagerly sought by red squirrels which consume the seeds along with those of Scots and Corsican pines.

5. Twenty species of **dragonflies** and **damselflies** are recorded annually on the island throughout the season. Four of these are nationally scarce: small red damselfly, downy emerald, ruddy darter and hairy dragonfly.

its safe wilderness. After a chequered history in which it was occupied by the military, a pottery magnate, smart society and an elderly recluse, the island was acquired by the National Trust and opened to the public in 1963. It attracts over 110,000 visitors annually who come to enjoy its quiet attractions and wildlife: it has the UK's largest population of red squirrels, sika deer have made their home here, and the lagoon (leased and managed by the Dorset Wildlife Trust) is filled with common and Sandwich terns in the summer and a large flock of avocets in winter.

The island came into the ownership of the National Trust following the death of Mrs Bonham-Christie in 1961. She had bought the island for £125,000 in 1927 and lived a very solitary life, allowing the land to revert to wilderness, until she died aged 98. The Brownsea Island Appeal Committee was formed following rumours that the island might be developed as a marina. The Treasury agreed to accept the island in lieu of death duties and the National Trust agreed to take responsibility for it, providing a £100,000 endowment was raised. This was achieved by a variety of donors, large and small, including the John Lewis Partnership which has leased Brownsea Castle from the National Trust every year since as a retreat for its employees.
Poole Harbour, Poole, Dorset BH13 7EE (01202 707744)

Left: Brownsea Island.

Leave the quayside to discover the Lily Pond set in the woodland at Brownsea.

Right: Peacock

This glamorous bird with its fantastic plumage is one of a small population of peacocks on the island.

Name that fossil

The Jurassic Coast is rich in fossils found at the base of cliffs after rockfalls. Especially good fossil hunting is to be found on the beach at Charmouth, which has a visitor centre offering guided fossil walks. Here are some that the eagle-eyed fossil hunter might come across on the Jurassic Coast:

1 **Ammonite.** This marine animal lived in vast numbers 240–65 million years ago and became extinct along with the dinosaurs. It belonged to a group of predatory molluscs known as cephalopods, which propel themselves by squirting water out of their bodies. They lived in deep water and modern living relatives include the octopus, squid and cuttlefish. Look out for a ridged, coiled spiral. They vary greatly in size but the most likely finds will be about the size of a 5 pence piece.

2 **Brittle star.** Closely related to the starfish, there are over 2,000 species of brittle stars living today. Most are found in deep water. Not many fossils exist, as brittle stars tend to fracture after death, but if you find one it will have five long, flexible arms up to 60cm in length. It used these to move, unlike the starfish, which has hundreds of tube feet.

3 **Nautilus.** Another cephalopod, the nautilus has changed very little over the last 500 million years, but the number of species has reduced: only six remain from what were once hundreds. Dissected, the nautilus fossil looks like a chambered spiral.

4 **Ichthyosaur vertebrae.** One of the spinal vertebrae from a giant marine mammal that resembled a dolphin, this fossil is small, round and flat with an indent in the centre.

5 **Belemnite guard.** Another cephalopod, now extinct. The soft parts of the belemnite weren't fossilised but the hard parts, the guard and the phragmocone, were. Guards are found more frequently than phragmocones. Look for a long bullet, tapered at one end.

6 **Crinoid.** This marine animal has branching arms around the top of a globe-shaped structure containing the main body of the animal. They are sometimes referred to as sea lilies because of their resemblance to a plant. The most frequently fossilized part is the stem, which has a screw-like thread.

How to look for fossils

Before embarking on your fossil-hunting adventure, there are a few things to keep in mind:

1 As long as you are not in a protected area, you can pick up small fossils that are lying on the ground. Sarah Kennedy, ranger in Dorset says, 'The best, and safest, way to look for a fossil is on the beach, where the sea has washed them out and left them for you to find.'

2 Do not remove fossils from rocks or cliffs. It's best to go collecting on the shore on a falling tide to ensure that you don't get caught out by the sea.

3 Leave large fossils alone so that everyone can enjoy them.

4 Report any rare finds to museums or the closest visitor centre.

5 If you are collecting in a Site of Special Scientific Interest (SSSI), follow any rules they might have: they are there to protect geology for future generations.

Burton Bradstock and surroundings

The picturesque village of Burton Bradstock, with its thatched cottages and fourteenth-century church, is one of the main gateways to the Jurassic Coast and the South West Coast Path. Nearby, Freshwater Beach is backed by vertical sandstone cliffs that rise up to 49m and the coarse, sandy Hive Beach is a popular place for families and dog walkers. Stop for refreshment at the Hive Beach Café where you can eat seafood while gazing across Lyme Bay, or catch the annual Spring Tide Food Festival selling the best of local produce. To the east is Cogden Beach, surrounded by farmland, which is popular with anglers who fish from the shore for bass, dogfish and whiting, depending on the season. Burton Cliff has a curious ridged formation of alternate hard- and soft-layered rock, which turns golden in the sunlight.

'Burton cliff has a curious ridge formation of alternate hard and soft-layered rock'

Right: Freshwater Beach

The distinctive striated red sandstone cliffs on the beach rise up to 45m high.

Golden Cap

Named after the golden Greensand rock at its summit, this rocky outcrop, at 191m, is the highest point not only of the Jurassic Coast but of the whole of the south coast. No surprise then, that it offers spectacular views across Lyme Bay to Dartmoor, and is well worth the 40-minute walk from Seatown. Golden Cap is part of 809 hectares (2,000-acres) owned by the National Trust which, as well as truly dramatic coastline, comprises hills, fields, sunken lanes and ancient hedgerows, all within an Area of Outstanding Natural Beauty. There are 25 miles of footpaths around the estate including a circular trail through Langdon Hill Wood, home to large numbers of common blue, marbled white and pearl-bordered fritillaries in summer. Drop into the National Trust information point (also a bunkhouse) housed in a Second World War radar station to discover more and to visit the shop. There is also a popular National Trust shop situated on the esplanade in nearby Lyme Regis. **Golden Cap Estate, Morcomblake, Bridport, Dorset**

Ringstead Bay

Five miles east of Weymouth, this quiet stretch of the coast away from the more obvious attractions of Durdle Door and Lulworth Cove is worth exploring for its cliff-top paths and safe shingle beach. Walk from the National Trust car park and descend via steep, ancient tracks once favoured by smugglers, to the beach which has rockpools, sandy stretches and an offshore reef at low tide. Nearby, the chalk cliffs of White Nothe have great views of the Isle of Portland lying along the horizon like a giant marine mammal. **Ringstead, near Weymouth, Dorset DT2 8NQ**

Below: Golden Cap Estate

The view west from the top of Golden Cap with the cliffs curving away in the distance.

Right: Golden Cap

Looking along the beach from St Gabriel's Mouth to Golden Cap with the sun catching the rock face.

Left: Birdwatching

The Rees Cox Hide overlooks Little Sea, Studland, and is a great place to spend an hour or so with a pair of binoculars.

Opposite: Colourful windbreakers

With its long, sandy, gently shelving beach and surrounding dunes, Studland is a popular summer destination.

Studland Beach

On a summer's day there are few better places to be than Studland Beach. With 4 miles of white sand backed by dunes and heathland, there is plenty of space to roam and plenty of things to do. The long curve of sand is made up of South Beach, Middle Beach, Knoll Beach and Shell Bay. All have warm, shallow waters and are protected from the strong easterly winds so are ideal for swimming, snorkelling, kayaking and other watersports – kit can be hired from a shack on Knoll Beach. It is also a perfect spot for naturists who have their own 900m designated section of the beach, clearly marked with green-topped posts and blue signs.

The National Trust-run Knoll Beach Café serves food sourced from as many local producers as possible, including Currendon Farm, a Trust volunteer allotment 2 miles away.

Studland Heath, situated behind the dunes, is also owned by the National Trust and includes Little Sea, a freshwater lake that was cut off from the sea in 1880 by natural processes. This wildlife haven is inhabited by teal, mallard, little egret and heron, as well as 20 species of dragonfly. The Heath, which, with the beach and dunes, and Godlingston Heath, form a National Nature Reserve, is also an important habitat for reptiles: sand lizards (see page 178), common lizards, slow worms, grass snakes, adders and smooth snakes all live here. These were seriously threatened in August 2013 when a fire ripped through the heathland killing some lizards and destroying the habitat of others. It could take 30 years for the burnt heathland to return to its pre-fire status.

The Trust's Discovery Centre at Knoll Beach is the place to find out more about this and Studland's wildlife in general. Five hundred and fifty metres from the sea, it was built with sustainability in mind and is heated by a wood-burning stove, insulated with old phone directories and has composting toilets. **Studland, near Swanage, Dorset**

Holiday Cottage

Seaview, Studland, Dorset. This former tennis pavilion is the perfect place to return to after a day on the beach or walking the Coast Path. Its wide, wrap-around verandah is an ideal spot in which to sip a drink in the cool of the evening while watching the light dim over the ocean. South Beach is a 180m stroll across the large enclosed garden,

Red squirrels (*Sciurus vulgaris*)

Small, shy and tawny coloured with tufty ears, the red squirrel is one of nature's most charming creatures. Which means that its nationally decreasing numbers are especially dispiriting. The arrival of the more resilient grey squirrels from America, which often carry squirrel pox but are immune to it (red squirrels are not), has meant that numbers of this UK native have reduced to 140,000, compared with 2.5 million grey squirrels. More than 200 red squirrels live on Brownsea Island, a safe haven rich in the food they love and with plenty of tree canopy to hide and nest in (and free from grey squirrels). Here are five things you may not know about them:

1. Their nests are called dreys and are often found in forks of tree trunks.

2. Red squirrels are mostly solitary, only coming together to mate, but sometimes share their dreys in winter for extra warmth.

3. Red squirrel's young are called kittens. There are usually 2–3 kittens in each litter but there can be as many as 6.

4. They are seed eaters, especially those found in pine, larch and spruce trees. They also eat some fungi, shoots, and fruits of shrubs.

5. You are most likely to spot them in autumn as they hunt for seeds and nuts on the woodland floor.

and Studland Village with its friendly pub is a short walk away. Inside, tongue-and-groove walls, iron bedsteads and rattan furniture give it a gracious, faintly colonial vibe. For more information see www. nationaltrustcottages.co.uk.

Corfe Castle

Enid Blyton visited Corfe Castle in 1940, and it's thought the towering ruins gave her the idea for Kirrin Castle, which appears in her Famous Five books. The thousand-year-old fort withstood two Civil War sieges (defended by the brave Dame Mary Bankes) before being partially destroyed by Parliamentarian forces in 1646. It continues to provide fuel for the imagination today, with its 'murder holes' and resident ravens. Don't restrict your visit to the castle; the National Trust also looks after much of the beautiful coast and countryside that surrounds it. Explore Corfe Common and Hartland Moor nearby on a Wildlife Walk and keep your eyes peeled for common lizards, pyramidal orchids and common blue and meadow brown butterflies. **The Square, Corfe Castle, Wareham, BH20 5EZ (01929 481294)**

Below: Outer Gatehouse

This is part of Corfe Castle's defensive system of walls and mural towers.

Right: Corfe Castle

Rising out of the dawn mist, the castle looks suitably romantic.

Kingston Lacy

Following the demise of Corfe Castle, this grand seventeenth-century mansion was built as the Bankes family's new ancestral home. It was extended and adapted in the early 1800s by William Bankes, who added Italianate features such as the Carrara marble staircase. His travels through Europe and the Middle East resulted in the largest private collection of Ancient Egyptian artefacts in the UK, such as the 6.5m obelisk in the grounds. The opulent decorative scheme complements the works of old masters, such as Rubens, Titian and Tintoretto. Outdoors, the grandeur continues through the Edwardian Japanese tea garden and 3,440-hectare (8,500-acre) estate with its Iron Age hill fort and water meadows.

Wimborne Minster, BH21 4EA (01202 883402)

'The opulent decorative scheme complements the works of old masters'

Below: The Parterre Garden

The formal garden is one of several fascinating areas to explore in the 3,440-hectare (8,500-acre) estate.

Right: Kingston Lacy

This grand seventeenth-century mansion was built as the ancestral home of the Bankes family.

Shore-spotter's Guide

1

'**Oystercatchers** (*Haematopus ostralegus*) always make me smile when I see them,' says Ranger Robin Cottrell. 'They always seem immaculately groomed come rain or shine. Their striking orange bills contrast with their smart black and white feathers. I often see them in pairs "fishing" together and noisily calling to one another with their beautiful "*pe pe pe pe pe*" calls. They are always a welcome sight.'

2

'The great thing about the **Brent goose** (*Branta bernicla*), is that it acts almost as a barometer in terms of the changing of the seasons. The birds winter over here, so when they arrive we know that we have reached autumn. Similarly, when they leave we know that spring is around the corner. And then there's the sight of them flying in V formation: impressive at any time of the year.'

3

'My favourite sight is **bottlenosed dolphins** (*Tursiops truncatus*) moving across the bay. They can sometimes be seen through our telescope at Middle Beach, breaching the bow wave of passing boats as they leave Poole harbour. A wonderful sight if fortunate enough to spot them.'

4

'My favourite flower selection is quite broad: it is the heathland behind the sand dunes at Shell Bay. During the summer when the heath is in flower, it is a mass of vibrant purples and violets. I love to stand on top of the dunes looking across as the sun sets. Such landscapes are unfortunately becoming rarer and rarer across Dorset due to mismanagement and/or development.'

(5)

'We are lucky enough to have all six native UK species of reptile at Studland and the **slow worm** (*Anguis fragilis*) is probably my favourite. Although it looks like a snake, it is actually a lizard without legs. They are beautiful little creatures with strikingly shiny skin and can often be seen basking in the early morning or evening sun.' Insects abound, including sizeable populations of **grayling** (*Hipparchia semele*) and silver-studded blue (*Plebejus argus*) butterflies, and Purbeck's own specialist biting fly, the black deerfly (*Chrysops sepulcralis*).

As recommended by Beach Ranger
Robin Cottrell *(Studland)*

Old Harry Rocks walk

BEGINNER GRADE

Distance: 3.5 miles (5.5km)

Time: 1 hour to 2 hours

Breathtaking views of the Jurassic coast and unique rock formations await you on this circular pub walk.

Terrain

This is a fairly gentle walk, normally with good conditions underfoot. One steady climb up to Ballard Down. Beware of sheer cliff edges on and approaching Old Harry. Dogs welcome under close control.

Directions

1 From the car park walk down the road past the Bankes Arms pub and turn left by the public toilets on to the path signed for Old Harry. Look out for rectangular earthworks in the woods near Old Harry – they are the remains of fields used by Celtic farmers.

2 From Old Harry follow the Coast Path up a gentle rise, keeping well back from the sheer cliff edge. Old Harry and the remains of Old Harry's Wife, have been carved by the action of the waves. Together they form one of Dorset's most famous landmark. Savour the fine views across Poole Bay to Bournemouth, Hengistbury Head and the Isle of Wight.

3 At the first gate, keep to the cliff-top path. There's a good variety of chalk grassland flowers in the short turf, but you'll need to go down on hands and knees to best appreciate them. Look back to enjoy a fine view of the Pinnacle stack. Also look out for peregrine falcons circling high above.

4 Go through a farm gate and head straight on past the earthworks and along Ballard Down.

5 Just before the stone bench marked 'Rest and be thankful', where the main paths cross, turn right down the hill back towards Studland.

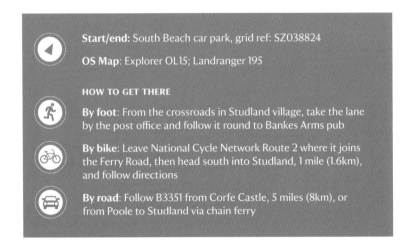

Start/end: South Beach car park, grid ref: SZ038824

OS Map: Explorer OL15; Landranger 195

HOW TO GET THERE

By foot: From the crossroads in Studland village, take the lane by the post office and follow it round to Bankes Arms pub

By bike: Leave National Cycle Network Route 2 where it joins the Ferry Road, then head south into Studland, 1 mile (1.6km), and follow directions

By road: Follow B3351 from Corfe Castle, 5 miles (8km), or from Poole to Studland via chain ferry

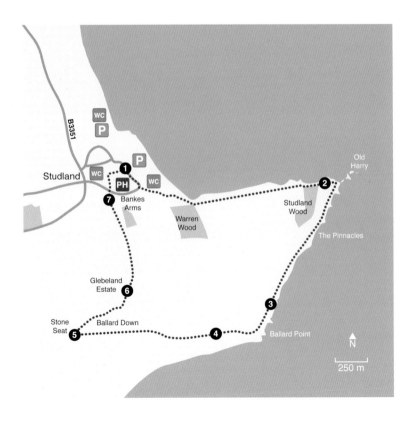

6 Follow the road down through the Glebeland Estate.

7 Go straight on at the crossroads, following the sign for the church. On your right is the village cross, which was erected in 1976. The carvings depict a range of images both ancient and modern.

8 At the end of the lane, go through the gate into the churchyard. Pass the church on your right then turn immediately right and follow the footpath back to your starting point.

Above: Old Harry Rocks

Old Harry and his Wife (now just a stump) lie just off Handfast Point.

The coastal path

From schoolboys' plunge pools to shingle spits and mudflats, an abiding love of walking the British coast has led **Christopher Somerville** to some incredibly atmospheric places.

There was no coast where I grew up. You didn't catch the smack of salt or the cry of herring gulls in the flat country of the River Severn where the great river began to snake and broaden out towards Gloucester. But each spring, King Severn would rise from his bed and come visiting, advancing across 2 miles of medieval ridge and furrow into our village, drowning roads, floating hedges, islanding cattle and houses. It was a whisper, dilute but seductive, from the far-off sea.

That sea-less childhood in the Severn Vale planted the seed of my abiding love of walking the coasts of Britain. A strong naval tradition in my family gave me a romantic attachment to the sea, something salty and undeniable in the blood, even in the face of my abject incompetence in any kind of boat. And the love affair was sealed by the sort of reading an imaginative small boy would do – *Swallows and Amazons* at Pin Mill on the Suffolk coast, *Tarka the Otter* battling a harsh Devon winter on Braunton Burrows, smugglers slipping by moonlight through the Essex mudflats or into a Cornish cove. Creeks and coves, guts and pills, saltings and dunes: I had no idea what such exotic things were, but I knew they'd be wonderful and magical once I found them.

The first time I actually met the sea, I met it literally head-on, diving at eight years old into the swimming pool at Dancing Ledge on the Isle of Purbeck. The Isle isn't really an isle; it is a quarry-scarred peninsula on the coast of east Dorset. And Dancing Ledge's so-called swimming pool is a rough-edged hole that was blasted out of a flat rock pavement at the sea's edge a hundred years ago to make a tidal plunge for local schoolboys. You have to walk to get there, at first over stony fields, then along a slippery quarryman's path above the sea. Crimson sea anemones and acid-green sea lettuce cling to the sides of the pool, and the water emanates a wavery green-blue light, beguiling and strange.

Above: Dancing Ledge, Isle of Purbeck

This beguiling landscape was the first coastal path walked by Christopher Somerville.

'Grey sky, black rocks and green sea – crouching on the tapering ledge, I wanted nothing more than this.'

Lonely shores and the quiet progress of nature

Since I first walked at Dancing Ledge I must have wandered thousands of miles on foot by the sea margins of these enchanted islands of ours. If there is such a wild variety of geography, geology, natural life and human history packed into such a manageable compass anywhere else in the world, I'd be astonished. And it has always been the lonely parts that have most strongly drawn me – the bony ribs and the out-jutting elbows of the coast. Crunching across the pebble ridges of Orford Ness, a great angular shingle spit that lies off the Suffolk coast, you come to a scatter of buildings, Chinese pagodas by appearance, their slanting roofs heaped with flint cobbles tossed there by storms. They are the hulks of abandoned laboratories, where atomic bombs were experimented upon in dead secret at the height of the Cold War. Walking here under a heavy October sky and looking round at the empty beach, the level clouds and dark horizontal coast, I might be the last man in a post-apocalyptic world.

Another location that does not feature on any chocolate box is the Durham coast, once blighted and fouled by coal-mining spoil. I used to bike out there from Durham city as a student, part appalled and part captivated by the black beaches and grey waves thick with sea coal and sewage. Skeletal gantries spewed showers of spoil into the sea, to be washed back onto the beaches where it formed a cliff of compacted pit waste, taller than a man, known to locals as 'minestone'. Now this forgotten coast with its bird-haunted denes or limestone canyons has been painstakingly cleaned up and regenerated as a wildlife haven and walkers' delight. You can wander the trails down Hawthorn Dene in spring through pungent drifts of white-flowered wild garlic, watching tree creepers patter up the ash trunks in search of insects, and emerge among early purple orchids in the little cove of Hawthorn Hive where the sea is gradually nibbling the minestone cliff to nothing. The sight of nature quietly and inexorably undoing the handiwork of man in this way is a salutary one, and reassuring at a time when ecological angst continually hums its ominous background note.

Between the sea wall and the enormous sky

Some coastal walks are more edgy than others. A couple of years ago I was walking a stretch of National Trust coast on the peninsula of Islandmagee in County Antrim. I went off track, partly by design and partly by accident, and found a secret doorway in the cliff, a black arch labelled in large, faded gold letters 'The Gobbins'. Beyond, a rough rock-cut stairway led up to a precarious shelf where salt-rusted iron stanchions had once supported a safety rail. It was all that remained of a Victorian marvel, a walkway of cast-iron bridges and cliff flywalks where ladies with parasols could teeter out in delicious fear above the waves that smacked against the rocks a hundred feet below. Grey sky, black rocks and green sea – crouching on the tapering ledge, I wanted nothing more than this.

I think in the end it's loneliness I search for when I walk at the edge of the sea – loneliness and strangeness, a proper sense of being 'out there'. Maybe that, too, is a legacy of a childhood spent roaming the fields and orchards

Above: Horden Beach

The Durham coast has been cleaned up and regenerated as a wildlife haven.

of an out-of-the-way corner of ground. I love the bleakness of the Essex coast, out beyond Rochford and Maldon, out where the Saxon chapel of St Peter-ot-the-Wall stands guard over the Brent geese and sandpipers picking along the tideline, and the brown seals loll like fat old bathers on the mud flats. Something calls to me there as nowhere else, a proper sense of myself as a very tiny organism, only a part of a huge whole. There between the sea wall and the enormous sky I find what I am looking for.

Christopher Somerville has spent 25 years writing and broadcasting about country walks and other rural matters. He is the author of several books including Somerville's 100 Best British Walks, *and* Britain and Ireland's Best Wild Places.

Seaside things to do in Dorset

1 Go beach riding at Studland

One of the most thrilling ways to experience the 4-mile expanse of Studland Beach – also a prime spot for swimming, kayaking, kite surfing and diving – is on horseback. Riders can drink in the views out to Old Harry Rocks and the Isle of Wight while trekking along the tideline. Then there's the network of bridleways to explore through the heathland behind and chalk ridge above, overlooking the Jurassic Coast. Daily permits are available for beach riding (www.nationaltrust.org.uk) between 1 October and 30 June. Always respect other beach users and the environment, and check tide tables beforehand. For more information see www.nationaltrust.org.uk/studland-beach.

Below: Horse riding

A network of bridleways runs through Godlingston Heath, Studland.

2 Build a den at Brownsea Island

Brownsea Island is the go-to place for families to re-engage with the natural environment. From self-guided orienteering trails to overnight camping, there are all kinds of opportunities for an outdoor escapade, and to take a break from hi-tech living. Pick up a free tracker pack from the visitor centre for a ready-made child-friendly tour of the site. Or, for something a bit different, join the rangers for one of their regular den-building days – these are designed for parents and children to take part in together, using natural materials found on the island. For dates and more details see www.nationaltrust.org.uk/brownsea-island or call 01202 707744.

3 Catch a fish at Hive Beach

Framed by Jurassic cliffs, the shingle strand of Hive Beach at Burton Bradstock is a picture-perfect launchpad for aspiring sea anglers (and is popular with more experienced fisherfolk, too). You can fish from the shore here, using a net or a rod, and also at Cogden, heading eastwards along Chesil Beach. Mackerel are the most sought-after catch during the summer months (note: always return rare, endangered or undersized fish to the sea). Then, after a hard day's casting, you can hang up your tackle and try some local seafood at the Hive Beach Café. The National Trust recommends keeping away from the busy area in front of the café when angling – use the area towards Cogden instead – and asks that you take all litter home with you. For more information see www.nationaltrust.org.uk/burton-bradstock.

4 Take a wildlife walk at Purbeck

A coastal walk through the Purbeck countryside has an added frisson, due to the presence of various fork-tongued creatures. All six native species of British reptile (including adders and slow worms) can be found in the area: keep an eye out for rarities such as the sand lizard and smooth snake. The best time for spotting them is April/May, when they emerge from hibernation and are still relatively slothful. (This is also when the male sand lizard turns vivid green to attract females.)

Check out sunny spots on the dunes and heaths, where they like to bask in the warm rays. The birdlife here is another big draw, and there are hides on the heathland and overlooking Poole Harbour for eyeing avocets, meadow pipits and stonechats. Take your pick from more than 20 walks designed by the Trust through this wildlife-rich landscape. For more information see www.nationaltrust.org.uk/purbeck-countryside.

⑤ Sail around Weymouth and Portland

In the wake of the Olympics, the Dorset coast has become one of the UK's top spots for sailing, and you'll get the best views of the striated cliffs and show-stopping geological features, such as Lulworth Cove, from a boat. It's possible to take RYA courses, for all ability levels, at the Weymouth & Portland Sailing Academy, which was the host venue for the London 2012 sailing events. Visiting boat owners, meanwhile, might want to make use of Portland Marina. At the National Trust beach at Studland, where the sheltered waters also make for ideal sailing conditions, there is a selection of boats available for hire from Studland Watersports, some suitable for beginners, others for more seasoned sea dogs.

⑥ Find out about fossils on the Jurassic Coast

Following Mary Anning's famous 1811 discovery of the first complete ichthyosaur at Lyme Regis, the town has attracted many fossil hunters, with the rocks yielding all manner of prehistoric flora and fauna, from

Above: Camping on Brownsea

Pitching a tent is just one of the outdoor activities to be enjoyed at Brownsea Island.

fossilised fish, wood and ammonites to a long-necked plesiosaur. To find out more about the shoreline's sizeable history, and to have a go at fossil collecting yourself, join in one of the regular expert-led walks run by either Lyme Regis Museum or Charmouth Heritage Coast Centre. Who knows what you might come home with? See pages 19 and 182 for advice on collecting fossils.

Island of adventure

Head Ranger Reuben Hawkwood's favourite things to see and do on Brownsea Island.

1 Go for a stroll. 'There are 8 miles of trails crisscrossing the island, and we are constantly trying to improve them. For the 50th anniversary in 2013, we cut a winding path into pine trees in the middle of the island. We call it The Maze. It's magical.'

2 Climb a tree. 'There's a tree-climbing trail on the island which is a lot of fun. We are also building a natural play area near the heath: stepping stones and ropes. The opportunities to explore – just like Enid Blyton's Famous Five – are endless. Enid Blyton refers to Brownsea as both Whispering Island and Kirrin Island.'

3 Watch a play. 'Every summer there is a three-week Shakespeare theatre run on the field by the church put on by Brownsea

Open Air Theatre (BOAT). In 2013 our volunteers put on *Pericles* and *A Midsummer Night's Dream*; 4,000 people came to the performances. '

4 Enjoy the beach. 'There are three cracking beaches on Brownsea – Castle Beach, which belongs to the castle, South Beach and Maryland. Hardly anyone ever seems to spend much time on Maryland but it's glorious. In summer we get up to 2,000 visitors a day but Maryland is never, ever busy.'

5 Have a snack. 'Our local Villano café has stunning views across Poole Harbour. A new manager took over two years ago and the food really is fantastic and draws on lots of local produce. I'm a vegetarian but I'm told the venison stew is out of this world. They serve hot and cold lunches, sandwiches, cakes and their famous cream teas throughout the day.'

Somerset
and Devon

Devon stretches across the south-west of England, the only county to boast two quite separate and quite distinct coastlines. In this chapter we travel along the north coast first and marvel at its giddying sea cliffs and headlands riven by forested valleys, dropping in on the Victorian resorts of Ilfracombe, Lynmouth and Lynton as we go. To the east, Somerset's coastline of mudflats, estuaries, vast beaches and shingle shores continues to be shaped by the huge tides that funnel down the Bristol Channel, often causing severe flooding. Huge volumes of water, such as those that hit Somerset in the winter of 2013/14, present challenges for the National Trust, which prefers to manage the situation using natural processes; for example diverting surface water and planting wet woodland, rather than building man-made defences.

We then move to South Devon, which is all about rose-coloured cliffs, elegant seaside architecture and the palm trees and grand hotels of the English Riviera. This is a coastline that caters for many different tastes: head to Sidmouth for mind-clearing coastal walks; Brixham for a fresh fish supper; and Torquay for sub-tropical plants and yachts moored in the harbour.

Somerset and North Devon: where the Bristol Channel meets the ocean

In haste to get to the more popular counties of Devon and Cornwall, many ignore the beauty of the Somerset coastline. Unfurling into the Bristol Channel from the Severn Estuary, it possesses wildlife-rich mudflats and saltmarsh, yawning expanses of sandy beaches, dramatic cliffs dropping to shingle shores, wooded valleys and delightful, old-fashioned resorts.

This is a shoreline shaped by the power of the ocean as it funnels its way into the 50-mile long estuary. Huge tides sweep along the estuary's length, creating strong currents and whirlpools, then power back again towards the Atlantic, exposing vast areas of glistening mud (which become sand near Weston-Super-Mare) as they retreat. In some places a 2-mile stretch of sand is revealed at low tide while, inland, a web of drainage ditches reclaims land from the sea.

These huge tides – up to 50ft under the Severn Bridge – mean that the tidal range here is the second highest in the world (second only to the Bay of Fundy in North America). During the spring and autumn equinoxes, high tides can reach 9ft and surge up the River Severn creating the famous 'bore', a wall of water big enough to be surfed. Knowledge of the tides is essential for all seafarers if they are to avoid being swept out to sea or stranded in the mud. The seabed is littered with the wrecks of vessels that didn't make it.

The flat landscape of the Somerset Levels, a coastal plain and wetland area in central Somerset, suffered severe flooding during the winter storms of 2013/14. Lying only 6m above sea level, they have always been prone to flooding from fresh water and, less often, the sea. Heavy rainfall caused the River Parrett to overflow and the water sat on the clay levels covering 6,879 hectares (17,000 acres) of land for over a month.

A city and a resort

Bristol, situated near midway along the estuary, is a city founded on seafaring. One of the world's greatest ports in the seventeenth and eighteenth centuries, its fortune was made through the trading of sugar, rum, slaves and tobacco. Maritime commerce is still very much in evidence in the harbour, which was the original Port of Bristol and is now the cultural hub of the city. Galleries, restaurants and arts centres may have replaced warehouses and workshops, but historic boats, including the SS *Great Britain* designed by Isambard Kingdom Brunel,

Right: Porlock

The groynes are part of the old (failed) coastal defence. The National Trust prefers to work with nature not against it.

Below: Clevedon Court

Built for Sir John Clevedon in 1320, this is one of the few houses of the period that has survived intact.

'The poet Samuel Taylor Coleridge lived nearby and walked the hills'

are permanently berthed there. Brunel also designed the suspension bridge, which opened in 1864 and spans the Avon Gorge. Nearby, in Clifton, elegant eighteenth-century buildings were once residences of wealthy merchants and ship owners.

Clevedon, further along the coast, saw its fortunes change when wealthy Bristol merchant Sir Abraham Elton bought Clevedon Court in 1709. What had been a fishing village became a fashionable destination as smart society came to visit. The resort continued to expand into the nineteenth century with the addition of elegant buildings and a splendid pier, now Grade I-listed, which opened in 1869.

Weston-super-Mare is a town that teaches patience: at low tide, the sea is a mile from the seafront. Although most of the beach is sand, mudflats are exposed the further the tide ebbs, and it's risky to venture that far out. Better instead to wait for its return and go for a swim, or stay on the beach and enjoy the new Grand Pier (built in 2010 to replace the previous one which had been destroyed by fire) and the annual Sand Sculpture Festival.

Sweeping sands

Burnham-on Sea faces Bridgwater Bay along the shore from Weston. Here the coastline changes as the Severn Estuary becomes

the wide-open Bristol Channel. Low tides reveal 7 miles of sand, which sweep along to the National Trust-owned Brean Down (see page 210) and seabird-friendly mudflats (see feature, below) where the River Parrett joins the Channel. The Mendip and Quantock Hills frame the coastline, which is fringed with small bays. Once a popular resort, Burnham (which has the shortest pier in the country) boasts a 9-legged lighthouse and views of the Welsh coast.

Clean, flat sand really begins at Minehead, the basis for its popularity as a holiday destination and its mile-long promenade. The tide still goes out a long way – 1.5 miles – but here the shore is free from mud; instead there is sand, scattered pebbles and the possibility of seeing the exposed stumps of fossillised trees from ancient forests.

Nudging the Devon border, the village of Porlock is set in a deep hollow flanked by hills and is reached by descending steep gradients and tricky bends. The poet Samuel Taylor Coleridge lived nearby and walked the hills with William Wordsworth: their route is commemorated as the Coleridge Way. Porlock is now landlocked but Porlock Weir, a harbour protected by a shingle spit, is popular with families off to catch crabs and to paddle.

Above: Coleridge Cottage

The Somerset home of the poet Samuel Taylor Coleridge between 1797 and 1800.

Opposite: Porlock Bay

Part of the Holnicote Estate, this farmland coastline includes new saltmarsh habitat created from coastal realignment.

What's special about mudflats?

Bridgwater Bay National Nature Reserve is one of the biggest intertidal mudflats in Britain. But what are mudflats and why should we value them?

Mudflats are generally found in sheltered bays and estuaries where sediments such as silts and clays are deposited by tides and rivers. The action of tides, waves and currents prohibits the sediment rising high enough for plants to establish and grow, but the high organic content washed in by the sea and rivers provides food for wildlife. Consequently, mudflats have no vegetation but plenty of marine life.

The days when mudflats were reclaimed from the sea and drained for use as agricultural land are largely over. The value of these stretches of wetland for wildlife and biodiversity is now recognised and many are nature reserves and carefully managed. They are also recognised for the part they play in preventing coastal erosion: their long, low, sloping profile causes waves to lose energy gradually and peter out before reaching dry land. However, they are still under threat from rising sea levels, pollution, dredging and land claimed for urban development.

What lives in a mudflat? Worms such as lugworms and ragworms; shrimps, prawns, mud shrimp; crabs; shellfish such as cockles, mud snail and laver spire shell. Migratory birds such as godwits, knots, spotted redshanks and curlew sandpipers come here to feast on these worms and shellfish.

Other mudflats: the Wash, the Solway Firth, the Mersey Estuary, Strangford Lough, Morecambe Bay.

Vertiginous cliffs and rugged headlands

The North Devon coastline is where lofty and expansive Exmoor drops dramatically and raggedly to the sea. The cliffs on the western edge of Countisbury Common – 302m above sea level and said to be highest in England – unfailingly startle as you motor around an acute bend and find the land in your peripheral vision falls away entirely.

These series of lofty, gorse-clad cliffs and headlands are interspersed by deep, forested valleys and roads that wriggle towards the sea. Lynmouth, a sheltered harbor, is reached either by a 1-in-4 road or a water-powered funicular railway (see page 230), which propels you vertically down the cliff (and back up again) from Lynton. Percy Bysshe Shelley eloped to this fishing village with his 16-year-old bride Harriet (who later drowned herself after he deserted her for Mary Wollstonecraft). Enchanted by steep, leafy, sunken valleys, Shelley and other Romantic poets sung its praises, and the Victorians named it 'Little Switzerland'. Its gorge-like valleys were the town's worst enemy, however, when in August 1952, 90 million gallons of rainwater fell in a single night and funnelled towards the sea, carrying away buildings and claiming many lives.

Below: Romney sheep

These animals, which graze at Morte Point, are an important element in heathland management.

Limitless horizons

The National Trust owns most of the coast between Ilfracombe and Woolacombe, and as a result, it is largely undeveloped. After it sweeps past the Victorian resort of Ilfracombe and around the lighthouse at treacherous Morte Point and the surrounding grassland, gone are the rocky coves and shingle beaches, replaced instead with mile-upon-mile of mind-clearing, expansive sand. Three fine beaches – Saunton Sands, Croyde Bay and Woolacombe Beach – are where dogs run free, sandcastles are built, windbreaks protect sunbathers, and surfers spend the day waiting for the right wave. At low tide, big skies and limitless horizons are reflected in glistening sand. So much space means that the beaches rarely seem crowded or noisy – the only sounds to be heard outside the summer months are the boom of the Atlantic Ocean and the squawk of a gull.

Alongside this expanse of sand, runs one of the country's largest dune systems, Braunton Burrows, which forms a spine along the back of Saunton Sands. Running for 3 miles with dunes of up to 30m high, it has been designated a UNESCO Biosphere and Area of Outstanding Natural Beauty (AONB) and is rich in wild flowers and migratory birds. The River Taw Estuary, whose muddy creeks run into the sea beside it, is home to large flocks of waders and waterfowl.

Writers and darlings

Beyond Westward Ho! (named after an adventure story by Charles Kingsley and the only place name in Britain with an exclamation mark) lies Bideford Bay, a coastline of cliffs, valleys and ancient woodland that inspired Rudyard Kipling who attended college in Westward Ho!. National Trust-owned Peppercombe Valley is car-free and attracts visitors looking for orchids, butterflies, deer and badgers as they head towards its secluded beach. Also look out for The Cabin, an artistic retreat at the fishing village of Bucks Mills kept in its original condition by the National Trust.

'... gorse-clad cliffs and headlands are interspersed by deep, forested valleys'

The annual Herring Festival in the village of Clovelly is a strong reminder of its fishing past when the 'silver darlings' were a prime source of income. Fresh fish is still sold in this enchanting village, whose cobbled streets (paved with pebbles from the beach) fall away down the side of a valley to the sea, but it now relies on its visitors for revenue. It's traffic-free, so leave the car at the visitor centre and amble down the steep narrow streets, past window boxes billowing with flowers, white-washed cottages until you reach the pretty harbour and what feels like a different era entirely.

Above: Morte Point

Woolacombe and the village of Morthoe can be seen in the distance.

Explore National Trust places on the Somerset coast

Brean Down, near Weston-super-Mare

Protruding into the Bristol Channel, this 1.5-mile long limestone headland – described as Somerset's greatest natural pier – is the place to head for a blustery walk with panoramic views across the Somerset levels and sand flats. Its 64 hectares (159 acres) have been owned by the Trust since 1954 and boast a Palmerston Fort at the tip. Built in 1867 against a potential French invasion, the fort housed 50 men before being abandoned in 1900 following a magazine explosion.

Follow a steep path down to the beach and the Cove Café for refreshments, keeping an eye open for feral goats clambering about on the rocks and peregrine falcons hanging in the sky above. In high summer, the white rock rose, dwarf sedge and Somerset hair grass festoon turf on the southern slopes, an almost unique community of vegetation.

The Down's history also stretches much further back in time: the remains of a Roman temple were excavated here on the second highest point in 1964 and were dated to around AD 340. Its foundations are just visible. And those mounds and bumps you may come across as you walk the south side of the Down are burial mounds dating to the Bronze Age (1900–800 BC). **Brean, North Somerset**

Sand Point and Middle Hope, near Weston-super-Mare

Smaller than Brean Down but no less lovely, this headland north of Weston-super-Mare offers a shortish walk to the end of the point and back, with views across Sand Bay (which earns its name at low tide when the sea retreats for more than a mile). Nearby is Woodspring Priory, a handsomely restored medieval building that belongs to Landmark Trust and is available to rent. There are plenty of birds to spot on the headland: alongside seabirds, keep an eye out for

Left: Brean Down

The ancient church of St Nicholas looks out across the Down to the Somerset Levels and sand flats.

Above: Horner Wood

One of the largest blocks of entirely semi-natural woodland in England, situated on the Holnicote Estate.

swallows, greenfinches and skylarks who nest in the scrub. The scrub also provides an ideal habitat for butterflies such as gatekeepers and skippers and the hummingbird hawk-moth which feeds from the flowers of lady's bedstraw. **Brean, North Somerset**

Holnicote Estate, near Minehead

Set within Exmoor National Park, the coastal paths, pretty villages and saltmarshes of Holnicote are ideal for outdoor enthusiasts. Over 100 miles of footpaths, including one around Hurlstone Point (perfect for a spot of sunset-watching over the Bristol Channel) will keep ramblers occupied, and those who wish to relax can enjoy picnics on the shingle beach or a cream tea in the village of Selworthy.

Horner Wood on the Estate is an ancient wood pasture that was once used to produce wood for fuel and fodder for stock. It still has several oak pollards (trees cut back regularly to encourage foliage) that are 400 years old. The dead trunk of a former pollard is known as a hulk, and is valuable for wildlife. **Near Minehead, Somerset**

The challenges of flooding in Somerset

As sea levels rise, coastal habitats are subject to flooding and erosion, especially where they lie in front of man-made sea defences. Sometimes this is good news: in Porlock Bay the breaching of the shingle bar by a severe storm in 1996, created a new habitat: saltmarsh and lagoons that now attract waders, ducks and plants that had previously been rare or even completely absent.

The National Trust works with nature rather than against it. It prefers to manage the huge volumes of water created by severe flooding (as hit Somerset in the winter of 2013/14) by respecting natural processes to slow the water down rather than by man-made defences. On the north coast of Somerset, the villages of Bossington and Allerford are vulnerable to flooding from water cascading down from the uplands of Exmoor into Porlock Bay. A major Trust project is working to reduce run-off from moorland by blocking ditches, creating catch pools and diverting surface water from paths and tracks. Planting of wet woodland in the paths of rivers also helps slow the progress of water, and allowing fields to flood in winter creates water meadows which in turn encourages the return of wildfowl. Where necessary, large earth bunds (embankments) hold water temporarily during intense rainfall, then releases it slowly into rivers.

Explore National Trust places on the North Devon coast

Watersmeet

Watersmeet, which lies within Exmoor National Park, 2 miles north of Lynton, is one of Britain's deepest river gorges, and is named after the meeting of the valleys of the East Lyn River and Hoar Oak Water. Over 40 miles of footpaths will take you along the East Lyn river to Lynmouth through woodlands of oak, ash and wych elms. Watersmeet is delightful in summer as the sunlight dapples through the trees and sparkles on the water, gorgeous in autumn as the leaves change colour, and dramatic in winter when the river is in full spate, pummelling its way over Devonian rock and sandstone before finally reaching the mudstone of the coastal plateau. Look out for otters, red deer and buzzards as you ramble along. Anglers can fish for sea trout, brown trout and salmon with the necessary permit available from Watersmeet House. Cream teas are also available at this National Trust-owned Victorian fishing lodge, which has been serving refreshments to passers-by since the 1900s.

The high, rocky cliffs of Countisbury Bay and Foreland Point tower over Lynmouth and are Devon's most northerly point. Reached from the South West Coast Path out of Lynmouth (there is also a small car park at Countisbury), this is the place for panoramas: views extend to Porlock Bay and North Hill. High brown fritillary butterflies lay their eggs on the dog violets, which are the main food source for the caterpillars. **Watersmeet Road, Lynmouth, Devon, EX35 6NT**

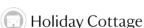 Holiday Cottage

The Lighthouse Keepers' Cottage, Lynton, North Devon. Situated on Foreland Point, Devon's most northerly spot, and surrounded by crashing waves and wheeling peregrines. Little beats this holiday cottage for a remote and memorable getaway. The lighthouse was established in 1900 to support ships heading towards the Severn Channel and although originally manned, it became automated in 1994 (the light flashes four times every 15 seconds). For more information see www.nationaltrustcottages.co.uk.

Heddon Valley

With tree-fringed coves (Woody Bay, secluded and great for a wild swim), towering sea cliffs (Hangman Hill), unspoilt heath (Holdstone and Trentishoe Downs) and moorland views over the Bristol Channel, it is little wonder that this stretch of coast was favoured by the Romantic poets. Robert Southey, Samuel Taylor Coleridge, William Wordsworth and Percy Bysshe Shelley all walked through this landscape, which is within Exmoor National Park and remains largely unchanged since their time. Follow the River

Opposite: Watersmeet

The tea garden in the nineteenth-century fishing lodge provides a welcome pause when exploring over 40 miles of footpath.

Above: Woody Bay

Looking down at the beach at Woody Bay, which is a favourite place for wild swimming.

Heddon down a wooded valley to the sea at Heddon's Mouth beach, enjoying shade from sessile oaks as you go, or ride there along one of several bridleways. Look out for the dark green and silver-washed fritillary butterflies along the sea cliffs where you will also find seabirds including razorbills, guillemots and kittiwakes and if you're lucky spot a school of porpoises on a clear summer day.

Rangers at Heddon Valley hold regular family fun days when kids can make a bow and arrow, race a raft and build a campfire. Stop for an ice cream at the Heddon Valley shop, which also has a wide range of produce from Exmoor and Devon. **Parracombe, Barnstaple, Devon, EX31 4PY**

Baggy Point

It is easy to forget you are so near the bustling surf town of Croyde when you take a stroll along the headland at Baggy Point. A comfortable walk (see pages 228-229) takes you from the National Trust car park on a circular route around the Point with eye-popping views all the way. Look out for Lundy Island in the distance, then enjoy views of the glistening beaches at Saunton Sands and Bideford Bay sweeping before you, and the sea peppered with surfers. Finally reward your endeavours with a stop off at the Sandleigh Tea Room, metres from the slipway to Croyde Beach.

Baggy Point is designated a Site of Special Scientific Interest (SSSI) because of its geological formations, particularly the Devonian sandstone formed here 417–354 million years ago. Overlying the Devonian rocks are raised beach and periglacial deposits from the Quaternary Period. North Devon is famous for a number of large glacial erratics (boulders made from rock not found in the area). One of the most well-known is nearby on Saunton Beach – a pink granite boulder that weighs 12 tons; the nearest outcrop of similar rocks occurs in western Scotland.

Lundy Island

Swathed in stories of pirates and smugglers and home to the fantastical puffin, Lundy exerts an irresistible, romantic pull. A two-hour boat trip from Ilfracombe or Bideford will take you to the island, which lies about 10 miles off the coast of North Devon. Administered by the Landmark Trust which works with the National Trust and Natural England to preserve and protect the wildlife, it is a place to go for peace and quiet (there are no cars), to walk and observe nature (the island is 3 miles long and half a mile wide, so quite manageable) and even to stay (the Landmark Trust has 23 holiday properties there). The waters around Lundy are also a Marine Conservation Zone, and attract many different marine creatures such as the grey seal and the spiny lobster.

> ‘A two-hour boat trip from Ilfracombe or Bideford will take you to the island.’

Left: Lundy Island

The ruins of Quarry hospital, built in the 1860s on the east side of the island.

Right: Granite stacks

The waters around Lundy are a Marine Conservation Zone and attract many marine creatures including the grey seal.

South Devon: deep estuaries, crumbling cliffs and lively resorts

Cliffs of pinky-red sandstone edge the town of Sidmouth, still elegant with its Georgian and Regency architecture, reappear at genteel Budleigh Salterton, then run all the way along to Exeter. The cliffs with their expansive views of the ocean (and tendency to crumble: hikers beware!) are part of the East Devon Heritage Coast and make for great coastal walks, with possible stopovers at busy little resorts (Shaldon and Teignmouth) and picturesque villages (Topsham and Lympstone).

At Exmouth, where the River Exe meets the sea, sandy beaches alternate with steep shingle banks, and the shore is lined with Georgian houses and beach huts. The National Trust owns 51 hectares (126 acres) of land here, which extend to Sandy Bay and its towering headland.

The South Devon Scenic Railway, built as an extension to the Great Western Railway by Isambard Kingdom Brunel in 1843, runs from the Exe Estuary along the coast and up the Teign Estuary to Newton Abbot, stitching together the towns of Exeter, Dawlish Warren, Teignmouth and Newton Abbot along the way. The journey takes you inches from the sea through five tunnels and along a 4-mile sea wall and is a thrilling way to experience the beauty of the coastline. During the storms of February 2014, part of the track was left dangling when the sea wall was breached. It reopened in the April at a repair cost of £35 million.

Palm trees and fishing fleets

The arc of Tor Bay encloses the resorts of the English Riviera, Torquay and Paignton, and the fishing harbour of Brixham. This huge, sand-rimmed bay began attracting visitors at the end of the eighteenth century reaching the heights of fashion during the nineteenth. Devotees included Lord Tennyson who declared Torquay the 'loveliest sea village in England'. Its spacious harbour, dotted with yachts, palm trees and sub-tropical plants, lend it a Mediterranean air that still feels glamorous. A recent addition to

Above: A La Ronde

Looking past this unique 16-sided, eighteenth-century house, towards the sea at Exmouth.

Right: Brixham

This picturesque harbour, with its replica of Francis Drake's *Golden Hind*, still functions as a fishing town as well as a popular place for visitors.

the town's attractions is Living Coasts, a coastal zoo based around seabird and other coastal wildlife, with a penguin beach, artificial tidal estuary and a tropical mangrove swamp.

Brixham is a rare thing these days: a picturesque harbour that still functions as a fishing town. Once England's major fishing port, largely due to its powerful trawlers, it still has one of the largest fishing fleets in the UK and is busy with trawlers offloading catch to sell at the fish market on the quayside.

Nearby, Berry Head nature reserve, a limestone promontory with views over Tor Bay, is well worth visiting for its views (880 square miles of sea are visible from its tip) and its wildlife, including a guillemot colony.

A shingle bar and a drowned village

The Dart Estuary weedles its way inland through rolling farmland past Dartmouth, Greenway (see page 225) and Dittisham to Totnes. At its mouth, Start Bay, with shingle beaches, sandy coves and steep cliffs (some more than 134m high), sweeps magnificently round to Start Point. Slapton Sands is a shingle bar 2 miles long, bordered by water on both sides – encroaching sea and a freshwater lake,

Above: Dittisham

This attractive village sits at the water's edge 2 miles upstream from Dartmouth.

Below: Salcombe Estuary

A popular destination for sailing enthusiasts, the estuary also hosts a diverse ecosystem.

Slapton Ley – and is vulnerable to change as it tries to roll landward in the face of rising sea levels and storms. The Sands were also the location for Exercise Tiger in 1943–4, a large-scale rehearsal for the D-Day invasion of Normandy marred by poor communication and co-ordination. An Allied convoy positioning itself for landing, was attacked by E-boats of the German navy, resulting in the deaths of 946 American servicemen. As the operation was top secret, it was not reported at the time, so the general public were unaware until after the War and local people were sworn to secrecy.

The nearby village of Torcross is also perilously surrounded by water and, if proof of the vulnerability of this stretch of coastline were needed, a few ruined cottages at the foot of a low cliff are the only remnants of Hallsands, a fishing village with a population of 100 people, which was swept away by a high tide in 1917 after the protective shingle beach had been removed to provide material for the construction of Plymouth Breakwater.

Boats, sea slugs and sea tractors

The National Trust looks after more than 200 hectares (500 acres) inside Salcombe Estuary: from the coastal slopes of Rickham

Common to Snapes Point, which hangs over the town of Salcombe, and the estuary woodland of Halwell, tucked into Frogmore Creek. The upper reaches of Salcombe's creeks are estuarine but the middle and lower reaches are entirely marine. This creates a diverse ecosystem, including a sea slug thought to be unique to the estuary, seagrass beds, rare seaweeds and sponges and corals. Salcombe is one of the country's finest natural harbours and a popular destination for sailing enthusiasts. The local yacht club holds a competitive and lively regatta every August. For a fine view of this Jurassic coastline, take a walk around National Trust-owned Salcombe Hill, from where you can see Sidmouth and, on a good day, Portland Bill in Dorset.

Between the promontories of Bolt Head and Bolt Tail, cliffs with grassy summits rise 122m above the sea before the coast changes as tidal estuaries run inland between the fields and woodland of South Hams.

At low tide it is possible to walk to tidal Burgh Island from Bigbury-on-Sea; at high tide, guests are ferried to the Art Deco hotel, which dominates the island, in a sea tractor.

Explore National Trust places on the South Devon coast

South Milton

South Milton is Thurlestone's most popular beach and you can see why: reddish-golden sands and crystal-clear water are backed by lush fields and wetlands, which are home to many different species of wildlife. Offshore, Thurlestone Rock, a natural arch, is a popular landmark for kayakers and windsurfers to navigate around. See the feature opposite for what the Neptune Coastline Campaign has helped to achieve in South Milton. **Thurlestone, near Kingsbridge, Devon, TQ7 3JY**

Orcombe Point, Exmouth

The summit of Orcombe Point, noteworthy as the western gateway to the Jurassic Coast and its most westerly point, is marked by the Geoneedle, a 5m-high stone sculpture made from all the rocks found along the Jurassic Coast. **Exmouth, Devon, EX8**

Dart Estuary to Brixham

A walk along ancient woodland beside the eastern shore of the River Dart rewards with views of the village of Dittisham and a stop off at Woodhuish, a recently renovated nineteenth-century cider press and organic farm with traditional breeds such as North Devon cattle and Hebridean sheep, farmed to graze and manage the coastal heathland.

Overbeck's

Perched high on the cliffs above Salcombe is the seaside home of scientist Otto Overbeck. Built in 1913, it is a joyful combination of exotic gardens, eccentric inventions and eclectic collections of natural and maritime history. Its warm microclimate means that rare and tropical plants such as banana plants, citrus and olive trees all thrive here, as well as acers, magnolias and cornus and plants from South Africa and Australia. **Sharpitor, Salcombe, Devon, TQ8 8LW**

Left: Thurlestone Rock

Lying off South Milton Sands, the rock arch is a dramatic destination for windsurfers and kayakers.

Enterprise Neptune in South Devon

Wembury Point. This former naval gunnery range at the mouth of Plymouth Sound had been closed for reasons of national security since 1940. Situated in the heart of the South Devon Area of Outstanding Natural Beauty, it included Great Mewstone Island, a popular site for nesting seabirds.

English Nature invoked rarely used powers to force the Ministry of Defence to invite bids from a conservation body to buy it. In 2005 the National Trust launched an appeal to raise the money to save Wembury Point as part of the 40th anniversary celebrations of its Neptune Coastline Campaign. The fear was that if the public appeal had not been launched, the site, which is prime land, would be bought up by developers.

The money was found through a very successful appeal that raised over £2 million, enough to pay for the land and an endowment to look after it in perpetuity. In 2006, the National Trust paid the MOD £1.4 million to secure 56 hectares (138 acres) of cliff top. Acquisition meant that public access along the coast was once again permitted and the risk of further development of the Sound was averted.

Visitors to Wembury Point these days enjoy walks along a flat coastal footpath with views of the Great Mewstone, secluded coves and cliffs, home to nesting seabirds, to a sheltered woodland walk overlooking the Yealm estuary. The rocky shoreline, slate reefs and wave-cut platforms make good habitats for marine plants and animals as well as excellent rock pools.

South Milton Sands. The National Trust worked with the local South Hams community to solve the problem of its rotting wooden sea defences. A stakeholder group worked with the Parish Council to put forward a plan to local people. Once agreed, the car park was moved, rotting timbers were removed and the area was re-landscaped to form dunes, which were stabilised by planting marram grass. The Sands were restored to their original state and continue to be a haven for wildlife, including migratory birds in the spring, dragonflies and damselflies in summer, insect-eating birds such as swallows and wagtails in autumn, and wildfowl such wigeon, teal, mallard and shoveler in the winter.

However, the winter storms of 2014 did a lot of damage to the reinstated dunes and much material was removed, and the access road was washed away. Following the principle of 'roll back', the road has been relocated landwards and the dunes will be allowed to re-establish naturally and no further interventions are planned.

Salcombe to Hope Cove

Follow the South West Coast Path to honey-coloured sands at Soar Mill Cove or take a trip inland up the Salcombe Estuary to watch the yachts and sailing ships. Better still, paddle your canoe along the coast with the aid of a National Trust map-guide and discover shipwrecks, coves and wildlife from a seafarer's viewpoint. **Salcombe, Devon, TQ8 8LW**

Above: Overbeck's

Salcombe Estuary seen from the garden of the house of scientist Otto Overbeck who lived here from 1928 until 1937.

Right: Branscombe

A blacksmith hammers hot iron in the thatched working forge – the oldest in the country.

Branscombe: the Old Bakery, Manor Mill and Forge

Some of the houses in this historic seaside village are over 400 years old. The National Trust looks after the oldest working thatched forge in the country here as well as a nineteenth-century water mill, now restored and working, and the Old Bakery, now a tea room. Stroll through the village to Branscombe beach, part of the Jurassic Coast. This is the site of the notorious beaching of the container ship *Napoli* in January 2007. **Seaton, Devon, EX12 3DB**

Coleton Fishacre

The country home of the D'Oyly Carte family sits at the top of a valley which runs down to the sea. Rupert and Lady Dorothy D'Oyly Carte spotted the valley as they sailed past in the 1920s and thought it looked

Above: Coleton Fishacre

The garden of the country retreat of the D'Oyly Carte family was originally planted by Lady Dorothy Carte.

the perfect setting for a house to entertain in style. The house, which was built in 1923 to the design of architect Oswald Milne, has an Arts and Crafts exterior but its interior is a masterpiece of Art Deco. Much of the fittings and furnishings have been re-created by the National Trust since it took ownership, and have been carried out according to original designs and photographs. The garden

'Catch a riverboat to Greenway from Dartmouth to see the house as Agatha first saw it'

has a rill, which runs down to the sea and is the perfect place for a picnic. **Brownstone Road, Kingswear TQ6 0EQ**

Greenway

Agatha Christie, the much-loved crime writer, described her holiday home as 'the loveliest place on earth' and you begin to understand why as you look around the estate. Set in sweeping gardens with views across the Dart Estuary, it is a generous, well-proportioned house. Furnished as it was when Agatha lived here, and filled with many of the family's collections, it is a rare glimpse into the writer's life and interests. Catch a riverboat to Greenway from Dartmouth to see the house as Agatha first saw it – from the water. **Greenway Road, Galmpton, near Brixham, TQ5 0ES**

Halwell Woods

Situated on the Kingsbridge estuary near Salcombe, this National Trust newly acquired woodland is a great place to stop and explore if you are walking the South West Coast Path. It brims with bluebells and wood anemones in spring and looks out over meadows on to the creeks of the estuary and all its wildlife. **South Pool, Kingsbridge, TQ7**

Left: Coleton Fishacre

A rill runs through the garden down to the sea at Pudcombe Cove.

Right: Greenway

Crime writer Agatha Christie's described her home near Brixham as 'the loveliest place on earth'.

Shore-spotter's Guide

Despite being a particularly hardy breed, the **Dartmoor pony** is now an endangered species with only about 800 living wild on the moors. They are looked after by the South Devon National Trust rangers. You can see them all over Exmoor and in particular, grazing on the cliffs at Wembury.

The **peregrine falcon** (*Falco peregrinus*) population dropped significantly in the 1960s but numbers have increased considerably in recent years. This large and powerful bird of prey is one of the world's fastest species, flying consistently at 60mph and diving at speeds of up to 200mph. It is increasingly found in large cities as well as on the more familiar territory of coastal cliffs and northern uplands, such as the cliffs of North Devon near Lynton, and near the mouth of the Salcombe Estuary on the rocky cliffs. The National Trust maintains a special peregrine viewing point at Plym Bridge, near Plymouth.

The **pyramidal orchid** (*Anacamptis pyramidalis*) get its name from the cone, or 'pyramid', of tightly packed pink flowers it produces between June and August. Flowering is unpredictable as the seeds of the orchid do not contain enough nourishment to produce leaves and flowers and so the it relies on fungus in the soil to provide the root nourishment. See them at Woolacombe Warren and South Milton Sands.

Horner Wood on the Holnicote Estate has as many as 330 different species of lichen, including some rare types. Lichens are composite organisms and come in many different forms and are an indicator of clean air. On the nearby heathy slopes, the rare **heath fritillary** butterfly (*Mellicta athalia*) has a major stronghold, abounding in some of the combes during June.

The quality of the water and the seagrass beds in the Salcombe Estuary create the perfect habitat for both species of our native seahorse the **spiny seahorse** (*Hippocampus histrix*) and the Atlantic or short-snouted seahorse (*Hippocampus hippocampus*). Seagrass plants can reach almost 2m in places but are vulnerable (as are seahorses) to damage from boat anchors and propellers.

A rare relative of the yellowhammer, the **cirl bunting** (*Emberiza cirlus*) is found in the fields and hedges of south Devon, near to the coast. It is slightly larger than a robin with a short beak and pink legs. The female is brown and black with cream and yellow feathers and the male is similar but brighter. One of the better known sites to see it in South Devon is Prawle Point, Devon's most southerly point, and also on the Yealm Estuary.

Baggy Point, North Devon, easy access walk

Distance: 2 miles (3.2km)

Time: 1 hour

This is an easy walk that's great for families, taking you along the west side of Baggy Point, with far-reaching coastal and sea views. This is also an excellent route for bird watching and, if you have a keen eye, you may see seals. Also, at certain times of the year you can watch rock climbers scaling the cliffs. The area is designated a Site of Special Scientific Interest (SSSI) for its geological features. Contact 01271 87055, baggypoint@nationaltrust.org.uk

Terrain

This easy access walk follows a graded, well-surfaced, almost level path to the end of Baggy Point and back. It is suitable for wheelchairs, all-terrain mobility scooters and pushchairs almost all the way to the end of the headland. Dogs welcome but please keep on a lead, due to the proximity of the path to the cliff-top and livestock in surrounding fields. No litter bins.

Directions

1 Go out of the car park by the kiosk and turn right up the asphalted lane, signed Baggy Point 1 mile. Be careful as there can be traffic on this section.

2 Go through the gateposts to the fingerpost at the fork in the path; go left here. (On your left is the only dog-waste bin in this area.) Follow the asphalted track past the houses. Keep an eye out for peregrines flying overhead.

'This is an excellent route for bird watching'

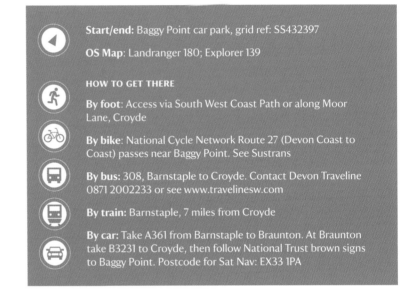

Start/end: Baggy Point car park, grid ref: SS432397

OS Map: Landranger 180; Explorer 139

HOW TO GET THERE

By foot: Access via South West Coast Path or along Moor Lane, Croyde

By bike: National Cycle Network Route 27 (Devon Coast to Coast) passes near Baggy Point. See Sustrans

By bus: 308, Barnstaple to Croyde. Contact Devon Traveline 0871 2002233 or see www.travelinesw.com

By train: Barnstaple, 7 miles from Croyde

By car: Take A361 from Barnstaple to Braunton. At Braunton take B3231 to Croyde, then follow National Trust brown signs to Baggy Point. Postcode for Sat Nav: EX33 1PA

Left: Baggy Point

A short walk that suits bird watchers, seal spotters and anyone seeking exhilarating views.

③ Keep to your left at the next fork (on your right here is a driveway to a modern house). About 28yd (25m) further look at the whale bones on the right side of the path. These bones are all that remains of a large whale that was washed up on Croyde Beach in 1915. They were preserved here for the benefit of visitors by the Hyde family who gave Baggy Point to the National Trust in 1939.

④ Follow the mostly level, graded track to the end of the headland. Look out to your left across the bays to Hartland in the far distance. As you walk along, look for wild flowers in the spring and summer, bright yellow gorse and a variety of fungi in the autumn, and lichens and moss all year round. Be careful not to touch any of the fungi as many of them are poisonous.

⑤ As the path curves slightly to your left, look for three steps up to your right where you'll find a pond that has been restored to create a valuable wildlife habitat. It was built by the Hyde family, who were keen conservationists and protectors of Baggy Point. The water here is deep so please keep your children and dogs under close supervision. Return to the path, passing through the gorse to the gate. Stop a while here and look at the memorial stone, set into the dry-stone wall, to Henry Williamson (1895–1977), writer, English

naturalist and farmer known for his natural and social history novels. He won the Hawthornden Prize for literature in 1928 for his book *Tarka the Otter*.

⑥ About 33yd (30m) past the gate you'll come to a fingerpost. Carry straight on, signposted Baggy Point ½ mile. There's a detour off this path that leads down to the rock pools – if you do decide to take a look, please be careful as the path and the rocks can be slippery. Look out for grey seals along the shoreline, especially in the summer. On a clear day you can see Lundy Island, 20 miles due west, where the Atlantic Ocean meets the Bristol Channel (see page 214).

⑦ When you reach the headland do take time to stop and absorb the view – it's magnificent at any time of year and in any weather. The west-facing cliffs of Baggy Point are a popular nesting place for a wide variety of sea birds including herring gull, fulmar, shag, cormorant and occasionally peregrine. On clear days, and when the sea birds aren't nesting (March–June), you may also have the chance to watch the many rock climbers who come to Baggy Point. You can also see the headland at Morte Point, also owned by the National Trust.

⑧ Retrace your steps back along the path to return to the car park.

Seaside things to do in Devon and Somerset

❶ Fish for shrimps on Saunton Sands

At low tide, shrimps lurk in rock pools on Saunton Sands underneath clumps of bladderwrack seaweed. Pick up a prawning net, put on some old shoes, tie a plastic bag to your waist to collect them in and you're all set. Brown shrimps generally hang out in numbers so are easy to scoop into a net. Back in the kitchen, boil in water, peel and demolish with a slice of brown bread.

❷ Rock pool ramble at Wembury Point

The rocky shore, slate reefs and wave-cut rock platforms around Wembury make ideal rockpooling territory. Boasting some of the best rock pools in the country, it is the perfect place to head at low tide to immerse yourself in its fascinating underwater world. The shallow waters teem with life, including limpets, sea anemones, crabs and starfish. Learn more about local marine life at The Marine Centre, situated on the South West Coast Path, which runs regular rambles (bring your own fishing nets, they will supply buckets). Then have a refreshing cup of tea at the charming Trust-owned Old Mill Café on the beach.

❸ Take a train up the cliff

You could reach the picturesque harbour town of Lynmouth by foot or by driving down a 1-in-4 road from Lynton and hoping for a place to park. More fun is to be had, though, by leaving the car in Lynton and catching the Cliff Railway. Built in 1890 to replace ponies, which had struggled up the hill carrying deliveries and paddle-steamer passengers, it is gravity powered by a 700-gallon water tank fitted to each of the two cars. As the water is discharged from the lower car, the heavier top car makes its 152m descent down a 1:1.75 gradient. It's a delightful way to travel and an excellent way to get a panoramic view of Lynmouth and its coastline.

Above: Cliff Railway

The Lynton and Lynmouth Cliff Railway connects the two seaside towns and is powered by a 700-gallon water tank.

Right: Croyde

The beach between Woolacombe and Saunton Sands has the perfect conditions for surfers.

❹ Canoe around the Salcombe-Kingsbridge Estuary

The creeks and inlets of the estuary (actually a tidal inlet formed as river-cut valleys were flooded by post-glacial rising sea levels) are perfect for paddling a kayak or canoe. The best time to go is mid–high tide when the entire estuary is accessible by canoe and you can explore quieter sheltered creeks such as Bowcombe and Frogmore. Allow 2–5 hours for a round-trip paddle from Kingsbridge to Mill Bay; 2–3 hours for North Sands to the Saltstone and remember to pay your harbour dues at Salcombe Harbour Office before you set off. For more information and a canoe map, go to www.nationaltrust.org.uk.

❺ Cycle the Tarka Trail

The disused railway tracks between Braunton and Meeth are now a 30-mile cycle path. Much is flat and off road so entirely suitable for a family outing. The route passes alongside the Taw Estuary (look out for wintering wildfowl such as curlew, redshank and Brent geese), the coastal town of Bideford, to the River Torridge and out into open country with views of the Dartmoor National Park. Information boards and sculpture accompany you as you peddle through the landscape popularised by Henry Williamson in his novel *Tarka the Otter*.

❻ Learn to surf in Croyde

The setting of Croyde beach – facing the Atlantic Ocean and in a sheltered bay between Woolacombe, Putsborough and Saunton Sands – makes it perfect for surfers. Waves are funnelled towards the beach by the rocky outcrops of Baggy Point and Saunton Down and break quickly on the sloping sands. Numerous surf schools offer lessons, which are strongly advisable until you get your feet, especially as

there are rip currents near the rocks at either end. The shallower water near the beach is full of wetsuited surfing acolytes bobbing about in groups and grappling with their boards while further out the more experienced wait patiently for the perfect wave.

Also try: Wembury – a consistently good beach for surfing – Seacombe Sands, Ayrmer Cove and Soar Mill Cove, all National Trust beaches.

Wildlife to look out for in Somerset and Devon, recommended by National Trust Rangers

Julian Gurney, Head Ranger, West Exmoor

'Look out for wild flowers at Watersmeet like the rare Irish spurge, bright yellow Welsh poppies, wood anemone and heath spotted orchid in the spring. You can often see grey wagtails, dippers, butterflies, brown trout and salmon, which, although still elusive, are beginning to reappear in greater numbers here. In the summer, porpoises and dolphins can sometimes be seen off Heddon's Mouth, Woody Bay and Foreland Point, and a wide variety of sea birds. You may also be lucky enough to see peregrine falcons or the occasional red kite. The lovely Heddon Valley is also one of the best places in Britain for the spectacular but rapidly declining high brown fritillary, which flies over bracken slopes from mid-June to late July.

Jonathan Fairhurst, Head Ranger, Croyde, Woolacombe and Mortehoe

'Look out for pyramidal orchids which flower in their thousands in the summer in Woolacombe Warren. These native, but rare, plants have colourful, dense spikes of pink or pale purple flowers, and look among the sand dunes. In the spring, when the days get longer, and the weather warms up, migrant birds start to come back to Mortehoe: swallows, wheatears and chiffchaffs signal the start of summer. My favourite view is from the tip of Morte Point for its rocky wildness, especially on a stormy day when the sea birds are driven close to shore and the waves are crashing over the rocks.'

Lorna Sherriff, Ranger, South Devon

'In winter keep a look out in hedges and fields along the Yealm Estuary for cirl bunting (see page 227), a nationally rare bird which successfully breeds in this area. You may also see a peregrine falcon (see page 226) soaring overhead. 'The boundary stone walls are a vital habitat for lizards, spiders, snails and many mosses, ferns and lichens.'

Cornwall

Blessed with warm seas, mild temperatures and vast, sandy beaches, the long peninsula of Cornwall has attracted holidaymakers since the railways first brought them in early Victorian times. Before the arrival of these summer visitors, this south-western corner of the country was dependent on other forms of income: fishing, tin and copper mining, farming and quarrying. Reminders of these activities can be seen throughout the county, from the tall chimneys of the abandoned engine houses of the mines, to the picturesque fishing villages overlooking harbours now busier with tea shops than fishing boats.

The long strips of sand and rolling waves attract surfers who ride the curls of sea whipped up by winds that once drove ships on to the treacherous rocks, reefs and stacks that line much of the county. The coves and caves created by the relentless battering of the sea on the rocky cliffs of the shoreline were heaven for smugglers whose names and exploits now join the mythical characters in the book of Cornish legends.

The National Trust cares for hundreds of miles of Cornish coastline (almost 36 per cent of the total for the county), including some of the best beaches, farmland, heathland and cliffs.

Previous pages: Hemmick Beach, an unspoilt cove situated on the south coast of Cornwall, near St Austell.

Left: Towanroath Shaft Pumping Engine House, part of the Wheal Coates mine on the cliffs near St Agnes.

Cornwall: a wild and rugged coastline wreathed in legends

Just across the border from South Devon and ignored in the rush to get down to more popular areas of Cornwall, the Rame Peninsula is often overlooked. It is well worth a detour: bordered by Plymouth Sound to the east, the estuary of the River Lynher to the north and the English Channel to the south, it has both wildlife-rich creeks near Torpoint and a great sweep of beach at Whitsand Bay. It takes its name from Rame Head, a rocky headland surmounted by an eleventh-century monk's chapel dedicated to St Michael. It is also where you will find Antony House, an eighteenth-century mansion owned by the National Trust (see page 254).

The 4 miles of sand at Whitsand Bay are reached by zigzagging down steep paths close to vertiginous cliffs that you need to take care on. Upon arrival, the sea may look tempting but it is not safe for swimmers: strong currents are treacherous and, combined with stiff south-westerlies, have wrecked many ships along the shore.

The villages of Looe and Polperro were once alive with fishing fleets spilling their morning's catch onto the quayside. Although some fishing still continues, especially in Looe, most activity comes from visitors who drift around their narrow streets, peer into the windows of fishermen's cottages and listen to tales of when smugglers hid their booty in local caves and pilchards were abundant.

Headlands, estuaries and Daphne du Maurier

To appreciate the secluded bays of Lantivet and Lantic to the full, walk to Pencarrow Head whose highest point is 137m above the sea. There you will see Lantic Bay to your right, a low tide beach reached on foot after parking at the Trust car park east of Polruan. To the left is Lantivet Bay, a secluded south-facing beach near the hamlet of Lansallos. Look out for the remains of the pilchard palace, once an active fish-pressing cellar.

Cutting deeply into farmland, the Fowey Estuary frays into tributaries along its length. Once part of the sea, it is a ria – a drowned river valley or network of valleys – created 10,000 years ago at the end of the Ice Age when sea levels rose. The creeks of Pont and Penpoll are quiet backwaters best explored in a kayak. The natural harbour at Fowey at the head of the estuary has been a harbour since the Middle Ages and still attracts a variety of boats, from local ferries to yachts and even

Right: Lantic Bay

The white sands of Lantic Bay can be reached on foot via a steep path down the cliffs – it is well worth the effort.

Below: Power kiting

The secluded location of Lantic Bay with its high cliffs is a perfect place for power kiting.

'The villages of Looe and Polperro were once alive with fishing fleets spilling their morning's catch onto the quayside.'

tall ships. Author Daphne du Maurier lived and wrote in Fowey, and was inspired and informed by her surroundings – the spirit of the place and of Cornwall haunts her books such as *Jamaica Inn* and *Rebecca*. The Coast Path from Fowey to craggy Gribbin Head skirts Menabilly where Daphne du Maurier lived and which is said to be the original Manderley in *Rebecca*. Gribbin Head is literally unmissable: it is crowned by an 26m high, red-and-white striped daymark to alert mariners of the jagged rocks below.

Charlestown, which sits at the heart of St Austell Bay, takes its name from Charles Rashleigh a local mine owner who financed its build in 1790. Created as a port to export copper, it was designed by John Smeaton, the builder of the third Eddystone lighthouse. When supplies of copper ran out, it became an

Above: Gribbin Head

The daymark tower is just visible in this view of Gribbin Head taken from the Coombe. A return to cliff grazing on the headland has allowed the return of a diversity of wild flowers.

important outlet for the export of china clay from workings near St Austell. It is now owned by a company that sails a small fleet of tall ships, often found moored up in the harbour.

Cornwall is a county of many dramatic headlands and the highest on its south coast is Dodman Point, which has the added attraction of a massive Iron Age earthworks. Nearly 666m long and over 6m high, this earthworks encloses the headland and may have been a settlement over 2,000 years ago. There are great views across Veryan Bay from here towards the Roseland Peninsula.

Creeks, beaches and hamlets

There is some disagreement about where the Roseland Peninsula starts but it is safe to say that a walk to Nare Head from the Trust car park above Kiberick Cove, offers a good view of the sweep of its southern edge. However, there is little debate that it is bounded by the sea on one side and River Fal on the other and intersected by the River Percuil and its tributaries. Within this boundary are wooded creeks, quiet beaches, hamlets folded into farmland and ancient churches (thirteenth-century St Just-in-Roseland is particularly atmospheric). Walks crosshatch the Roseland and take the curious

along the river to the headland and nineteenth-century lighthouse at St Anthony's Head. From there, a tiny passenger ferry at nearby Place shuttles back and forth to St Mawes, a dignified resort whose setting and mild climate has earned it the title 'Cornish Riviera'. Smart hotels and fish restaurants attract a well-heeled crowd but for those on a tighter budget, wet fish is sold most days from a van on the harbour wall.

Frequent ferries sail from St Mawes across the expansive waterway Carrick Roads to the natural harbour of Falmouth. It is an uplifting way to arrive at the lively town, which boasts a high street packed with independent shops, a fascinating National Maritime Museum, a glamorous marina, and Rick Stein's fish and chips restaurant, Fish. Learn about Falmouth 'packets' at the Maritime Museum; these fast, two-masted sloops carried mail to Europe and the West Indies for 150 years until replaced by steamboats. Pendennis Castle sits sternly on the headland overlooking the entrance to Carrick Roads, a companion castle to St Mawes Castle on the opposite bank. Both were built for Henry VIII in 1539–45 to defend the large inland expanse of water against invasion from Catholic France and Spain, and form part of a chain of coastal defences known as Device Forts.

Right: Carrick Roads

The Carrick Roads, seen from Trelissick Garden (see page 254), is a drowned river valley created at the end of the last Ice Age which leads to the Fal Estuary.

Bucolic peace and quiet

Daphne du Maurier made Frenchman's Creek, a tributary of the Helford River, famous in her book of the same name. It is one of several enchanting creeks that meander away from the Helford, cloaked with trees and busy with small boats. Even at the height of summer, these creeks are the place to go for peace, quiet and bucolic walks. Further up the river, Gweek, once a busy port, is now known principally for the Cornish Seal Sanctuary which raises and tends orphaned baby seals and sick and injured adults, before releasing them back into the sea.

'The geology allows a rich and unusual botany not found on any rock type elsewhere'

The quay at Tremayne was built for a visit by Queen Victoria which never happened: it is said the Queen cancelled due to rain. Her great grandson, Edward, later Duke of Windsor, did visit in 1921 when he was Prince of Wales. The woods and quay were bequeathed to the National Trust in 1978 by the Vyvyan family of Trelowarren and are now enjoyed by walkers, sailors, anglers and young crabbers. A passenger ferry service has crossed the river, between Helford Passage and Helford, since medieval times and still operates from Good Friday until 31 October.

A remote peninsula and an unusual rock

The Lizard is a land shaped by its complex geology. The combination of hard and soft rocks has led to the sea sculpting all manner of caves, cliffs and arches into its coastline. The geology allows a rich and unusual botany not found on any rock type elsewhere, including the Cornish heath, only found on the Lizard, cross-leaved heath, the black bog rush and very rare dwarf rushes.

The southernmost point of mainland Britain, Lizard Point with its wind-lashed rocks, is reached by a single road and then a lonely

Left: The Lizard

Shetland ponies are used for conservation grazing on the coastline near Beagles Point, Coverack.

Serpentine: the Lizard's lustrous mineral

Caerleon Cove, a National Trust-owned beach in the Poltesco Valley on the Lizard, is not only a delightful place to spend a couple of hours but also a reminder of Cornwall's once-thriving serpentine industry.

This unassuming-looking rock was used to build homes until, in 1828, a Mr Drew discovered that when polished, it shone with a rich and luminous lustre. He began to fashion objects from it and sell it commercially from his premises in Penzance. A rival factory was built in Caerleon Cove in the 1830s, close to the source of the stone to process and polish the mineral and turn it into jewellery and larger pieces such as fireplaces and decorative building materials.

Business really took off when Queen Victoria and Prince Albert stopped off at the Lizard during their Cornish cruise in 1846 and bought several pieces for their house at Osborne on the Isle of Wight (see page 148). Serpentine became fashionable with sales further boosted when pieces were shown at the Great Exhibition of 1851. The Lizard Serpentine Company (LSC) was founded in 1853 and the company's initials can still be seen on the warehouse building in Caerleon Cove. For many years Jabez Druitt, owner of the company, lived at Caerleon House overlooking the works, which closed in 1893 when serpentine fell out of favour. A few craftsmen still work with the stone, creating lighthouses, paperweights and other decorative objects which can be bought direct from the maker in Lizard village.

footpath to the lighthouse and feels suitably wild and remote. The lifeboat station, recently rebuilt, is testament to the number of lives saved by its crews from the treacherous waters. Serpentine (see feature, left), shaped into paperweights and ornaments, is sold nearby.

Kynance Cove is a medley of cliffs, stacks, pinnacles, arches and a sandy beach that is revealed for only a few hours each day at low tide. No wonder, then, that it has always attracted artists, including Pre-Raphaelite William Holman Hunt, as well as holidaymakers and even royalty: Prince Albert brought his children here in 1846. 'Kynans' means gorge in Cornish, and the cove sits among 60m cliffs and is reached via a steep path. The National Trust took over the café in 1999 and turned it into an environmentally friendly place. The roof is clad with photovoltaic cells cunningly disguised as slate. The building is insulated with Hardwick sheep's wool and the toilet has a self-contained sewage system.

Poltesco on the east of the peninsula was home to the Lizard Serpentine Company, which employed nearly 100 people who turned the dark green mottled stone into mantelpieces, urns and even shop fronts. The neighbouring village of Cadgwith is a favourite subject for artists charmed by its thatched cottages squeezed into a narrow valley that runs down to a shingle cove where lobster pots are heaped up on the tiny harbour.

There are splendid walks all along the shoreline of Mount's Bay. The Coast Path over Mullion Cliff to Predannack Head, which rises 79m

Below: Mullion Cove

Coasteering allows visitors to really engage with the dramatic coastline of the Lizard, exploring caves, scrambling over rocks, and leaping from cliffs.

above the sea, is exhilarating with sweeping views of Mount's Bay. Mullion and Poldhu Coves are both popular holiday destinations. There are surf competitions at Poldhu, a sandy beach crossed by a small stream and sheltered by steep slopes. Marconi also conducted experiments at Poldhu Cove, including the first transatlantic signal transmission in December 1901. Find out more about that historic day by visiting The Marconi Centre at Poldhu.

Mullion Cove has a small harbour and a natural tunnel that leads through the rocks to the beach at low tide. It suffered a fair degree of damage during the winter storms of 2013/14 to both arms of the harbour wall. The fifteenth-century church of St Winwaloe is tucked into the lee of a rocky headland at Church Cove, a sandy beach that feels more open and less hemmed in than its neighbours.

At a mile long, Loe Pool is the largest freshwater lake in Cornwall, cut off from the sea by a broad shingle bar, formed in the thirteenth century when a natural sand bar dammed the River Cober. Legends surround this mysterious place, notably that it was home to the Lady of the Lake and King Arthur's sword Excalibur. The lake is the centerpiece of the 648-hectare (1,600-acre) Penrose Estate owned by the National Trust, and many paths explore its farmland and woodland.

'St Just was the centre of Cornish tin mining during the Victorian era'

Praa Sands is one of West Cornwall's most popular beaches and offers family-friendly simple fun; there are no amusement arcades, just a mile of flat golden sand (perfect for sandcastles), clean water and good swimming.

At the furthermost western end of Mount's Bay, a tidal causeway at Marazion leads to its most famous landmark, St Michael's Mount (see page 256), a granite island rising 91m above the sea and topped with a fourteenth-century castle.

The foot of the country

Land's End, the south-western tip of the British mainland, pulls the crowds who come to be photographed by the famous sign and to look through telescopes out across the Atlantic. A short walk or drive in either direction, though, and the throng is left behind as the landscape expands to breathtaking views from sheer cliffs over rocky coves and moorland. Sennen Cove is tucked around the corner at Whitesand Bay and is a stretch of golden sand popular with surfers, dolphins and basking sharks. The headland Cape Cornwall, near St Just, has as much drama as Land's End but is quieter and can only be reached on foot from the car park. It was given to the National Trust by H. J. Heinz and Co. Ltd in 1987, as commemorated in a small plaque in the shape of a baked beans tin label set into the granite base of a chimney on the headland.

St Just was the centre of Cornish tin mining during the Victorian era and the countryside around it is littered with evidence of that time, from derelict engine houses, to closed-down mine shafts and shale heaps. In 2006, Botallack Mine near St Just, which ceased working in 1895, was given World Heritage Site status by UNESCO, testament to the importance of Cornish mining internationally. Between 1815 and 1915 over 250,000 people left to work in other mining areas, and its estimated that there are 6 million people of Cornish descent globally. Until 1991, when the last mine closed, the coast and moorland had been mined for tin and copper for over 2,000 years.

The Neptune Coastline Campaign has helped the National Trust acquire some 4 miles of the coastline around St Just, protecting such beautiful areas as Kenidjack, Ballowall Common and Nanjulian Farm, and preserving important features such as the Levant Beam Engine (a steam-powered engine still on its original mine site perched on the edge of the cliffs).

Penzance was once a major port, but these days its harbour is full of smaller vessels, although the Scillonian ferry departs for the Isles of Scilly from its quay. The town is full of interest, with attractions including the Morrab Gardens, planted with subtropical plants, and the Jubilee Pool, the UK's largest seawater lido and an exemplar of Art Deco seaside architecture.

Below: Levant Mine and Beam Engine

Part of the Cornwall and West Devon Mining World Heritage Site, this is the only Cornish beam engine that is still in steam on its original mine site.

Opposite: Botallack Mine

The abandoned beam engine houses of the Crowns section of Botallack Mine near St Just.

The Isles of Scilly

Historian Charles Thomas described a time when the Isles of Scilly were part of the same land mass as Cornwall, before sea levels rose and engulfed most of it. The result was the 'drowned landscape' we now see: over 100 islands about 28 miles south-west of Land's End. The largest of these is St Mary's, where light aircraft land and the Scillonian ferry discharges its passengers. Hugh Town is the heart of the archipelago and has the majority of hotels and restaurants and a supermarket. The other main islands, St Agnes, St Martin's, Tresco and Bryher, are reached by a network of small ferries, and each offers its own particular attractions. St Agnes is linked to Gugh by a sand bar and both are littered with archaeological sites, including a stone labyrinth. St Martin's has long sandy beaches and a flourishing flower farm, and Tresco is home to Abbey Gardens, a subtropical paradise of rare plants.

Neighbouring Newlyn is a rare thing: a Cornish town that still depends on fishing for its livelihood. The fish market along with several fishmongers sell the daily catch at reasonable prices. The fishing community was the subject of many paintings by the Newlyn School of artists, a colony of artists resident in the town from the 1880s. The lives of fishing folk were chronicled in their work, much of which can be seen in the Penlee House Gallery and Museum in Penzance. The artistic tradition continues at Newlyn

Art Gallery, which shows the work of contemporary artists, focusing on painting and drawing.

Mousehole was Cornwall's main fishing port for years until Newlyn took its trade in the nineteenth century. It is a quintessentially pretty fishing village of stone cottages clustered around a neat little harbour that is especially charming during the Christmas period when it sparkles with festive illuminations.

As theatrical settings go, little can beat the Minack Theatre in Porthcurno for natural drama. Built from granite blocks by one woman, Rowena Cade, with the help of two gardeners, it sits above a gully jutting out into the sea.

The 14 miles of coastline from Pendeen to St Ives has been described as one of the most beautiful in the UK. With cliffs reaching over 90m high at Zennor Head, and the moors of West Penwith topped with tors behind, it is a thrilling stretch of coastal path to step out on.

The perfect seaside town and miles of sand

As seaside holiday destinations go, few beat St Ives. Once Cornwall's busiest pilchard port in the nineteenth century, it is now one of its biggest tourist spots. And it's easy to see why: four sandy beaches group around its headland, St Ives Head, which shelters two of them, Porthgwidden and Porthminster. The art gallery Tate St Ives looks out on Porthmeor Beach and on surfers sitting on their boards waiting for the next wave, and Harbour Beach is lined with restaurants and cafés and people sinking pints in the sun outside the ancient Sloop Inn. The town's particular light, bounced from the sea, and its narrow streets of whitewashed cottages with lichen-covered roofs have always attracted artists, most notably Barbara Hepworth, Bernard Leach and Ben Nicholson. Their work can be seen in the Barbara Hepworth Museum, The Leach Pottery and in Tate St Ives.

The scoop of St Ives Bay begins with the soft sand of family-friendly Porthminster Beach and continues through Carbis Bay, similarly sandy and less crowded, before sweeping past the Hayle Estuary and

Right: Porthcurno Beach

Close-up view of the white sand and turquoise waters of Porthcurno in the far west of Cornwall, The Minack Theatre is perched above it with outstanding panoramic views.

on to the vast beach running up to Gwithian Towans and Godrevy Point. Banks of turf-topped dunes ('towans' in Cornish) sprinkled with chalets and surf shacks and rich with wildlife and flowers, back the 3-mile beach, which stretches endlessly at low tide. The waves at Godrevy, whipped up from the Atlantic, are popular with surfers and surfing instructors can be seen throughout the year shepherding their pupils into the shallows for their lesson.

The lighthouse on Godrevy Island, a craggy islet at the end of St Ives Bay, was the inspiration for Virginia Woolf's *To the Lighthouse* and was erected in 1859 in response to the high number of shipwrecks. Godrevy Point is peppered with seabirds stopping off on their migratory flights or nesting on the steep cliffs.

The National Trust car park at Godrevy and the access road to the headland is vulnerable to coastal erosion and landslip. Early estimates gave the road some 15 years of life but the winter storms of 2013/14 have possibly halved that figure. The National Trust faces the challenge of managing the fragile coastal grassland and archaeological remains, and providing space for visitors to park and to enjoy the headland and beaches.

Beyond Godrevy, heading north to Portreath and to St Agnes Head, the coast, much of which is managed by the National Trust, is a continuous line of steep cliffs punctuated by sandy coves reached by narrow lanes. The South West Coast Path runs along its length, and with constantly breathtaking views and level terrain, makes for perfect walking.

Left: Godrevy

Enjoying the surf off Godrevy at the far end of St Ives Bay. The lighthouse sits about 300m off Godrevy Head on the largest rock of the Stones reef.

Right: Bedruthan Steps

Spectacular cliff-top view of the sea stacks that line a beach that is only accessible at low tide. The granite rocks are said to be the stepping-stones of the giant Bedruthan.

Chapel Porth, another vast sandy beach revealed at low tide, is also a popular surfing spot and the site of the World Bellyboarding Championships held every September, which attract competitors of all ages and abilities for a day of high-spirited fun (see page 268). The village of St Agnes was once a mining community with over 100 tin and copper mines. Remains of engine houses, perched right on the edge of the cliffs, can still be seen. St Agnes Beacon and surrounding cliff tops are all that remain of a huge tract of heathland, which once spread across Cornwall and is now a valuable habitat for wildlife and wild flowers.

Watersports and a slippery path

Newquay has become a destination for young would-be surfers and hedonists who flock to its surf pods and clubs in the summer as a rite of passage. The grand Victorian hotels on its headlands are a reminder of its earlier status as genteel destination for holidaymakers arriving by train. But to see it merely as a playground for kids is to miss much of what it has to offer. When Fistral Beach gets too congested with surfers, nearby Crantock is a wide and empty beach surrounded by dunes at the mouth of the River Gannel, which runs along its northern shore. Holywell Bay is another, vast sandy beach backed by the largest dune system owned by the National Trust, with the added attractions of a grotto-like cave and a rusty wreck which are both exposed at low tide.

Watersports enthusiasts flock to Watergate Bay, which, with 2 miles of sand at low tide, is ideal for surfers, kite surfers and even polo players (Polo on the Beach is held every year). The path from the cliff edge down to Bedruthan Steps is not for the faint-hearted: steep and often slippery, it tumbles towards the beach at an alarming pitch. It's worth the peril, though: on arrival the glittering beach, revealed at low tide, is studded with craggy rock stacks that have been shaped by a relentless sea (legend has it that these stacks were once the stepping-stones of a giant). The terrain along this stretch of the coast is constantly changing and visitors are advised to keep away from the crumbling cliff edge and to check tide times to make sure they don't get trapped at high tide.

Neighbouring beach resort Mawgan Porth is less wild and romantic but altogether safer. Sheltered by an enclosing valley and with soft white sand, it is ideal for new surfers and swimmers. A number of bars and hotels provide convivial perches from which to watch the sunset.

'… it is studded with craggy rock stacks that have been shaped by a relentless sea'

Left: The Rumps

The Rumps headland between New Polzeath and Port Quin is a prehistoric site. Its location across a thin strip of land or isthmus was exploited during the Iron Age when the local people built a series of ditches and ramparts to defend against landward attack.

Right: Boscastle

Tucked into a deep-sided valley, the village of Boscastle boasts a charming natural harbour and fifteenth-century cottages.

A wide and interesting estuary

North Cornwall's wall of cliffs is broken by the River Camel whose wide, sheltered estuary and tributaries were created by melting ice after the last Ice Age. On one of the creeks sits Padstow, a traditional fishing town now principally a tourist destination. Visitors come to eat pasties on the harbour wall and watch the boats, to amble through the narrow streets and to eat at one of Rick Stein's many seafood restaurants. The townsfolk come out in full force on 1 May (Beltane in the Celtic calendar) when the 'Obby 'Oss, a man wearing a fearsome mask and a black cape suspended from a circular frame, cavorts through the town preceded by teasers and followed by dancers dressed in white. Supposedly a fertility festival, it ends with the Oss being 'done to death' by onlookers.

The Camel Trail, an all-ability route for walkers, cyclists and horse riders, follows the track bed of the old Bodmin and Wadebridge Railway and is a pleasurable way to explore the area. A ferry sails across the estuary to Rock, a centre for sailing and water sports that has acquired a reputation for popularity among weekenders from London.

The wild and rugged Pentire Peninsula has views of Padstow Bay and the headland Trevose Head in the distance. The Rumps, an excavated Iron Age settlement is reached by crossing an isthmus, and the island of The Mouls can be seen from its ramparts. The Mouls were visited during the First World War by the poet Laurence Binyon, inspiring him to write his poem, with the familiar memorial lines, ' They shall not

grow old, as we that are left grow old; Age shall not weary them, nor the years condemn.'

Lundy Bay, set in a sheltered valley, is lush with wild-flower meadows and butterfly glades. It also has a spectacular natural arch created when the roof of a cave collapsed many years ago. A path from the car park to the beach will take you to Markham's Quay, a narrow natural fissure used by smugglers to hide their contraband.

King Arthur was here!

Cornwall is rich in legend and nowhere more so than at Tintagel. The ruined medieval castle, which spreads dramatically along a cliff-top 91m above the sea, has been linked with King Arthur and the Knights of the Round Table since Geoffrey of Monmouth in the twelfth century wrote that Arthur was conceived in Tintagel and had his power base there. These romantic notions unfortunately have little to substantiate them, although the wild and dramatic setting does much to keep the legend alive. The castle and the remains of a Celtic monastery sit on a narrow headland connected to the mainland by a finger of land, the crossing of which can feel like an epic adventure itself.

Barras Nose, the headland north of King Arthur's Castle was the first piece of English coast to be acquired by the National Trust in 1897, as a result of widespread concern about the number of houses and hotels springing up in Tintagel because of the Arthurian connections. In so doing, the National Trust managed to rescue one of the last vernacular

buildings, the Old Post Office, a fourteenth-century open hall house (see page 256).

With its stone cottages, tea rooms, Museum of Witchcraft, and Elizabethan quay, Boscastle is lively with visitors during the summer months. Throughout the nineteenth century, however, it was busy with boats. This was the time before railways when goods were moved by sea and, as one of the few natural inlets for 40 miles of coastline, Boscastle was the only place where a harbour could be built. Even so, it was not ideal: sailing vessels found it difficult to enter unless the sea was still, and the entrance was obstructed by the island of Meachard. As a result, they had to be towed in by row boats called 'hobblers' manned by eight oarsmen.

The floods of 2004 brought the town to the nation's attention when cars and buildings were swept into the harbour. Water funnelled down the deep Valency valley set between steep cliffs, and 91 people had to be rescued, although fortunately none had serious injuries. The National Trust owns 128 hectares (317 acres) of land in and around Boscastle, including the harbour and river, and was significantly involved in working with the local community to rebuild and adapt the village to future flooding, in keeping with its character and history.

This treacherous coastline claimed many victims during the age of sail. One beach called, ominously, The Strangles, saw 20 vessels wrecked on its shore during one year in the 1820s. The graveyard in St Genny's church in the tiny port of Crackington Haven has the graves of 14 sailors lost in two wrecks at the end of the nineteenth century. A good vantage point to experience this dangerous but thrilling shoreline is High Cliff, Cornwall's highest cliff, standing at 223m high.

The Cornish coastline ends in some style at Bude. With its extensive sands and white-topped waves, it is a major surfing destination, particularly the beaches at Summerleaze, Crooklets, Widemouth Bay and Sandymouth.

Left: Port Gaverne

The shingle inlet of Port Gaverne, near Port Isaac is the starting point of the 'Big Swim Cornwall' (see pages 268–269).

Right: Sandymouth Beach

The vast expanse of golden sand at Sandymouth makes it an ideal place to go horse riding.

Explore National Trust places on the Cornish Coast

Antony

This grand, two-storey house stands on a peninsular surrounded by the rivers Lynher and Tamar and the sea. Its 10 hectares (25 acres) of gardens, landscaped by Humphry Repton, run down to the banks of the River Lynher and include a knot garden and a formal garden with topiary. Unsurprising then, that Tim Burton chose it as a setting for his film *Alice in Wonderland*. The house was built for Sir William Carew between 1711 and 1721 and generations of the Carew family have lived here since, donating the house and garden to the National Trust in 1961. The gardens not only have the National Collection of daylilies but some pieces of modern sculpture including a water sculpture by William Pye. **Torpoint, Cornwall, PL11 2QA**

Trelissick Garden

The best way to approach Trelissick is by sailing up the Carrick Roads to the quay at the foot of the gardens (ferries sail from St Mawes and Falmouth). The white stucco of the house (not open to the public) can be seen sitting proudly above 12 hectares (30 acres) of garden, which roll down to the water's edge. The gardens were donated to the National Trust by Mrs Ida Copeland in 1955. Mrs Copeland, with her husband, planted many of the subtropical plants that still flourish in its warm micro-climate: canna, rhodendrons, camellias, ginkgo and ginger lilies, as well as numerous trees that make up the woodland walk. The National Trust has built on this horticultural heritage and added a Cornish orchard planted with 68 different

Left: Antony

The wrought-iron gates at the south front of Antony. The house is considered to be one of the finest surviving Queen Anne buildings in the West Country.

Left: Trelissick Garden

The Water Tower at Trelissick Garden was probably erected in the 1820s to provide water pressure for the house and garden. Today it is a one-bedroom holiday cottage.

Above: Glendurgan Garden

The cherry laurel maze at Glendurgan Garden was built in 1833 by Alfred and Sarah Fox to entertain their children.

species of mostly Cornish apple trees and a small sensory garden in what was the vegetable patch. There is also a gift shop, second-hand bookshop and six holiday cottages in the grounds. **Feock, near Truro, Cornwall TR3 6QL**

Glendurgan Garden

Ships arriving from the Americas, the Far East, Africa and the Antipodes in the 1820s and '30s provided Alfred Fox with a source of rare and exotic plants from around the world for his new garden. Grown in a lush valley in Cornwall's temperate climate, species such as the weeping Mexican cypress, Japanese loquat and magnolias, flourished. Giant gunnera gave the lower valley a jungle-like feel and spiky cacti and agave basked in the sun on the upper slopes. Cuthbert and Philip Fox gave the garden to the National Trust in 1962 and a period of restoration followed. The serpentine cherry laurel maze, planted by Alfred and Sarah Fox for their 12 children in 1833, was carefully coaxed back to its former glory, as was the 'Giant's Stride', a pole with ropes to swing from – always popular with children.

At the bottom of the valley garden is the hamlet of Durgan, which sits on the banks of the Helford river, and is the ideal place to watch birds, go boating, skim stones and go rock-pooling. **Mawnan Smith, near Falmouth, Cornwall TR11 5JZ**

 Holiday Cottage

Hemmick Cottage, St Austell. The beauty of this cottage is its simplicity. It sits in splendid isolation overlooking a sandy beach and the sea surrounded by farmland. Built in the mid-nineteenth century on the site of a demolished fishing hamlet, it may be small but it is perfectly constructed and simply furnished.

It would be hard to imagine a more idyllic and picturesque spot for a holiday than Hemmick. The beach is ideal for sandcastle building, and rock pools are revealed a low tide. A two-tier garden at the front has a picnic table and access to the beach and the Coast Path runs right outside the front door with walks across National Trust land. The nearest pub and shops are in Gorran Haven a mile and a half away. For more information see www.nationaltrustcottages.co.uk.

St Michael's Mount

Rising from the sea and reached only by a tidal causeway, St Michael's Mount, especially when enveloped by sea mist, has an enchanted look about it. So it's surprising to learn that it is still the home of James and Mary St Aubyn and family, who live in the castle surrounded by armour and antiques. In 1954 Francis St Aubyn gave most of the Mount to the National Trust, plus an endowment for its upkeep, but he also retained a 999-year lease to enable the family to live in the castle. They share the rocky island with 30 islanders including a head gardener, who maintains the terraced gardens that burst with subtropical plants. The island is topped by a fifteenth-century church that sits alongside the castle and gives the Mount its gothic silhouette: it is open from March to November. It is best reached by walking across the causeway at low tide, although a boat is also an option. It is also worth bearing in mind that it lies on one of Britain's most prominent ley lines, so may well be enchanted. **Marazion, Cornwall, TR17 0HS**

Tintagel Old Post Office

With its tumbledown roof and garden full of colourful blooms, this medieval yeoman's farmhouse has a fairy-tale feel about it. Set back from Tintagel's high street, it was acquired by the National Trust in 1903 and was its first built property in Cornwall. Its name dates from the Victorian period when it held a licence to be a letter-receiving station – there is a display of postal equipment inside. Take time to have a good look around the sensitively restored interior. There are many pieces of antique furniture to see and a traditional Cornish

Below: The Old Post Office

The front of the Old Post Office buildings off the main street through the centre of Tintagel village.

Right: St Michael's Mount

The causeway disappears beneath the water at high tide, and instead a small boat transports visitors to and from the island.

'It is best reached by walking across the causeway at low tide'

cloam oven built into the side of the chimney which is still used to bake bread and cakes. Don't miss the slate wall topped with turf built around the front garden: this is a fine example of a traditional wall built from slate quarried locally in a chevron design or 'curzyway'.

Fore Street, Tintagel, Cornwall, PL34 0DB

 ## Holiday Cottage

Guy's Cottage, Port Quin. Sitting yards from the beach, this stone cottage is one of two former fishermen's cottages located just off the South West Coast Path. There are sea views from the bedrooms, a wood-burning stove and stable doors that open on to a private walled terrace. Port Quin is a small hamlet set in a secluded cove between Polzeath and Port Isaac. For more information see www.nationaltrustcottages.co.uk.

Trengwainton Garden

This 10-hectare (25-acre) garden oasis harbours international species such as Tasmanian tree ferns, tropical banana plants and Chinese magnolias, while from the terrace, there are views of sparkling Mount's Bay. Central to its design is the walled Kitchen Garden, built by past owner Sir Rose Price to the dimensions of Noah's Ark, which is full of interest year-round. Look out for toads in the pond in springtime and vibrant autumn colour in the pumpkin patch.

Madron, near Penzance, TR20 8RZ

Below: Trengwainton Garden

The Kitchen Garden at Trengwainton was created around 1814 with raised sloping beds to combat cold weather, and the Head Gardener's cottage was built into the north wall.

Being a National Trust volunteer

The National Trust relies on its army of volunteers to help maintain its special places, and in return volunteers learn new skills and meet new people. Whether it's assisting with the pruning at a garden, guiding visitors around a house or helping with conservation work at the coast or country, the work is generally useful and rewarding. Steve is a full-time volunteer ranger in South East Cornwall:

'Being a full-time volunteer for the National Trust is a fantastic opportunity to get first-hand experience in practical environmental conservation. Employment in this sector is highly competitive, and volunteering is an excellent way of learning and practising some of the essential skills needed.

'I am part of a team that works within some of the country's most beautiful areas. In my six months so far, I have been involved in all aspects of the work that goes on here, and I feel that my work has been valued and has counted towards the management of countryside and coast around Fowey, Polruan, Polperro and Looe.

'A lot of my time is spent taking care of the coastal path that runs through our patch. This involves many things, from strimming to replacing steps and installing benches. There is always something different to learn each day.

'As a ranger I get to work at open days where I really engage with the public and help to promote these special areas. These are not just the places where I'm based, but also other parts of the country where I can see how other teams work.

'All in all I would thoroughly recommend volunteering. I see it as the first step in my goal to work in this sector. It's fun and enjoyable, but most importantly it's rewarding and you feel like you have made a difference.'

For more information see www.nationaltrust.org.uk.

Cotehele Estate

In the nineteenth-century Cotehele Quay bustled with vessels loading and unloading cargo: the River Tamar was the principle route to the sea for the surrounding area. Paddle steamers came upriver to see the valley's orchards and small boats carried market-gardening produce down the river for sale at Devonport Market. These days, a restored sailing barge *Shamrock* is moored at the quay – built to carry cargo up and down the river, it is a reminder of the area's mercantile past. Find out more about Cotehele Quay at the Discovery Centre.

The fortified manor house of Cotehele, the seat of the Edgcumbe family for six centuries, stands on high ground above the quay surveying the river. It is filled with fascinating artefacts, among them tapestries and suits of armour. Venture into the wild Valley Garden to see the sixteenth-century dovecote. Go online for details of riverside and woodland walks through the estate, and historic Cotehele Mill. **St Dominick, near Saltash, PL12 6TA**

St Anthony Head

The St Anthony Lighthouse lies at the southernmost tip of the Roseland Peninsula, an unspoilt headland perfect for walking (the South West Coast Path passes along here) and for views of the Fal Estuary. The lighthouse guards the entrance to the natural harbour of Falmouth and was built in 1834 to keep boats safe from the Manacles rocks. Its old officers' quarters are now converted into holiday cottages. Nearby are two sandy beaches: Great Molunan and Little Molunan, and a bird hide from which you can see shags, fulmars and grey seals.

Holiday Cottage

Bar Lodge, Helston. Built by Captain John Peverell Rogers of Penrose more than a century ago, this handsome house is approached via a winding track through the woods. Perched above Loe Bar, with views of the sea, from the high cliffs of the Lizard to the south to the Land's End Peninsula in the distant west, and with Loe Pool (the largest natural freshwater lake in Cornwall) just behind, there are endless opportunities for adventure. The lodge has a roof terrace with table and chairs overlooking the sea, and a multi-fuel stove in the living room. For more information see www.nationaltrustcottages.co.uk.

Below: Cotehele

The north-west tower on the estate amidst the spring daffodils. It was built at a later date than the house in 1627.

Right: St Anthony Head

A view along the cliff at St Anthony Head from above Great Molunan beach, near Falmouth.

Everybody's gone surfing…

Cornwall, with its shallow, sandy beaches and mighty waves, is the country's most popular coastline for surfers. As the National Trust owns and manages many of these beaches, it is keen for people of all ages to get out in the water to catch a wave. One of the best ways to get people 'stoked' about surfing is to meet those who live and breathe the sport: the National Trust Surf Ambassadors. Champions such as Alan Stokes and longboarder Ben Skinner help National Trust rangers at eco-surf events and spread the word about the joys of surfing wherever they can. Find out more about them at www. nationaltrust.org.uk.

If you are keen to learn to surf, then a lesson with a National Trust licensed surf school is the place start.

Top National Trust surfing beaches in Cornwall:

1. **Sandymouth:** ideal surfing conditions but beware, the beach almost vanishes at high tide, concealing rocks. Learn to surf at the Sandymouth Surf School.

2. **Holywell Bay:** popular spot away from the busier Newquay beaches. There are two National Trust licensed surf schools here: Cornwall Surf Academy and Holywell Bay School of Surf.

3. **Godrevy:** a popular beach at the north end of St Ives Bay. There are two National Trust licensed surf schools: Shore Surf School and Gwithian Academy of Surfing.

4. **Crantock:** good for all abilities. Learn to surf at Crantock Bay Surf School.

5. **Poldhu Cove:** surf suitable for all abilities. Learn to surf at the Dan Joel Surf School.

6. **Whitsand Bay:** 4 miles of surfing on this busy beach.

Above: Looe Bar

A vantage point on the Penrose Estate that overlooks the shingle bar and freshwater lake trapped behind.

Penrose

The Penrose Estate enfolds Loe Pool, Cornwall's largest natural freshwater lake, which is cut off from the sea by a broad shingle bar heaped up by the Atlantic. The estate is a mixture of farmland and woodland and is threaded through with paths and cycle tracks, from Helston to Porthleven. Stroll through the woods, keeping eyes peeled for butterflies, dragonflies and moths, which teem around the tributaries running into the Pool. Alternatively, walk around the perimeter of Loe Pool (a 6-mile hike), watch migrant birds in the winter from hides, and re-imagine Arthurian legends.

'Stroll through the woods keeping eyes peeled for butterflies and dragonflies.'

Sandymouth

The eastern tip of north Cornwall, between Bude and Morwenstow, has several beaches that are perfect for rockpooling and surfing. One of these is Sandymouth, which is enclosed by sheer cliffs made of stony clay rock. Take the dog here for a serious romp on the miles of sandy beach (dogs are allowed all year) and then head to the Sandymouth Café for refreshments.

Above: Sandymouth Beach

Taking the dogs for a walk on the cliff top above Sandymouth, looking down on its wide beach and sheer cliffs.

Shore-spotter's Guide

1

The return of the **chough** (*Pyrrhocorax pyrrhocorax*) to Cornwall in 2001 and the Lizard Peninsula in particular, is especially cheering as it has become a symbol of the county, even appearing on its coat of arms. Destruction of its preferred habitat – grazed heath and cliff land – had led to a decline in numbers. Grazing by sheep, cattle and ponies kept vegetation short and open, revealing insects such as cranefly larvae, dung beetles and ants for the birds to feed on. The National Trust has worked with farmers and landowners to re-introduce Highland cattle and Soay sheep to the coastal cliffs and has been rewarded with the sight of 118 chicks fledging from Cornish nests.

2

Deserted mine shafts in Polzeath, Pentire Points and The Rumps provide perfect habitats and hibernation spots for the **greater horseshoe bat** (*Rhinolophus ferrumequinum*): it was originally a cave dweller. One of the largest British bat species, it has soft, fluffy fur, is between 57mm and 71mm long, on average, and has a distinctive noseleaf. Numbers of the greater horseshoe bat have declined by 98 per cent in the last 100 years in the UK – those that remain are mostly found in south-west England.

3

The West Pentire Fields, west of Newquay, has been designated as an Important Plant Area by Plantlife and are a good place to find **Venus looking glass** (*Legousia hybrida*). With blue, violet or white bell-shaped flowers, it has a long calyx that resembles a mirror's handle (hence its name). Becoming increasingly rare due to modern farming methods, this herb belongs to the bellflower (Campanulaceae) family. Other flowers to look for here are small-flowered catchfly, weasel's snout, pyramidal orchid and carline thistle.

4

Look out into the ocean from the cliffs at Godrevy and you may just spot a **basking shark** (*Cetorhinus maximus*). The second largest living fish after the whale shark, it is a slow-moving filter feeder and it has a huge jaw (up to 1m wide), long gill slits and gill rakers and a pointed snout to feed on plankton. Also look out for dolphins and seals, all common visitors to warm Cornish waters.

5

You will only find **Cornish heath** (*Erica vagans*) growing in one place in the UK: on the Lizard Peninsula. The unusual geology here (basically an exposed section of the Earth's oceanic crust called ophiolite) gives rise to the alkaline, nutrient-poor soil it favours. Cornish heath was voted the County Flower of Cornwall in 2002 by the wild flora conservation charity Plantlife. The Lizard is a rich botanical area generally: wild flowers including squill, campion and thrift thrive here, as do dropwort, lady's bedstraw, milkwort and self-heal. Around the lighthouse, you will see an exotic-looking plant with pink and yellow flowers and fleshy leaves. This is the hottentot fig which is actually a bit of a bully and can smother native plants.

6

When walking the headland at Zennor or Rinsey near Breage, look out for a tangle mass of spaghetti-like plant. This is **dodder** (*Cuscuta*) a parasitical plant that produces no chlorophyll of its own but obtains all nutrients from the host plant it lives on. These plants are often found on gorse, heather and wild thyme growing on coastal heath. There are many different species of dodder but it is almost always yellowish-orange and has no leaves.

Lizard Point walk

BEGINNER GRADE

Distance: 1 mile (1.6km)

Time: 30–40 minutes

This scenic walk around Britain's most southerly point offers a chance to find rare plants, see Cornish choughs and enjoy a cream tea to finish. The Lizard Lighthouse was first built in 1751 and altered in 1903. The electric lantern has 150,000 candlepower and casts its beam for more than 20 miles. It also has one of the world's loudest fog horns, which you'll definitely hear on a foggy day.

Terrain

There are some steep steps on this walk, as well as stiles and the path goes close to cliff edges in places. Dogs are welcome.

Directions

1 Start at the National Trust car park next to the Lizard Lighthouse. The lighthouse, one of the largest in the world, was automated in 1998 and its engine rooms are now open to the public during the summer months.

2 Walk down to Lizard Point, following signs to the most southerly point. Look out for seals in the cove. The succulent plant growing here is the hottentot fig, an import from South Africa which has been steadily encroaching in areas, smothering some of the rare plants that grow on these cliffs, like the prostrate asparagus, which has been growing here since at least 1667.

'Look out for some Cornish choughs on the way'

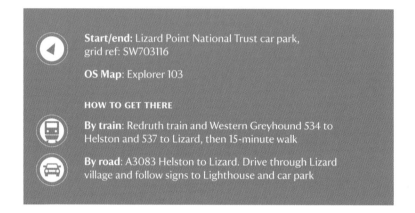

Start/end: Lizard Point National Trust car park, grid ref: SW703116

OS Map: Explorer 103

HOW TO GET THERE

By train: Redruth train and Western Greyhound 534 to Helston and 537 to Lizard, then 15-minute walk

By road: A3083 Helston to Lizard. Drive through Lizard village and follow signs to Lighthouse and car park

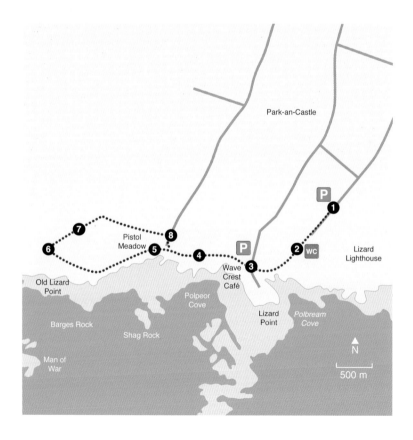

Left: Lizard Point

The lighthouse was built in 1751 and altered in 1903. It has one of the world's loudest fog horns.

Above: Wild asparagus

Wild asparagus growing in June on the coastline near Cadgwith, on the Lizard Peninsula.

⑤ Take the steps down to Pistol Meadow, the burial site of over 200 people when the *Royal Anne* troopship went down on the off-lying reefs in 1720. In keeping with the tradition of the day, the troops were denied a Christian burial and put into a mass grave at the valley bottom. Climb out of the valley on the Coast Path up the slope towards Lizard Head.

③ At the Point bear right and join the South West Coast Path in front of the Wave Crest Café. Look out for some Cornish choughs on the way. They are easily distinguished from other members of the crow family by their red bills and legs, and their distinctive 'cheeow' call.

④ Follow the Coast Path above Polpeor Cove. As excise duties increased, smuggling became an industry in Cornwall, and perhaps nowhere more so than on The Lizard. Luxury goods such as tobacco and brandy were shipped from France and were landed on the quiet coves of the peninsula from where pack horses quickly took the barrels to hiding places.

⑥ From the top of Old Lizard Head, looking west, you can see out towards Kynance Cove and beyond. Our hardy band of Shetland ponies and our tenants' cattle help maintain the rich flora and fauna of the coastal slopes, which make an ideal habitat for feeding choughs.

⑦ Take the footpath inland over the stile built into the dry-stone wall and walk across the field back towards Pistol Meadow.

⑧ Carry on over another stile into Pistol Meadow field and re-join the Coast Path to return to Lizard Point. If you want to avoid the stiles, retrace your steps from route point 6 along the Coast Path.

Seaside things to do in Cornwall

① Coasteer around the Lizard

To experience the coast from a new perspective – and to get up close and personal with Lizard's unusual pink and green serpentine rocks – why not have a crack at coasteering? This relatively new adrenaline sport (devised in the mid-1980s) involves scrambling, swimming and jumping your way around the shore – and getting absolutely soaked in the process.

Other National Trust places to coasteer: Stackpole Quay, Pembrokeshire; Boscastle, Cornwall; Polzeath Beach, Cornwall.

② Try bellyboarding

Every September a colourful bunch of enthusiasts take to the surf at Chapel Porth as part of the World Bellyboarding Championships.

All you need to participate is a plank of wood (well a surfboard-shaped plank made from ply) and a swimsuit. No wetsuits, leashes or swim fins are allowed. Organised and hosted by the National Trust, the championships attract contestants of all ages eager to plunge into the waves and be 'hooshed' ashore before tucking into tea and cucumber sandwiches. Chapel Porth itself, and its surrounding landscape, has changed little over the past 50 years, providing a perfect vintage atmosphere for the champs. For more information see www.bellyboarding.co.uk.

③ Paddle, snorkle or do the 'Big Swim'

Dippers and divers will delight in the saltwater bathing opportunities around this coast. Top of the list has to be Treyarnon Bay, near Padstow, for its warm, natural plunge pool (effectively a giant rock

Left: Coasteering

There are several great places to try this exhilarating sport including here at Mullion Cove on the Lizard Peninsula.

pool, above the beach). Crackington Haven and Porthminster (St Ives) are perfect for paddling, and Poltesco on the Lizard for snorkelling. Keen swimmers might like to compete in the Big Swim Cornwall, an annual beach-to-beach race supported by The National Trust. This takes place in August between the National Trust beach of Port Gaverne and Port Isaac, raising thousands of pounds for charity. Pick your event – from the Serious Swim of 1 mile to the Super Serious Swim (three times the distance). There's also a Little Swim for junior competitors.

④ See tin mines from the Coast Path

There are 300 miles of the South West Coast Path in Cornwall, nearly half its entire length, offering a wide range of routes for all abilities. More challenging stretches include the section between Boscastle and Tintagel, where tough cliff climbs are rewarded by the stirring sight of the legendary castle ruins (not National Trust but well managed by English Heritage) soaring above the sea. Or there's the 8-mile trek west from St Ives – a visual feast of Atlantic views across to 'Seal Island' and windswept Penwith moorland – landing in the ancient hamlet of Zennor. The best way to view Bedruthan Steps (seen from the National Trust site of Carnewas), or the industrial ruins of the Cornish Mining World Heritage Site (at St Agnes or St Just, for example), is on foot. And there's always the chance you'll catch sight of grey seals, dolphins or basking sharks en route. For routes see www.nationaltrust.org.uk.

⑤ Explore Cornwall's art colonies

The wild landscape and Mediterranean light of Cornwall has long drawn painters and sculptors here – and at the peninsula's south-western tip, two artists' colonies took root in the nineteenth and twentieth centuries. The Newlyn School of painters (such as Lamorna Birch and Walter Langley) flocked to this fishing village from the 1880s to paint local scenes *en plein air*. Their work can be seen at the Penlee House Gallery and Museum set within its own park, in Penzance. St Ives, of course, is synonymous with the Modernist pioneers (Barbara Hepworth and Ben Nicholson; Patrick Heron and Terry Frost), who set up home here in the early-to-mid twentieth century. Cornwall's 1993 landmark gallery Tate St Ives, overlooking Porthmeor Beach, regularly features works from this period, and combined tickets can be purchased for the gallery and Barbara Hepworth Museum and Sculpture Garden – a haven of tranquility in the town. The St Ives School of Painting, established in 1938, continues to run creative classes from the historic

Get under canvas

If you are part of the ever-growing band of camping enthusiasts, you might want to check out a National Trust campsite. All located in beautiful spots, they are a good option for an affordable, outdoor holiday. Take Highertown Farm Campsite on the south-east Cornish coast. Just off the South West Coast Path, the site is in the hamlet of Lansallos, just less than a mile from the beaches and coves of Lantivet and Lantic Bays and a short drive from the towns of Polperro, Fowey and Looe. Run with the environment in mind, it has solar-powered hot water, composting toilets and recycling facilities. The perfect get-away-from-it-all location for nature lovers, in other words. If tents are not your thing, the National Trust also has timber camping pods, yurts, bothies and bunkhouses. For more information see www.nationaltrust.org.uk or call 01208 265211.

Porthmeor Studios, where artists and fishermen have worked side by side for more than a century.

⑥ Visit the Isles of Scilly

Catch an early flight to Scilly from either Land's End or Newquay – or take the *Scillonian III* ferry from Penzance – and you can be enjoying a coastal walk around St Mary's, the largest island in the archipelago, by lunchtime. Explore the wild promontory of Peninnis Head, a notorious ship-wrecking site made up of rugged granite outcrops and boulders, then head for the Garrison, and sixteenth-century Star Castle (now a hotel), built in the wake of the Armada. Alternatively, make the short boat trip, around 10–15 minutes, from St Mary's to Tresco, and visit the subtropical Tresco Abbey Garden, founded by plant collector Augustus Smith in the 1830s. Then hop on a mid-afternoon sailing (or late afternoon flight) back to the mainland.

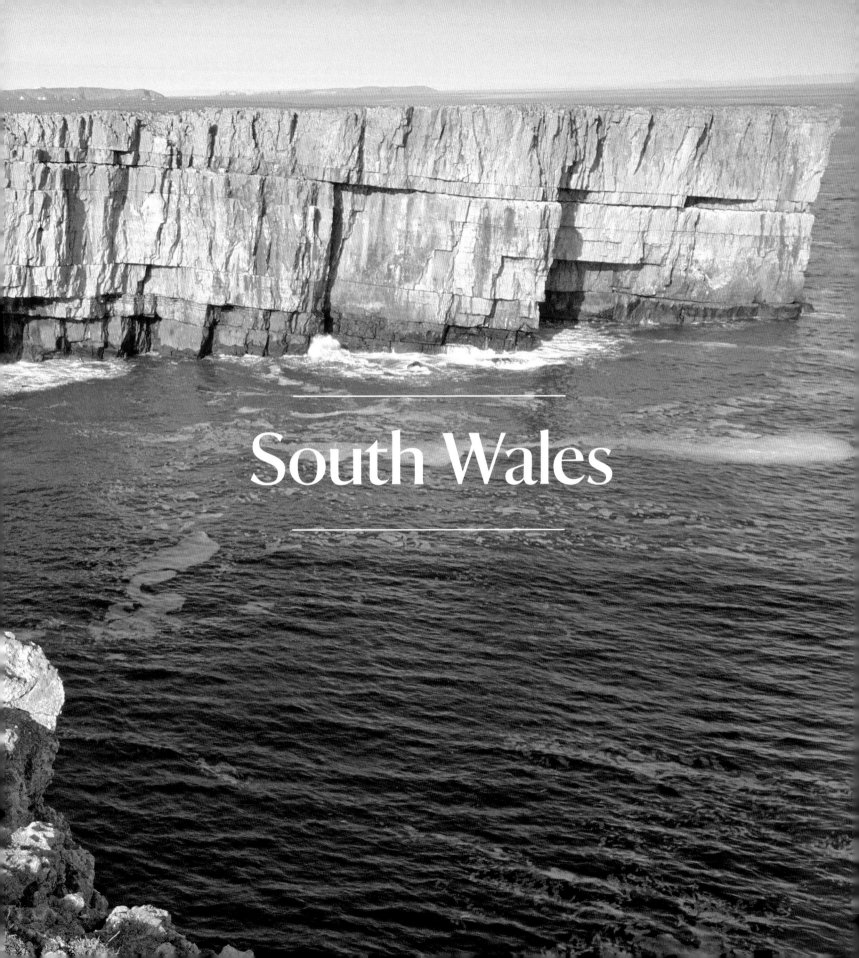

South Wales

One of the main purposes of the Neptune Coastline Campaign is to make as much of the coast as possible accessible to everyone. As the National Trust owns and manages 157 miles of the Welsh coastline (one third of Pembrokeshire, for example) it was able to further this aim by helping to enable the opening of the Wales Coast Path in 2012. This new path runs around Wales's coast from Chepstow to Queensferry, making Wales the only country in the world where you can walk the entire length of its coast. Established trails, such as the Pembrokeshire Coast Path, have been knitted together, and now walkers can enjoy the diverse shoreline with few interruptions.

And what a shoreline it is: South Wales's glorious stretches of award-winning beaches such as Barafundle, Rhossili and Pendine are guarded by spectacular cliffs rich with wildlife and generous with views. Small offshore islands such as Skomer and Ramsey chatter with the sounds of seabird colonies, and estuaries and inlets are dotted with small boats and watersports enthusiasts. Remote sections of the path have plenty of space for soul-searching escapists and pretty resorts offer plenty of options for those in a more sociable frame of mind.

Previous pages: Cliff scenery around Stackpole Head, Pembrokeshire.

Left: Looking from Carn Llidi on St David's Head towards Strumble Head in the far distance.

South Wales: post-industrial towns and unspoilt beauty

The coastline of South Wales starts with a story of declining export trade, industry and mining. The three cities of Newport, Cardiff and Swansea have all suffered from a decline in their economic fortunes. Fortunately this situation is being turned around as post-industrial sites are regenerated. Where once there were busy docks now there are marinas; and where once seamen disembarked for a night of carousing, now shoppers amble laden with carrier bags.

Newport once depended on the shipping of coal, mined in the nearby valleys, to keep its dockyards busy and its men in employment. When coal mining declined (1930 saw the filling in of the docks), the opening of the Llanwern Steelworks kept the town's fortunes afloat until 2001 when steel production ceased. Plans are afoot to regenerate the steelworks site, creating more housing and employment. Unique to the city is its 74m high transporter bridge, which moves cars across the river on a gondola above the water, the height necessary to avoid the masts of tall ships. Visitors who are brave enough can walk across the bridge on its upper deck for a vertiginous view of the city.

Cardiff, the capital city of Wales, was once one of the busiest ports in the world. Much of the credit for this must go to the 2nd Marquess of Bute who expanded the docks in 1839 and connected them to the pits and ironworks. But by the 1960s coal exports had virtually stopped and the docks went into decline. Following a regeneration programme that began in 1987, the waterfont has been reinvented. 'Cardiff Bay' is now home to the Welsh Assembly (the debating chamber is a fine modern building designed by Richard Rogers and known as the Senedd) and the Wales Millennium Centre arts complex. Visitors to the city come to attend sporting events and concerts at the Millennium Stadium and to shop in St David's Centre and in the Victorian and Edwardian arcades near the castle.

Penarth and Barry also suffered economically from the decline of the coal industry and they too have reinvented themselves. Penarth, billed as 'The Garden by the Sea' in Victorian times, is a holiday destination. Yachts drop anchor in the marina, formerly the dock. Barry was created by the coal boom in the late nineteenth century and enjoyed a period of intense activity when its harbour was used as docks and coal sidings. After the First World War, a slump in coal exports meant the boom was short lived. These days Barry is still a port but industry has shifted to manufacturing. The sandy beach at Barry Island, a peninsula linked to the mainland, has always drawn holidaymakers and is a thronging resort complete with a beachside pleasure park offering stomach-lurching rides.

Long strips of flat beaches run up the east coast of Swansea Bay. Access to Kenfig and Margam Sands is tricky because of the high dune systems that back them, but it's well worth the effort. Both are less visited than the more famous beaches on the Gower Peninsula, and feel remote and secluded, plus the surfing is good. Porthcawl is another example of port-turned-resort, and has a large caravan park, two Blue Flag beaches and an amusement park, Coney Beach Pleasure Park, which was built to entertain American troops – it was named after Coney Island in New York.

'Visitors who are brave enough can walk across the bridge on its upper deck'

Right: Newport

The famous Newport Transporter Bridge dominates the skyline. It operates as a suspended ferry, carrying vehicles across the river on a gondola.

A peninsula of unspoilt beauty

The enormous sandy beaches, high cliffs and saltmarshes of the Gower Peninsula are a world away from the city bustle of nearby Swansea. The Neptune Coastline Campaign (or Enterprise Neptune as it was originally named) acquired Whiteford Burrows in 1965 (the first acquisition under Neptune) and since then has supported the Gower: the National Trust now looks after 26 miles of Gower coastline, three quarters of which is an Area of Outstanding Natural Beauty, the UK's first.

Swansea Bay sweeps past Swansea – gradually shaking off the relics of its copper-based industrial past – to Mumbles Head and suddenly it feels like holiday time. Generous beaches are lined with hotels, B&Bs and seaside attractions that stretch from Swansea to the small town of Mumbles, known as the gateway to the Gower.

Beyond Mumbles Head, a series of bays (Langland, Caswell and Pwlldu) are reached by narrow roads and winding footpaths. Everything feels bucolic and secluded and surprisingly remote. Pwlldu Head is the

Dylan Thomas (1914–1953)

The Welsh poet known for works such as *Under Milk Wood* and *A Child's Christmas in Wales* was born in Swansea. He spent much of his life in the small nearby town of Laugharne where he lived in the Boathouse with his family, and wrote in a wooden hut above the River Taf. Both are open to the public (not National Trust). Thomas loved to gaze at the estuary from the hut, which is kept exactly as it was during his lifetime. Much of the view, including Mwche and Pentowyn directly opposite the Boathouse, is owned by the National Trust and Thomas described it as 'the mussel pooled and the heron priested shore' in his 'Poem in October'. He also wrote much of *Under Milk Wood* there.

Below: Three Cliffs Bay

Looking down onto the Pobbles with Three Cliffs Bay tucked in behind.

Right: Pennard Pill

The river, Pennard Pill, flows down the wooded valley and meanders into Three Cliffs Bay.

Port Eynon is a popular swimming spot and a pretty village with a sandy beach backed by dunes protected from westerly winds by the headland of Port Eynon Point. Burrowed into the headland are caves that were used as homes in prehistoric times, and the curious Culver Hole. This tall, narrow natural cleft in the cliff face has been sealed off by a 18m-high stone wall punctured with windows and a door, believed to date from the thirteenth or fourteenth century. Behind the wall are tiers of ledges thought to have housed pigeons (an important source of food) during the Middle Ages. Culver derives from the Old English word 'culfre' meaning pigeon or dove.

Follow the VW campervans down Gower's narrow roads and inevitably they will lead you to Rhossili Bay. This great curve of beach, acquired by the National Trust in 1967, faces directly west and the wind whips across the sea, forming crest after crest of crashing surf. Wet-suited surfers paddle out to catch the perfect wave and then ride back to

highest headland on the Gower and has great views of Pennard Cliffs, an important nesting site for chough and raven, and the Mumbles.

Walk from here to glorious Three Cliffs Bay for a real taste of what the Gower has to offer: unspoilt, wild beauty. Despite being popular with campers (it's one of the most scenic places in the country to pitch a tent) and climbers who feel their way up its sheer cliffs, Three Cliffs Bay can still be unexpectedly deserted. There is plenty of room to fling a Frisbee or run barefoot on its vast white sands, and dogs can charge up and down all year round. A scramble up from the beach through woodland reaches the romantic ruins of Pennard Castle, which is photographed almost as much as the bay itself.

Slightly inland, the dunes of Penmaen Burrows and Nicholaston Burrows are backed by heathland and woodland and fringed with cliffs, among which can be found the remains of a Neolithic burial chamber and a medieval church. You may spot the common lizard.

The village of Oxwich Bay is sheltered from the sea by the dunes of Oxwich Burrows that face 2 miles of sandy beach, which often ranks in magazine round-ups of the UK's best beaches. Less dramatic than its neighbours, Oxwich Bay is gentle on the senses with smaller dunes and a National Nature Reserve bursting with orchids, butterflies, lizards and all manner of birds. Shallow, calm waters mean it is safe to swim here, but watch out for small boats and jet skis.

Below: Worms Head

The colourful mixture of shells, pebbles and seaweed on the high tide line at Worms Head, Gower Peninsula.

shore. But there is more to Rhossili than surfing. The beach is wide –
3-miles long – bordered by mountainous dunes, and is generally
an invigorating place to be. Firm sand makes it ideal for walking
and a stroll here will take you past the skeletal remains of *Helvetia*,
a Norwegian ship wrecked in 1887, which still pokes through the sand
at the south end of the beach. Rhossili Down is a lowland heath and
home to a variety of birds and insects, including the rare black bog ant.
The South Gower coast hosts many rare plants and birds, including
yellow whitlow grass and choughs.

The scale and splendour of Rhossili is best seen from the cliff-top
path on Worms Head at the Bay's southern end. This spiny ribbon of

Above: Rhossili Bay

Looking out across the breathtaking Rhossili Bay
from the south as it sweeps around. This is an
ideal place for walking, surfing and rock climbing.

rock snakes out into the sea and can only be reached by crossing the
causeway at low tide (a young Dylan Thomas was stranded here one
night after misjudging the speed at which the tide sweeps in). The
Worm teems with birds from April to July as razorbills, kittiwakes,
fulmars and cormorants take residence. For views across the entire
Gower Peninsula over the sea to West Wales and the North Devon
coast, climb up to Rhossili Down and you will not be disappointed.

At the northern end of Rhossili Bay is Burry Holms, a tidal island crowned with an Iron Age fort, and beyond that is Whiteford Sands backed by Whiteford Burrows, see page 290. Much of the north coast of the Gower is saltmarsh, mudflats and tidal ditches, perfect feeding ground for wading birds and wildfowl, and for grazing sheep: saltmarsh lamb is a local delicacy. Cockles are another delicacy, which are raked from the sandy flats in the Burry Estuary near Penclawdd and sold worldwide. Try some for breakfast accompanied by laverbread (see feature, below), for a truly Welsh start to the day.

The River Tywi ends its 75-mile journey at a wide-mouthed estuary spilling into Carmarthen Bay. On the eastern side is Cefn Sidan Sands, which at 7 miles long, is one of Wales's biggest beaches. Favoured by kite buggies and kite flyers, who make the most of its wide, pancake-flat sand, it is also safe for swimming, although it's a long walk to the water's edge. On the western side, the hard flat surface of Pendine Sands, which stretches for 6 miles, made it a natural for land-speed attempts, most famously by Sir Malcolm Campbell and Parry Thomas, another racer, who died trying to break the record in 1927. Laugharne, a small town overlooking the River Taf, is where Dylan Thomas (see feature, page 276) famously lived and wrote. He is buried in the local churchyard.

A ragged coast of cliffs and coves

The Wales Coast Path continues to rollercoaster its way along a shoreline of estuaries, cliff tops and wide sandy beaches from Amroth in the south to St Dogmaels in the north. Although fishing and farming have shaped the landscape, the countryside is largely unspoilt and provides a taste of the wild and dramatic enjoyed by walkers striding out on the Coast Path. The less energetic can also benefit from Pembrokeshire's string of delightful resorts, accessible Blue-Flag beaches and ever-improving restaurants and hotels. Chief among these is Tenby. With its parade of Georgian houses the colour of Neopolitan ice-cream, long sandy beaches, sheltered harbour and position at the end of a rocky headland, it has it all. As artist Augustus John wrote of his home town: 'You may travel the world over but you will find nothing more beautiful. It is so restful, so colourful and so unspoilt.' The rocky promontory on which it is built

Left: Broadhaven South

The beach lies at the foot of the Bosherston Lakes, created 200 years ago to provide a backdrop to Stackpole Court.

'Another delicacy is cockles, which are raked from the sandy flats'

divides the town in two: one side (North Beach) is a sandy harbour facing the Gower; the other (South Beach) faces Caldey Island and the Atlantic ocean. Both are comfortable places to spend a day or two and, along with nearby Saundersfoot, make this stretch Wales's most popular seaside destination.

Visitors come to neighbouring Stackpole and Bosherston Lakes (see page 286), to enjoy the quiet beauty of Barafundle Bay and Broadhaven South beach adjacent to the Lakes. Reached by travelling along winding forest roads, then a 10-minute walk across fields, through a stone archway and down a staircase, to arrive at Barafundle – regularly featured as one of the Top 10 beaches in the world – is an adventure in itself. Backed by limestone cliffs, woods and dunes and sheltered from south westerlies by two limestone headlands, it is the perfect spot for a picnic or a day spent paddling in its shallow, sandy waters.

Further along, the Coast Path passes above St Govan's Chapel, a thirteenth-century hermit's house that looks as if it was created

A curious thing … laverbread

Described by Richard Burton as 'the Welshman's caviar', laverbread ('bara lawr' in Welsh) is a traditional dish made from seaweed. From the eighteenth century until the mid-twentieth, laver was collected daily from Pembrokeshire beaches and dried in huts along the shore. This cottage industry once boasted as many as 20 laver-drying huts at Freshwater West (the one on the cliff top has been restored) and provided income for many families. After it has been washed and dried, the laver is shredded, boiled for several hours and then puréed. The resulting black/green paste is the laverbread. This is eaten either raw or coated in oatmeal and fried. Served with bacon and cockles, it makes a hearty and nutritious breakfast (laver is rich in protein, iron and iodine). These days, laverbread is experiencing something of a revival as more people forage and as chefs cook with wild foods.

from the cliff face that surrounds it and, offshore, the enormous limestone pillars Elegug Stacks which are encrusted with colonies of guillemots, kittiwakes and fulmars.

The natural and industrial worlds sit side by side in the vast natural harbour of Milford Haven; this estuary has been used as a port since the Middle Ages. The town was founded in 1790, originally as a whaling centre, becoming a Royal Navy dockyard until 1814, when it became a commercial dock. It is still a busy port and also has several oil refineries. At the end of its 70 miles of sheltered coastline lie the high cliffs of St Ann's Head, Frenchman's Bay and Welshman's Bay and beyond them, the glorious Marloes Sands, where seals are born in Autumn, and Marloes Mere, an important wetland for waterfowl and birds of prey in the winter, whitethroats and sedge warblers in the spring, and reed bunting and marsh harriers in the summer. There are two hides from which to watch the action. The tip of the Marloes peninsula at Martin's Haven is the place to get a boat for the island of Skomer, another seabird haven, along with nearby Skokholm Island.

A holy peninsula and the end of the path

The Coast Path continues along the edge of St Brides Bay until it reaches the postcard-perfect beach at Newgale: 2 miles of wide, sandy expanse, which is ideal for surfing and safe for bathing. At low tide, the sea retreats a long way out, revealing the stumps of a prehistoric drowned forest.

The harbour at Solva is equidistant between Newgale and St Davids and is an excellent base to explore the coastline around both. A narrow, natural harbour, enclosed by steep hills on either side, Solva is a popular mooring for small boats. Waterside pubs, cafés and shops attract visitors and it is an ideal place to refuel before walking up to nearby headland The Gribin with its Iron Age fort and views across St Brides Bay, then onwards and down to Gwadn Beach tucked into a small bay. The National Trust owns most of the coastline from Solva to Newgale, including Dinas Fawr, a headland once mined for its lead and copper.

St Davids Peninsula, see page 288, is a wild, windswept headland with artists' studios and scenic campsites linked by winding roads that drop steeply down to lonely inlets and coves. It is great walking country: the twin volcanic peaks of Ramsey Island can be seen from the Treginnis Peninsula as can porpoises in the Ramsey Sound, and a climb from Whitesands Beach to the jagged peak of Carn Llidi

Above: The Gribin
The steep-sided ridge defines the east side of Solva Harbour and was the site of an Iron Age fort.

Right: St Davids Head
View from Carn Llidi down onto Whitesands Bay and across towards Ramsey Island.

passes the Neolithic tomb Coetan Arthur, a great place to sit and contemplate the view and the passing of time. Carn Llidi is an outcrop of 500-million-year-old volcanic rock, which makes up St Davids Head. The same rock appears again in the islands of Ramsey, Bishops and Clerks several miles out to sea. In late summer the coastal heath of St Davids Head turn bright purple and yellow as heather and gorse burst into flower, providing ideal habitats for butterflies, moths and beetles and birds including the stonechat and linnet.

Evidence of past industry is all around. In the village of Porthgain, granite was quarried and crushed in a plant overlooking the quay; there was also a brickworks, a by-product of slate quarrying. Surviving buildings now house restaurants The Shed and The Sloop. Slate was quarried until 1910 in what is now the Blue Lagoon in Abereiddy, a scooped-out seawater lake connected to the ocean by a channel blasted through the rock. These days it is popular with coasteerers (see pages 296-297) and is a venue for the Red Bull Cliff Diving Series. Ruins of quarrymen's cottages can be seen near the car park at Abereiddy Beach, also a good place to find graptolite fossils: small sea creatures from 470 million years ago.

The peninsula has also been a place of pilgrimage, most famously to the cathedral which qualifies St Davids as a city, but also to Ramsey Island where St Justinian, St David's confessor, lived in solitude. The island is now managed by the RSPB and boat trips sail around its precipitous cliffs daily, sometimes landing when the weather is good.

The cathedral dates from the eleventh century and houses the relics of St David, who founded a monastery and church here in the sixth century. A much more recent addition to the country's smallest city is Oriel y Parc Gallery and Visitor Centre, a semi-circular building which has won awards for its sustainable building practices – it has a grass and sedum roof and wool insulation, among other elements. Along with the National Trust Shop and Visitor Centre, it's a good place to get your bearings and find out more about the surrounding countryside and to see exhibitions by local artists.

Above: Pen Anglas

A stone obelisk stands on this rugged headland of basaltic rock known as Pen Anglas.

Right: Abermawr Beach

The currents at Abermawr can be hazardous, but this shingle beach with marsh and woodland behind is a great place to walk.

'Much of the coastline around Strumble Head was shaped by volanic activity'

The Coast Path ramps up a gear as it loops past the headland of Strumble Head and runs its ragged course around rocky coves and bays towards Cardigan. Much of the coastline around Strumble Head was shaped by volcanic activity including the six-sided balsatic rocks of Pen Anglas which resemble those of Giant's Causeway in Northern Ireland (see page 355) and the rocky outcrop of Garn Fawr which is topped by an Iron Age fort.

Once past the old fishing village of Fishguard (where ferries leave from Fishguard Harbour for Rosslare in Ireland) the cliffs become steeper and places of habitation fewer. It is wild, exhilarating walking all the way. Notable scenic spots include Pen y Afr and Gernos, the highest cliffs in Pembrokeshire and the most challenging section of the Coast Path; Dinas Island a promontory almost cut off from the mainland that provides a great circular walk (look out for chough and razorbills and guillemots nesting on Needle Rock), and Ciliau Mawr, a stretch of wet coastal heathland rich in bird life.

Cemaes Head is the final headland of the Pembrokeshire coast and overlooks the broad estuary of the River Teifi where it meets the open waters of Cardigan Bay. Tucked into the mouth of the estuary, Poppit Sands is an easily accessible and popular beach and Cardigan, a market town and resort further up the estuary, has a castle which was built in the time of Richard I and destroyed by Parliamentarians in the Civil War, but is now going through the process of renovation. It is also popular with geologists because of the range of rocks and structures revealed in the cliffs.

Below: Teifi Gorge

The ruins of the thirteenth-century Cilgerran Castle are still an imposing sight looming over the spectacular Teifi Gorge.

Explore National Trust places on the South Wales coast

Tudor Merchant's House, Tenby

Built in the late fifteenth century, this is the oldest house in Tenby and has been restored by the National Trust to replicate life in the town at the time. Tenby was a busy port and a centre of trade with Spain and Portugal. The merchant who lived in this three-storeyed house traded in cloth, vinegar, sea coal, pots and spices from his shop at the front of the house. Painted cloths behind the table in the hall show Tenby in its heyday, and the kitchen and latrine tower show what domestic life was really like. **Quay Hill, Tenby, Pembrokeshire, SA70 7BX (01834 842279)**

Stackpole, Pembrokeshire

Wander around Stackpole with its lakes, woodland, quay and beach and you get a sense of the scale of the vision of John Campbell II, 1st Baron Cawdor, who designed the landscape in the 1780s. Conceived as a setting for Stackpole Court, valleys were dammed to create the Bosherston Lakes whose water lillies and elegant bridges complemented the grand mansion before it was demolished in 1963. Under the National Trust's ownership, the gardens were opened up to reveal classic views that had become obscured by trees and shrubs.

Now the whole area is an internationally important nature reserve: the lakes are home to otters which feed on eels, pike, roach and tench. There are over 20 species of dragonfly and damselfly, and heron, kingfisher and other water birds have made it their home.

‘… the kitchen and latrine tower show what domestic life was really like.’

Above: Tudor Merchant's House

The exterior of the house in the heart of Tenby with its Flemish chimney.

Top right: Stackpole Quay

This tiny harbour is used by local fishermen and small pleasure boats.

Stackpole Outdoor Learning Centre, Pembrokeshire

At the heart of the 809-hectare (2,000-acre) Stackpole Estate, is the Trust-run Outdoor Learning Centre. Seven houses and cottages have rooms to suit all sizes of groups from single and double rooms to bunkhouse-style. The centre has won a Platinum Eco-Centre award for its environmentally friendly management: the restaurant serves seasonal vegetables from the walled garden, for example. Stay here to make the most of the outdoors: the surrounding woodlands, dunes, cliffs and lakes are the perfect setting for the best adventures. **Old Home Farm Yard, Stackpole, near Pembroke, Pembrokeshire, SA71**

Have a go ... at rock climbing

The sea cliffs of South Wales are a great place to learn to climb, or to improve your skills. Plus they have great views. Remember to climb safe: if new to the sport, make sure you climb with an experienced guide who will have all the correct safety equipment and knowhow. Also be aware of nesting birds and check first that there are none where you are climbing.

Here are three places to have a go:

1. The limestone cliffs and zawns at **Stackpole** have been described as a climber's paradise. There are seasonal voluntary climbing restrictions for nesting birds on many of the cliffs but some areas remain accessible year round. Check out the British Mountaineering Council (BMC) website (www.thebmc.co.uk) for information on restrictions and any recent new rules. For beginners, the Trust's team of education officers at Stackpole Outdoor Learning Centre can offer a basic introduction to climbing and abseiling techniques at Stackpole Quarry.

2. The sea cliffs at **Rhossili** overlook 3 miles of sandy beach. The crags are old quarried faces with a mix of bolted and traditionally protected lines. The Fall Bay area contains some of the best climbing on Gower. It has something for every climber from well-protected cliffs to steep, technical multi-pitch test pieces.

3. **Southgate** near the Bishopston Valley has the best selection of sport climbs on the Gower Peninsula, ranging from entry level to harder. The rock is mostly solid but the tops are often loose, so care should be taken when topping out.

Broadhaven South, at the foot of Bosherston Lakes, is a safe family bathing beach, and the 8 miles of Trust-owned coastline nearby includes Barafundle Bay, which can only be reached by a 10-minute walk from Stackpole Quay, itself a picturesque harbour still used by fishermen. The Boathouse at the Quay serves fresh local food and Pembrokeshire produce and a kiosk sells ice-cream and hot drinks. The name 'Stackpole' originates from the Norse for *stac*, meaning isolated rock, and *pollr* meaning inlet. **Stackpole, near Pembroke, Pembrokeshire (01646 661359)**

St Davids Peninsula

The best place to view the wide sandy sweep of Whitesands Bay is from Carn Llidi, a rocky outcrop on St Davids Head. This headland, with its scattering of Neolithic tombs, including Coetan Arthur,

a Neolithic chambered tomb, is 183m high and has 360-degree views. The National Trust looks after much of the peninsula on which Britain's smallest city, St Davids, stands. One way to see it is to follow the Monks' Dyke (Flos-y-Mynach), which was built, like Offa's Dyke, as a defensive barrier and runs across the peninsula from Morfa Common in the south to Penbeir on the north coast, passing three Trust sites as it does so. The National Trust Visitor Centre and shop is in the centre of St Davids opposite the Trust-owned medieval cross and sells a wide range of Welsh produce. **St Davids, Pembrokeshire (01437 720385)**

Marloes Sands and Mere, Pembrokeshire

The gentle arc of Marloes Sands is backed by sandstone cliffs and is the perfect place for a bracing walk. Skokholm and Gateholm Islands are clearly visible from the sandy beach, and boats sail from Martin's

Above: Marloes Sands

The Sands from the western end looking east with the evening light catching the sandstone cliffs.

Right: First earlies

Early potatoes grown at Trehill Farm, Marloes Peninsula. The potatoes are winners of a National Trust Fine Farm Produce Award.

Haven to the bird-rich Skomer Island. Slightly inland, Marloes Mere, a wetland in a shallow basin near the National Trust car park, is a great place for birdwatching, especially waterfowl and birds of prey in the winter. Watch the activity on the water from one of two hides that overlook the mere. And don't forget to pick up a bag of award-winning potatoes from Trehill Farm, which sells them from its gate in season. **Marloes, Pembrokeshire, SA62 (01348 837860)**

A beginner's guide to seaweed

Revealed in rock pools or scattered on the strandline at low tide, seaweeds with their strange forms and peculiar textures are the coast's most mysterious organisms. Unlike land plants, they have no branches, roots or leaves and produce no flowers (they are mostly brown algae). Instead they have fronds. Some of these have a ridge running down the centre and some have air-filled bubbles called bladders. Fronds release eggs and sperm into the sea for fertilisation. Each plant produces millions of eggs, although only a few germinate.

There are around 800 species of seaweed in the UK, broadly categorized into four main groups according to colour: green; red; brown and (rare) blue-green. Here are five seaweeds common on the UK coast:

1 **Bladderwrack** (*Fucus vesiculosus*) Easily recognised by its pairs of air bladders on branching fronds that grow up to 1m in length.

2 **Kelp** (*Laminaria digitata*) Grows in deep-water kelp forests and is only revealed during spring tides. Kelp has broad fronds that grow up to 2m in length.

3 **Dulse** (*Palmaria palmate*) Dark red and red-brown fronds with divided tips that grow up to 80cm in length and project from a holdfast on rocks. Can be eaten raw.

4 **Carrageen** (*Chondrus crispus*) Small purple-red seaweed that turns yellow-green when exposed to sunlight. Found on rocky shores and in rock pools, it has been used as a food thickener but there is some debate about its dangers to intestinal health.

5 **Sea lettuce** (*Ulva lactuca*) Found on rocks in sheltered bays, it has bright green ruffle-edged leaves that resemble lettuce.

If you collect seaweed to eat, make sure that you only gather it from clean and unpolluted water and rinse and/or soak it thoroughly before use. There is no common-law right to pick seaweed in the UK, but there is little harm in taking home a handful for tea. To be on the safe side, it's best to ask permission from whoever owns the beach first: it could be the National Trust, the local council or an individual.

Whiteford Burrows, llanmadoc, Gower

Whiteford Burrows, the dune system backing Whiteford Sands in North Gower, was Neptune's first purchase on the Gower Peninsula in 1965. Today it's a National Nature Reserve and Special Area of Conservation, and is rich with flora, insects and wading birds. The dunes join the extensive saltmarsh of Llanrhidian Marsh and the freshwater marsh of Cwm Ivy Marsh, a constantly shifting landscape, an important feeding ground for wading birds and wildfowl, and a lovely place to wander and daydream. The freshwater marsh is currently separated from the mighty Llanrhidian Marsh by a medieval sea wall, which is leaking badly. So the embankment is being converted into a causeway, allowing the tide in to create a huge new area of saltmarsh, one of the biggest coastal realignment projects in Wales. For a real get-away-from-it-all break, stay at National Trust Cwm Ivy Lodge Bunkhouse, a wooden lodge in the middle of the dunes, that accommodates 10 people and comes with a woodburner and campfire.

Right: Whiteford Burrows

A view across a rippled sandy area of the dunes at Whiteford Burrows with the pine plantation behind.

Holiday Cottage

The Old Rectory, West Gower, Swansea. This is one of the National Trust's most popular holiday cottages and it's easy to see why: it sits on a terrace overlooking Rhossili Bay. From the comfort of an armchair, your eyes can roam over miles of golden sand as far as Worm's Head and on to the horizon without a single interruption. The handsome, double-fronted house was built in the 1850s and is furnished in comfortable, traditional style. A very steep path leads down to the beach. For more information see www. nationaltrustcottages.co.uk.

Shore-spotter's Guide

 1

The sun-loving **green tiger beetle** (*Cicindela campestris*) likes sandy soil and can be seen between May and October running or flying fast over open ground at St Davids Head, Pembrokeshire. Its bright green body has cream-coloured patches and can be iridescent in sunlight.

2

Families of playful **otters** (*Lutra lutra*) have made their home at Bosherston Lakes, Stackpole. These aquatic animals have long slim bodies with short limbs, webbed paws with sharp claws, and long muscular tails. They can remain under water for up to 4 minutes and dive up to 90m in search of food. This is one of the best places to see otters in the UK, especially in early morning.

 3

Craggy Needle Rock off Dinas Island, Pembrokeshire, is a nesting site for many seabirds including a colony of **guillemots** (*Uria aalge*). This large auk comes to land only to nest and favours sheer cliffs where it gathers with other birds to form 'seabird cities'. The rest of the time it is at sea. It is easy to spot, with a black head, black wings with white underparts, a thin, dark pointed bill and a small rounded dark tail. (You can also see it at Stackpole.)

 4

Marloes Mere, Pembrokeshire is a great spot for birdwatching, especially to see waterfowl and birds of prey in the winter. **Snipe** (*Gallinago gallinago*) feed at the wet edges of the marsh and can be hard to spot, but the cold weather forces them out into the open. When disturbed, they zigzag wildly away with a sharp 'ketch' call.

5

One of over 600 species, the **corkwing wrasse** (*Crenilabrus melops*) lives in rocky inshore coastal areas all around the UK including Stackpole Quay, Pembrokeshire. Look out for a small fish with eye-catching colouring: mottled olive colour with wavy green and golden lines and a black spot on the tail.

6

You will probably recognize the bright pink flowers of the **bloody cranesbill** (*Geranium sanguineum*) as it is often found in domestic gardens. It also grows wild in the dunes at Penmaen Burrows at Nicholaston Burrows between Three Cliffs Bay and Oxwich Bay.

Dinas Island, Pembrokeshire, walk

MODERATE GRADE

Distance: 3 miles (5km)

Time: 2 hours

A circular walk with steep ascent and descent for some of the finest views anywhere on the Pembrokeshire coast. This is not a long walk but one to test your fitness, with plenty of reasons to stop and admire the scenery.

Terrain

Steep, rocky coast path, sharp gradients, steps, stiles and kissing gates. Dogs on leads welcome, although livestock nearby.

Directions

❶ From Pwllgwaelod Beach, turn right uphill following the Coast Path signs. At the cattle grid, turn left through a kissing gate.

❷ The path soon begins to climb sharply up 40 steps. You'll pass through heather and gorse on either side. After a stiff climb, you'll reach a stile and the path becomes easier. Your reward is fine views across Fishguard Bay.

❸ The path becomes steep again. As you round a corner you'll see the highest point of Dinas Island, Pen-y-Fan, ahead. Newport comes into view on your right. To your left, past Fishguard, is Carreg Wastad, scene of the last French invasion of Britain in 1797.

❹ Pause at the Ordnance Survey Triangulation Station to take a well-earned rest and enjoy the views north to the cliffs at Pen-yr-Afr and inland to the Preselis. Look for the rugged summit of Carningli above Newport.

'As you round a corner you'll see the highest point of Dinas Island, Pen-y-Fan.'

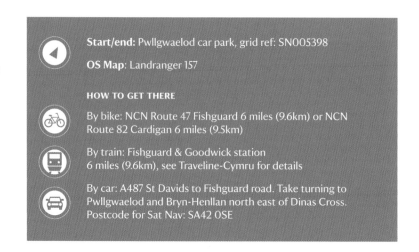

Start/end: Pwllgwaelod car park, grid ref: SN005398

OS Map: Landranger 157

HOW TO GET THERE

By bike: NCN Route 47 Fishguard 6 miles (9.6km) or NCN Route 82 Cardigan 6 miles (9.5km)

By train: Fishguard & Goodwick station 6 miles (9.6km), see Traveline-Cymru for details

By car: A487 St Davids to Fishguard road. Take turning to Pwllgwaelod and Bryn-Henllan north east of Dinas Cross. Postcode for Sat Nav: SA42 0SE

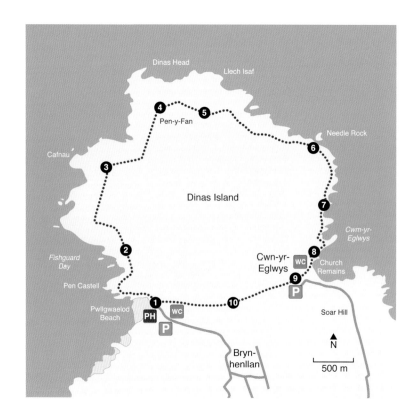

5 It's mostly downhill from here but steep. Follow the path downhill. 55yd (50m) beyond a kissing gate, the path divides. The main Coast Path plunges away to your left – you can see it snaking round the coast. If this looks too exciting, you can follow a broad path along the fence to your right. The two paths reunite further on.

6 Look for Needle Rock below you. Seabirds breed here in early summer.

7 The bay at Cwm-yr-Eglwys comes into view. Go through the kissing gate, which leads to a shady section of the path, but take care – it is rocky with tree roots.

8 A timber footbridge leads onto the road. Follow this down to Cwm-yr-Eglwys and past the public toilet on your right. Look at the remains of the church, destroyed in what became known as the Royal Charter Storm of 1859. Between 25 October (when the Royal Charter was lost) and 9 November a series of storms around the coast of Great Britain resulted in 325 ships being wrecked and 748 lives being lost.

9 Follow the path along the right-hand side of the boatyard, signposted Pwllgwaelod ⅔ mile, and walk straight ahead through the car park and alongside some caravans on your right. You'll see the footpath by a solid wood-panel fence in the far right-hand corner.

10 Walk back to Pwllgwaelod through the valley along a Tarmac path. As sea levels rise, Dinas Island will eventually become a true island.

Right: Dinas Island

Long view from the western edge of the island looking south across fields towards Mynydd Dinas.

A floating world

A lifetime's aquatic odyssey has led **Daniel Start** to journey around Britain swimming in its coves and caves and around its islands. He explains the irresistible appeal of plunging into the ocean.

That hot, sweltering summer was the beginning of my love affair with the sea. We were holidaying in far west Cornwall, on the wild and rugged coast around Zennor. I was only a boy but had a new bike and new-found freedoms and spent my time searching for secret coves and tiny inlets for snorkelling and jumping. Poring over my map in the evenings, I would locate little beaches that could be reached at low tide, then clamber down to explore them and swim from them. When I think back now, it conjures the scent of gorse and heather, the bright whiteness of the smooth shell sand, and the gentle ocean shimmering like a pool. That amazing summer was the inspiration for a lifetime's aquatic odyssey, journeying around Britain, searching for its most wild and wonderful coves, caves, and islands, while trying to understand what draws us to the ocean, and into the sea.

As an island race we have long been enchanted by the sea, from ancient legends of Cornish mermaids to tales of Scottish selkies and sirens. But our fondness for swimming and bathing, for health and leisure, is a relatively recent affair. It was at the end of the eighteenth century that the fashion for 'taking the waters' took off. In 1783 Dr Richard Russell wrote about the restorative qualities of bathing at the tiny Sussex fishing village of Brighthelmstone. The Prince Regent quickly rented a small farmhouse there, which in turn became a flamboyant pavilion and later the resort of Brighton. The more austere Royal Sea Bathing Infirmary in Margate was constructed at about the same time, offering treatment for complaints such as tuberculosis, skin conditions or jaundice. Professional 'dippers' were employed to thrust patients under the waves, though if you were wealthy you would enter the sea naked from the privacy of a bathing machine.

Today we have a better understanding of the health benefits of sea swimming. Cold-water dipping dilates the blood vessels and expels toxins from the body while at the same time releasing endorphins that elevate mood and libido. Regular dipping across the seasons leads to 'cold adaptation', which can strengthen the immune and cardiovascular systems. For me, sea swimming also provides a connection to the wild, and to beauty and immensity. Swimming in the ocean, everyday stresses dissolve and I feel alive and vital again.

A love of coves

The sheltered arc of a cove is my favourite place to bathe. Coves protect the swimmer from the worst of tidal currents and swells and make an easy, shelving entry point. In Britain we are fortunate to have a highly indented and convoluted coastline that provides endless inlets and coves. Football Hole on the wild Northumberland coast is spectacular, and just a short walk from the wonderfully preserved National Trust fisherman's village of Low Newton-by-the-Sea, with its fine inn and crab sandwiches. In the South West, Lantic Bay, close to where Daphne du Maurier lived and swam, is a wild and magnificent beach, and from here I like to swim round into Little Lantic cove, inaccessible except to the swimmer. When I splash ashore, jubilant and relieved, I imagine I am Robinson Crusoe arriving on his desert island after weeks at sea.

Coves seem to collect drifts of the most perfect white sands, some swept in from far-off climes by the Gulf Stream. At Whistling Sands in North Wales, on the dramatic Llŷn Peninsula, the perfectly formed sand grains sing harmoniously in the wind, and squeal underfoot as you run into the sea. But darker sands, such as those on the Hartland Devon coast, are a swimmer's friend too: swim at a high tide late in the afternoon, when the waters have risen over the hot grains, and water temperatures can reach 20°C or more.

The most perfect cove of all must be Lansallos, near Polperro. This is a true smugglers' cove. There are smooth silvery rocks from which to dive and warm up again on afterwards, and an enchanting walk down along a woodland stream. A hidden trackway has been carved out of the cliffs for carts and contraband and a quiet campsite above has views of the ocean.

Out into the ocean and into the cave

The most exciting swimming is often beyond the cove or beach, though. I remember my first visit to Abereiddy's 'Blue Lagoon' in South Wales. We arrived at dusk under a full moon and the huge pool, a great breached quarry since filled by the sea, was shimmering azure and indigo. We swam

' …in the ocean, everyday stresses dissolve and I feel alive and vital again. '

out beyond the old ruined winch tower, popular for those who like to jump, and out into the ocean, still and ethereal and filled with the heads of bobbing seals.

The sea has carved our coastline, and to enter a sea cave is to see its great power and history. I have explored Merlin's Cave under Tintagel Castle, and the vast labyrinth of cliff caves at Flamborough Head in Yorkshire. I have swum into the booming, coralline-encrusted sea chambers of St Non's Bay in Pembrokeshire, and the watery tunnels of the Witches' Cauldron in Cardiganshire. To swim under a sea arch is perhaps the ultimate rite of passage and Durdle Door in Dorset is the classic: as high as a cathedral and knotted and twisted as dinosaur skin. Nearby, between Dancing Ledge and Worth Matravers, you can find sea-level catacombs and lagoons and inlets left behind after quarrying removed stone for St Paul's Cathedral. On a hot day with calm seas you could be on a Greek island as people skin-dive in the perfect blue waters, leap from ledges and sunbathe on the golden rocks.

A seal-eye's view

Sea swimming is not, of course, without its risks. Even on a hot day never underestimate how cold water can sap your strength, so wear a wetsuit for any lengthy expedition, and make sure you can easily get out if you start to feel weak. Never swim alone and keep a watch on tides. Most importantly understand swell. It creates offshore rip currents on long beaches, and around the edges of smaller coves. If caught in an offshore rip, don't swim against it; swim parallel to the beach for a minute then return in on the surf.

Our 8,000-mile foreshore and its remote intertidal zone is perhaps Britain's greatest wilderness area left today. Yet cleaner waters, better footpath access and more affordable wetsuits and kayaks mean that more and more people are embracing the adventure and exploring it by swimming. So go beyond your usual beach, enter the water and explore the foreshore with a seal's-eye view. It's a completely new perspective on the seaside, and another world waiting to be discovered. Make a secret cove your destination today, and celebrate with a plunge.

Daniel Start is an award-winning travel writer, photographer and environmental consultant. He is the author of Wild Swimming, Wild Swimming Hidden Beaches, Wild Swimming France *and the* Wild Guide *and won the Writer's Guild Award in 1997. His most recent book is* Wild Swimming Hidden Beaches: Explore the Secret Coast of Britain *(Wild Things Publishing, 2014). For more information about wild swimming see www.wildswimming.com*

Left: Blue Lagoon
The lagoon at Abereiddy is a flooded former slate quarry, which is popular with swimmers, divers and coasteerers.

Seaside things to do in South Wales

① Walk barefoot on the Coast Path

You're spoilt for choice in terms of stunning shoreline walks along the 186-mile stretch of the Wales Coast Path through Pembrokeshire. To narrow things down a bit, one of the most well-loved and well-trodden trails is the 4-mile stretch between the Blue Lagoon at Abereiddy, a flooded former slate quarry (now a top spot for cliff diving), and the traditional fishing village of Porthgain. Or, for something new – and to connect with the landscape on a deeper level – have a go at barefoot walking. The National Trust has devised a 2-mile family-friendly barefoot-walking trail around the Pen Anglas headland, near Goodwick. The shoe-free section leads through coastal heathland, which should feel soft and peaty underfoot. And there are jaw-dropping views of the headland's volcanic rock formations and Cardigan Bay.

② Sail to Skomer, Skokholm and Grassholm

Catch the boat from Martin's Haven to discover the bird-rich islands of Skomer, Skokholm and Grassholm, off Pembrokeshire's Marloes Peninsula. Skomer (a 15- to 20-minute crossing) is a Marine Protected Area (MPA) and, during the breeding season, home to 6,000 pairs of puffins, 19,000 pairs of guillemots and 120,000 pairs of Manx shearwaters. A further 45,000 pairs of Manx shearwaters breed on nearby Skokholm. Both islands are satisfyingly wild places to explore on a day trip (or even an overnight stay), and are managed by the Wildlife Trust of South and West Wales. Further out, around 11 miles offshore, is Grassholm – the only gannetry in Wales, with 39,000 breeding pairs.

③ See dolphins in Cardigan Bay

Watching dolphins breach, or leap out of the water, is one of the most uplifting wildlife experiences you can have. And, as Cardigan Bay is home to the UK's largest semi-resident population of bottlenose dolphins, with more than 200 using the bay every summer, you might be lucky enough to see them from land. Mwnt Beach or New Quay are the two top sites to try to spot them. Keep an eye out when the water is fairly flat, and you should have more than a 50 per cent chance of a sighting. Of course, for an even closer view, there are dolphin survey boat trips operating from New Quay in season.

Below: Worms Head

Looking out to Worms Head across the causeway from Rhossili Cliffs.

'Immerse yourself in early Christian history at Britain's smallest city'

④ Follow the pilgrims to St Davids Cathedral

Immerse yourself in early Christian history at Britain's smallest city, St Davids, where the final resting place of the patron saint of Wales has been a place of worship since the sixth century. The present twelfth-century cathedral, built from local stone, stands on the site of a monastery founded by St David, and has been visited by hundreds of thousands of pilgrims, especially during the Middle Ages, when Pope Calixtus II decreed that two pilgrimages to St Davids Cathedral were equal to one to Rome, and three to visiting Jerusalem. See also the adjacent ruins of the once-lavish fourteenth-century Bishop's Palace (run by Cadw), and the medieval preaching cross at the centre of town, opposite the National Trust shop and visitor centre.

⑤ Enjoy camera-ready views of the Gower

The Gower AONB is celebrated for its unspoilt coastline and award-winning beaches, such as the 3-mile long Rhossili and Three Cliffs Bay. To enjoy the very best views of Rhossili, you have two options. Climb to the top of Rhossili Down – the highest point on Gower – for a dizzying 360-degree panorama, taking in Rhossili Bay, the Devon and Somerset coast and the Brecon Beacons. Alternatively, follow the rocky route out to the spectral promontory of Worm's Head, for a different perspective, looking back to shore. (Always

check tide times beforehand with the National Trust visitor centre.) Three Cliffs Bay, meanwhile, is best approached via the bridle path from Penmaen. Follow Pennard Pill stream down to the sand, to look up at the three limestone outcrops, shaped like giant dragon's teeth. For more information see www.nationaltrust.org.uk/rhossili-and-south-gower-coast/; www.nationaltrust.org.uk/penmaen-and-nicholaston-burrows/.

⑥ Go coasteering in Pembrokeshire

The North Pembrokeshire coast from St David's Peninsula to Cardigan has some of the best places for this relatively new activity, described by Lonely Planet 'as a bit of a superhero sport'. Coasteering is a means of exploring the coastline by climbing, jumping and swimming and is growing in popularity as more people discover its thrills. Inevitably there are some dangers involved, so it's never advisable to do it alone. Find a good outdoor activity provider who will have all the right equipment, including rescue and safety gear, and the necessary knowhow, preferably one that belongs to the Pembrokeshire Outdoor Charter. The Trust works closely with Preseli Venture Eco Lodge and Adventures along the Abereiddy-Abermawr Peninsula. For more information see www.preseliventure.co.uk.

North Wales

On 28 March 1895, 1.8 hectares (4.5 acres) of gorse-covered headland near Barmouth became the first property donated to the National Trust. A few months earlier, on 12 January, the National Trust had been founded by Octavia Hill, Sir Robert Hunter and Canon Hardwicke Rawnsley as a charitable organisation to preserve land and buildings of beauty or historic interest for the benefit of the nation. The land, Dinas Oleu, was given by Mrs Fanny Talbot, a friend of Octavia Hill and Canon Rawnsley. 'I have long wanted to secure for the public for ever the enjoyment of Dinas Oleu,' she said, 'but wish to put it to the custody of some society that will never vulgarise it, or prevent wild nature from having its way.' She told Octavia Hill that the National Trust had 'been born in the nick of time'.

The Trust has looked after Dinas Oleu ever since, retaining the wild nature that Fanny Hill so enjoyed. The same is true of the rest of the Welsh coastline in its care: often tucked away and little visited, the coves, cliffs and beaches of North Wales are there for the enjoyment of all forever, just as Fanny Talbot and Octavia Hill hoped.

Previous pages: Heather on the cliff top at Aberdaron at the westernmost tip of the Llŷn Peninsula.

Left: The enchanting Whistling Sands of Porthor on the north coast of the Llŷn Peninsula, where the sand makes a distinct sound when you walk on it.

North Wales: secluded coves, mountains, and impregnable castles

The west coast of Wales from Aberporth to Harlech runs up the country, edged with cliffs that are interrupted by coves and estuaries. The sea is not easy to reach – a tangle of lanes runs off main roads to cliff edges and vertiginous steps to the shore. There is no parking at Traeth Penbryn for example – cars have to be left a 10-minute walk away and the beach is reached down a high-banked, leafy lane. The rewards are more than worth it: this secluded sandy cove with low dunes backed by a wooded valley is one of Ceredigion's best-kept secrets. (For starry nights on the beach, see page 323.) Further north, the spectacular headland of Ynys-Lochtyn is worth the trek to see breakers crashing on the shore at its foot and for the chance to see porpoises surfacing out in the ocean.

New Quay had a thriving shipbuilding and repairing trade in the nineteenth century, but now its hilly streets and pretty harbour bustle with holidaymakers. (Dylan Thomas lived here in 1944.) Many of the handsome, ice-cream coloured houses that line Aberaeron's harbour were once owned by ship captains when the town was a port and shipbuilding centre. Created by Lord of the Manor Revd Alban Thomas Jones Gwynne from 1805, Aberaeron's Regency-style houses are laid out around a square, unusual for Welsh coastal towns.

West Wales's principal seaside resort is Aberystwyth. With two beaches, a wide promenade, Britain's longest electric cliff railway and views from Constitution Hill (which also has a camera obscura) across the wide sweep of Cardigan Bay, it has always attracted visitors. And now students: the University of Aberystwyth is here, as is the National Library of Wales, which holds the world's largest collection of books in the Welsh language.

The wide wooded estuary of the Afon Dyfi (River Dovey) is part of the National Nature Reserve at Ynyslas, which includes Cors Fochno, a swampy wilderness of semi-liquid peat, and the submerged forest near Borth whose ancient stumps have been preserved by acid anaerobic conditions and are revealed at low tide. Aberdyfi sits prettily in front of wooded hills, its pastel-coloured stucco terraces facing the mile-wide mouth of the estuary.

The mountain of Cader Idris and the other craggy peaks of South Snowdonia loom over the stone villages and beaches of Barmouth Bay. With the sea on one side and the mountains on the other, this

Right: Barmouth

Dinas Oleu, the gorse covered stretch of the fell that became the first property donated to the National Trust, seen from Barmouth Beach, Gwynedd.

Below: Aberystwyth

The town's promenade is one of the longest in Britain, at 1.5 miles long. This view shows North Beach and Marine Terrace with Constitution Hill behind.

'Llŷn still feels wild, remote and spiritual,
and a million miles from the commerciality
of the holiday resorts further north.'

is a wonderful stretch of shoreline. Mountainous tracks lead walkers off to discover waterfalls and ocean views and to Dinas Oleu, a gorse-covered hill (which was the first property donated to the National Trust in 1895), at the southern end of Barmouth Bay. Barmouth, at the mouth of the Mawddach Estuary and Cardigan Bay, is the starting point of the multi-sport endurance event, the Three Peaks International Yacht Race, held in June. Competitors have to sail to Fort William, stopping off to run to the top of Snowdon, Scafell and Ben Nevis on the way.

One of Edward I's monumental castles (see feature, page 310) dominates the town of Harlech. Built on a rocky bluff surrounded by a moat and a tidal creek, it was almost but not quite impregnable – in 1404 Owain Glyndwr captured it and made it the residence of the court until it was retaken by the English five years later.

The pilgrim's peninsula

Pilgrims to Bardsey Island had to travel the length of the Llŷn Peninsula to reach it, passing fields enclosed by *cloddiau* (earth banks) along the top of ragged and storm-battered cliffs. Llŷn still feels wild, remote and spiritual, and a million miles from the commerciality of the holiday resorts further north. Its two coasts are very different: the south has cliffs and coves reached by twisting roads and precipitous paths, and the north is all about stretches of sandy beaches enclosed by sheltered bays.

The peninsula starts with Porthmadog which sits on the Glaslyn Estuary behind a 1-mile long embankment (the Cob) built in the nineteenth century to reclaim 2,833 hectares (7,000 acres) of land from the mud flats. Once a centre for the export of slate from the nearby quarries of Blaenau Ffestiniog, it is now a popular holiday centre for watersports, rock climbing and horse riding.

Passing the castle of Criccieth, built by Edward I perched on a rocky promontory above the town, the coast arcs around to the market town of Pwllheli, the busiest town on the Llŷn Peninsula which

Left: Bardsey Island

Looking over farmland on Braich-y-Pwll with the island in the misty distance.

Above: Llanbedrog Beach

Elevated view of the beach at low tide on the Llŷn Peninsula.

also has generous sandy beaches and is the location for the annual festival of the sea, Wakestock, which combines pop music with wakeboarding. Then on to Abersoch, once a quiet fishing village and now a busy holiday centre: its two sheltered, sandy beaches backed by massive dunes are separated by a headland and attract sailors, and

For a panoramic view of the wild, unspoilt northern coastline of the peninsula facing Cardigan Bay, climb Mynydd Mawr. From the top of this mountain you can see the rugged coastline which heads north-east towards Porthor with its Whistling Sands (see pages 320-321 and 322) and the succession of cliff-backed coves that make up the shoreline. There is good surfing at Porthor but the best surfing in Llŷn is at Porth Ceiriad and Porth Neigwl on the south coast.

Porthdinllaen sits snugly behind a headland protected from the fiercer winds, although its position a few feet from the ocean means it is at the mercy of future sea-level rises. Once intended to be a major port for boats sailing to Ireland, it was overlooked in favour of the more accessible Holyhead on Anglesey. Under the ownership of the National Trust since 1994, it only has two dozen buildings, including the Tŷ Coch Inn (see page 322). Facing it, Nefyn has a sandy, crescent-shaped beach lined with beach huts and chalets. Further along the coast, the sixth- and seventh-century churches of St Beuno's at Pistyll and St Beuno's at Clynnog Fawr were both on the pilgrim's route to Bardsey.

The entrance to the Menai Strait is marked by Fort Belan, a blockhouse built by Lord Newborough as a defence against Napoleonic troops that is now an unusual holiday centre. Nearby, Foryd Bay attracts wildfowl and wading birds, but is potentially treacherous: quicksand and fast currents make bathing dangerous.

watersports and powerboat enthusiasts (there is also a motorboat exclusion zone).

The pilgrim's destination, Bardsey Island, lies 2 miles off the tip of the Llŷn Peninsula across the whirlpools and strong currents of the Sound (Bardsey's Welsh name is Ynys Enlli, 'the island of the tides'). Boat trips re-creating the final leg of the pilgrims' journey sail from Porth Meudwy near Aberdaron. Three pilgrimages to Bardsey were equivalent to one to Rome in terms of religious credit, so there was a lot of coming and going. Legend has it that 20,000 saints were buried there, making the Tombs of the Saints a holy site themselves. These days the island is run by the Bardsey Island Trust, and there are nine houses available as holiday accommodation.

Above: Aberdaron

The village is the last place of rest for the pilgrim on his way to Bardsey Island across the Sound.

Right: Porthdinllaen

Sitting at the water's edge, the fishing hamlet is situated in a perfect cove with fantastic views.

Left: Anglesey

The harbour at Amlwch in the north-eastern corner of Anglesey. From the port, copper was exported all over the world.

An island of outstanding natural beauty

Associated with druids, bristling with prehistoric sites and rich with geology, the island of Anglesey (Ynys Môn in Welsh) is rooted in ancient history. Its geopark GeoMôn, which covers 720 sq km of the island and 125 miles of coastline, boasts 100 different rock types spanning four eras and 12 geological periods.

Anglesey's entire rural coastline has been designated an Area of Outstanding Natural Beauty and has many fine sandy beaches as well as startling cliffs and small 'secret' coves often tucked away and hard to reach. Highlights include Llanddwyn Bay which has 4 miles of sandy beach to explore and an 'island' joined to the land by a narrow neck of beach; South Stack a tiny island off the north-western tip, joined to Holy Island by a small suspension bridge; Cemaes Bay which has five beaches, three of which are sandy, and a violent history of smuggling and shipwreck; Cemlyn near Cemaes, which has one of the UK's most important tern colonies; Red Wharf Bay which has a beach 2.5 miles wide at low tide, and Black Point with its old lifeboat station, castellated lighthouse and views of Puffin Island and Snowdonia beyond.

Also worth visiting is the Trust-owned Plas Newydd (see page 314), ancestral home of the Marquess of Anglesey. Many travellers miss all of this as they drive anxiously to catch a ferry to Dun Laoghaire and Dublin from Holyhead, the island's largest town.

A curious thing … sea salt

Sea salt is replacing mined salt in more and more households as chefs recommend its soft flakes, but it is far from new: it has been produced on British shores since before Roman and medieval times. In those days, large pans were filled with seawater and left in the sun to evaporate, producing salt crystals. These days Halen Môn in Anglesey produces it with more modern methods: seawater is drawn from the Menai Strait, heated until it turns into a salty brine which then crystallises into salt flakes.

Sea salt production isn't restricted to North Wales, however: Essex and Cornish coastlines are also rich sources for this now essential condiment, particularly Maldon, Essex, and the Lizard, Cornwall.

Castles and cable cars

A thin strip of water, the Menai Strait, separates Anglesey from the mainland and can be crossed by two bridges. Thomas Telford's Menai Bridge was built in 1826. Its 30m central span enabled fully rigged sailing ships to pass beneath it. Robert Stephenson's tubular railway bridge opened in 1848 but was burnt down in the 1970s. It was replaced by a two-deck bridge carrying road and rail traffic, which kept the original towers and abutments.

Caernarfon Castle looks over the Strait with considerable presence. The most significant of Edward I's castles (see feature, right), it took 37 years to build and its polygonal towers and solid masonry helped stamp his authority over the Welsh. Caernarfon was already a fortified town before Edward arrived: Celts had built a fort there and a Roman garrison, Segontium, was constructed nearby (see page 312).

The medieval walls and gateways of Conwy have survived almost entirely and it is still possible to walk along the ramparts. Another Edwardian castle dominates the town, which also has a suspension bridge by Thomas Telford spanning the River Conwy. One of the first road suspension bridges in the world, it's now pedestrian only, and is similar in style to the Menai Suspension Bridge.

From Conwy onwards, the North Welsh coast is mostly about pleasure seeking, starting with the Victorian town of Llandudno. Straddling an isthmus, it has the benefit of two beaches. West Shore is a sand-and-shingle beach backed by dunes, but North Shore is where all the action is: a 2-mile long promenade, a sandy beach, an ornate blue and white pier built in 1878, landscaped gardens, a cable-hauled tram and a cable lift. Both tram and cable lift run to the summit of the Great Orme, a limestone headland that offers panoramic views and a tea shop. The town was planned by Edward Mostyn and Owen Williams at the end of the nineteenth century and is built on a grid with a grand avenue linking the two beaches.

'Caernarfon Castle looks over the Strait with considerable presence.'

Edward I's coastal castles

As symbols of domination, the medieval castles of North Wales take some beating. The majority were built by Edward I of England who came to the throne in 1272 determined to unite Britain and particularly to subjugate the Welsh prince Llywelyn ap Gruffydd. He achieved this in 1282 after an uneasy truce ended with a Welsh rebellion. Llywelyn was killed in a chance encounter with an English knight (on such accidents the fate of a nation can turn) and Edward was determined to prevent further uprisings. He did this by constructing brutish castles in areas where rebellion might occur. Designed by military architect Master James of St George, they are characterised by having two walls of thick masonry, deep moats and fortified barbicans. Many were sited by the sea so supplies could come in by boat rather than cross a potentially hostile interior. Forbidding and impregnable, no expense was spared in their construction: it is testimony to their solidity and strength that so much of them survive today. To further establish his rule, Edward's son, the first English Prince of Wales, was born in Caernarfon Castle, and subsequent Princes of Wales have been invested there, including Prince Charles in 1969. The castles of Beaumaris, Caenarfon, Conwy and Harlech (along with the town walls around Caenarfon and Conwy) were collectively named a World Heritage Site in 1986.

Edward I's castles: Abersytwyth, Harlech (pictured), Criccieth, Caernarfon, Beaumaris, Conwy, Flint.

Colwyn Bay with its neighbours Rhos-on-Sea and Old Colwyn makes up 3 miles of beach which throng with holidaymakers enjoying attendant amusements including a miniature railway. A 5-mile promenade/ sea defence runs between Rhyl and Prestatyn, perfect for a bracing stroll or a cycle ride. Rhyl was once an elegant Victorian resort and is being regenerated after a period of decline, and Prestatyn has all manner of attractions including restaurants, bars, a swimming pool and Pontin's Prestatyn Sands Holiday Park. It is also the start of the Offa's Dyke Path to South Wales.

Above: Llandudno

The cable car ascending to the summit of the Great Orme above the seafront.

Explore National Trust places on the North Wales coast

Llanerchaeron, near Aberaeron, Ceredigion

We have to thank negligent past owners of this eighteenth-century Welsh gentry estate for its present state. Rather than demolish or repair the household service outbuildings, they let them languish. So, when the last owner, Mr John Powell Ponsonby Lewis, bequeathed Llanerchaeron to the National Trust in 1989, it was an opportunity to restore the buildings and walled garden and re-create the estate as it was originally intended. The result is a model self-sufficient complex: everything needed to provide for an eighteenth-century family is within the grounds, including spaces to brew beer, salt fish and meat, make cheese, and do the laundry. The garden has, among many other things, 75 apple trees (some 200 years old), and the organic farm has Welsh Black cattle, Llanwenog sheep and rare Welsh pigs. The house itself is the most complete early work by young architect John Nash and was built in 1795 for Major William Lewis. It is full of interesting collections, including taxidermy. **Ciliau Aeron, near Aberaeron, Ceredigion SA48 8DG**

Eifionydd, Llŷn Peninsula

Running from the foothills of Snowdonia down to the sea, the area has a mythical feel. It includes the age-old districts of Merionnydd with its ancient woods of the Vale of Maentwrog, Eifionydd with its unspoilt farmland, and Arfon, where the 3,000-year-old hill fort of Bwncan Dinas Dinlle can be found, said to have been the home of legendary hero Lleu Llaw Gyffes, as written about in Mabinogion, the ancient Welsh mythology.

Also look out for the wooded rocky knoll of Ynys Tywyn, the source of stone used to build the Cob embankment at Porthmadog (see page 307) – there is a sheer cliff on one side where it was quarried. The ancient, semi-natural woodland Coed Cae Fali is being replanted with native oak to replace the existing pine and has been classified as temperate rainforest – it is rich with ferns, lichens, liverworts and mosses. **Dinas Dinlle, Gwynedd**

Segontium, Caernarfon, Gwynedd

The remains of most of the buildings of the Roman fort, which was built in AD 78, have been preserved, so it is possible to walk around and get a sense of its scale. One thousand auxillary infantry were stationed here – the main fort in North Wales – to defend the Roman

Empire against the Welsh. The site on Llanbeblig Road shows the remains of the commandant's house, the underground strongroom where the pay for the troops was kept and the regimental chapel. 'Caer' is Welsh for fort, which explains why so many settlements nearby, not least Caernarfon, have it as part of their name.

Caernarfon, Gwynedd LL55 2LN

Plas Newydd Country House and Gardens, Anglesey

During the tenure of the 5th Marquess of Anglesey, the grand eighteenth-century Plas Newydd became a party house with members of society descending to enjoy theatrical antics and lavish living. Unfortunately the results of these extravagances bankrupted the family who were forced to sell their other homes and move here permanently. The 6th Marquess turned the estate's fortunes around and restyled the interior, getting rid of the theatre and inviting Rex Whistler to paint a mural in the dining room. The National Trust took on ownership in 1976 and today visitors can enjoy the results of the 6th Marquess's transformation – the house is much as it was then – as well as wonderful views of Snowdonia over the Menai Strait, an extensive second-hand bookshop and an Australasian arboretum.

The mansion is kept warm by Britain's biggest marine source heat pump, installed by the National Trust, which will provide all of its heating. Once a big oil user (consuming 1,500 litres of oil a day on cold winter days) it now runs on energy from a heat exchanger driven by sea water being pumped from the Menai Strait. This new clean energy will reduce bills at Plas Newydd by around £40,000 a year. The marine source pump was the first of five schemes to be completed in the

National Trust's £3.5 million pilot phase of its Renewable Energy Investment Programme, launched in partnership with Good Energy. **Llanfairpwll, Anglesey, LL61 6DQ (01248 714795)**

Penrhyn Castle, Bangor, Gwynedd

This grand country house sits magnificently between Snowdonia and the Menai Strait. Originally a medieval fortified manor house, it was transformed by architect Thomas Hopper between 1820 and 1833 into a mock Norman castle for the Pennant family. It was paid for by profits from the West Indies sugar trade and from money generated by the family's slate quarries around Bethesda in North Wales. Appropriately, it has a slate Grand Staircase, a slate floor in the Great Hall, and other pieces of slate furniture including a bed weighing 1 ton made for Queen Victoria. The interior is richly decorated with plasterwork and stone carving and is packed with art treasures, particularly Spanish and Dutch seventeenth-century paintings (including a Rembrandt portrait). The restored stable block houses a railway museum and there are 24 hectares (60 acres) of grounds to explore including a Victorian walled garden. **LLandegai, Bangor, Gwynedd, LL57 4HN (01248 353084)**

Above: Penrhyn Castle

The Drawing Room at Penrhyn Castle showing the oak chairs and sofa designed by Thomas Hopper, and the dazzling silk lampas (brocade) and curtains.

Opposite: Plas Newydd

Early morning view of the east front of the house on Anglesey, with the Menai Strait and Snowdonia beyond.

Bodnant Garden

This delightful 32-hectare (80-acre) garden in the Colwyn Valley was created by five generations of the same family, and juxtaposes formal, Italianate terraces with a wooded valley, stream and a waterfall. Famous for its international collections of plants (including rhododendrons, azaleas and redwood trees) collected over a century ago by plant hunters, it is also noteworthy for the nineteenth-century 'Poem' building, a family mausoleum, built by Henry Davis Pochin. The interior is decorated with marble, stained glass and a gold-starred ceiling, and is open to visitors on the last Tuesday of the month. **Tal-y-Cafn, near Colwyn Bay, Conwy LL28 5RE**

Conwy Suspension Bridge and Aberconwy House

When visiting Conwy, be sure to walk across Thomas Telford's pioneering 1826 suspension bridge, whose crenellations echo those of the ancient castle. Find out more about its genesis at the Toll House, styled as it might have been in the 1890s. Close by, Aberconwy House, dating back to the fourteenth century, is the only medieval merchant's residence to have survived the walled town's chequered history. **Conwy, LL32 8LD (01492 573282); Castle Street, Conwy**

Above: Bodnant Garden

The Canal Terrace and Pin Mill reflected in the water. Pin Mill was originally built as a gazebo in 1730 at Woodchester, Gloucestershire. It was moved to Bodnant in 1939.

Left: Conwy

The suspension bridge looking across the river towards Conwy Castle. The bridge was completed in 1826 by Thomas Telford.

The fantasy village of Portmeirion

Happen upon the coastal village of Portmeirion unawares, and you might think you had slipped through a portal to a different time and place. Architect Clough Williams-Ellis was so enchanted by the villages of Italy, especially Portofino on the Italian Riviera, that he wanted to re-create a village with a similar charm and spirit in his Welsh homeland. After much searching, he eventually found a piece of land where he could realise his vision. Between 1925 and 1975 he transformed a hollow on the sandy estuary between Porthmadog and Harlech from a scrappy overgrown wilderness into an architectural extravaganza. By rebuilding buildings ranging from weatherboarded houses to a seventeenth-century town hall and an Italian campanile, he created a uniquely picturesque place that drew artists and celebrities (Noel Coward wrote *Blithe Spirit* here). It became even more famous in the 1960s when it was used as a setting for The Village in the TV series *The Prisoner*, and continues to attract holidaymakers keen to book a room in its unique accommodation or to look around the subtropical garden.

Aberdaron

A good place to start your exploration of the Llŷn Peninsula is the new visitor centre, Porth y Swnt, in the fishing village of Aberdaron. Alongside information about walks and attractions, you will discover stories about local people, landscape and the area's history. **Henfaes, Aberdaron, Pwllheli LL53 8BE**

 Holiday Cottage

Moryn, Porthdinllaen, Llŷn Peninsula, Gwynedd. Yards from the sea, this cottage is the perfect seaside getaway. One of a string of houses in the fishing hamlet of Porthdinllaen (see pages 308 and 322), it has picture windows to make the most of the sea view and a generous roof terrace to watch the sunset after a day exploring the Llŷn Peninsula. Plus the centuries old, Trust-owned Tŷ Coch Inn is just a stroll away. For more information see www.nationaltrustcottages.co.uk.

Right: Aberdaron

Brown crab harvested from the clean waters around the Llŷn Peninsula for Aberdaron Seafood, a company run by local fishermen.

Shore-spotter's Guide

About 60 pairs of **chough** (*Pyrrhocorax pyrrhocorax*) nest in cliff crevices around the Pembrokeshire coast. Which is good news as this member of the crow family almost disappeared in 1973. Look out for its distinctive black plumage, red legs and red bill, especially at Stackpole and St David's. The Llŷn Peninsula is also a stronghold, and there are a few pairs in Anglesey. (See also Lizard Point walk, pages 266–267.)

Warming seas have led to new natives in our seas, the most striking of which is the **grey triggerfish** (*Balistes capriscus*), normally found in the warmer waters of the Atlantic and Mediterranean but now seen in waters off the coast of North Wales. Look out for this relatively small (less than 2.3kg in weight) drab grey fish in the sea at Porthdinllaen. It has become fairly common in South Wales, and may breed off the Gower. Porthdinllaen is one of the most northerly places where it has been spotted.

Waters off the Welsh coast are home to one of only two semi-resident UK populations of **bottlenose dolphin** (*Tursiops truncatus*). There are 130 or so of these grey mammals with a curved mouth that resembles a smile in Cardigan Bay. The best time to seen them is between April and September.

Other Welsh dolphin and porpoise hotspots: Cemlyn, Cemaes, Fedw Fawr, Anglesey; Uwchmynydd, Llŷn Peninsula; Ynys-Lochtyn and Marloes Peninsula, Pembrokeshire; Lochtyn near Llangrannog, Cwmtydu near New Quay and Porth Ceiriad near Abersoch; Mwnt, Ceredigion.

4

If you go for a walk along the beach at Porthdinllaen, Llŷn Peninsula, between April and mid-September, keep an eye open for **sand martins** (*Riparia riparia*) which nest in holes in the cliff face. These swift, agile fliers look similar to house martins and swallows and will dart in and out of their nests as they search for food.

5

Believed to be an ancient species that has remained unchanged for millennia, **golden hair lichen** (*Teloschistes flavicans*) is bright orange with branched, flattened lobes. ('Teloschistes' means 'split ends'.) One of the reasons for its disappearance elswhere is that it is extremely sensitive to air pollution. See it at Mynydd Mawr, Llŷn Peninsula.

6

The UK's smallest thrush, the **redwing** (*Turdus iliacus*) population is declining but can be seen on Bardsey Island during its autumn migration period. Look out for a small bird with a creamy stripe above the eye and orange-red patches on its flanks.

Porthor and the Whistling Sands, Aberdaron, Gwynedd, walk

Distance: 1 mile (1.6km)

Time: 30 minutes

The views are spectacular along this rugged coastline on the northern side of the Llŷn Peninsula. This is a great walk on which to absorb some of the history and heritage of the area.

Terrain

Moderately steep hill, four kissing gates, can be muddy. Dogs on leads are welcome. Route goes through some grazed fields.

Directions

1 From the car park follow the orange waymarker along the path between the toilet cabins, then through a cluster of willow trees.

2 There are great views of the Whistling Sands down on your right. Locals gave this crescent-shaped beach its name because of the squeak or whistling sound the sand makes underfoot. Follow the path until you come to a bench and a kissing gate on your left.

3 Go through the kissing gate and follow the path that winds along the coastline. The National Trust is restoring the cliff slopes to your right using aerial spraying to control bracken and returning to the tradition of grazing.

4 Keep a good look out here; you might be lucky enough to spot a seal, porpoise or even a dolphin swimming off the coast.

'Look out for the distinctive red rock, jasper, which used to be quarried here.'

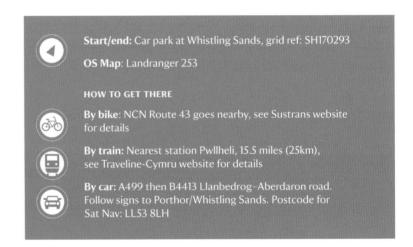

Start/end: Car park at Whistling Sands, grid ref: SH170293

OS Map: Landranger 253

HOW TO GET THERE

By bike: NCN Route 43 goes nearby, see Sustrans website for details

By train: Nearest station Pwllheli, 15.5 miles (25km), see Traveline-Cymru website for details

By car: A499 then B4413 Llanbedrog–Aberdaron road. Follow signs to Porthor/Whistling Sands. Postcode for Sat Nav: LL53 8LH

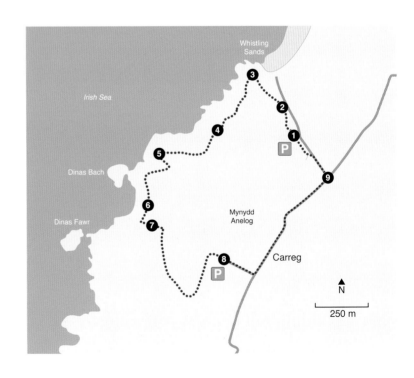

Above: Dinas Fawr

The island known as the 'large stronghold' lies to the south of Porthor.

5 The two islands down to your right are Dinas Bach ('small stronghold') and Dinas Fawr ('large stronghold'). Further along the coastline in the distance you'll see the peak of Mynydd Anelog rearing out of the Irish Sea.

6 Soon after you pass the first of the islands you come to a kissing gate with another immediately on your left. Go through both, following the waymarker up a gentle slope. Look out for yellowhammers and finches feeding on thistle seeds. The double fencing to the fields creates a wildlife corridor for all kinds of animals and birds.

7 Follow the waymarker around the edge of the field up to Carreg. Turn right through the last kissing gate and follow the orange marker past Carreg to the road. Look out for the distinctive red rock, jasper, which used to be quarried here. The circular tower at the top of the hill above Carreg Farm was built as a lookout point and used during the Second World War. It was topped with a glass dome to give shelter to the watchers as they peered out into the Irish Sea searching for enemy vessels.

8 When you reach the road turn left. After about 650yd (600m) you'll see a signpost for the Whistling Sands. Follow this lane back to your starting point in the car park.

Seaside things to do in North Wales

1 Swim (or stop for a pint) at Porthdinllaen

One of the most photogenic sights on the Llŷn Peninsula is the tiny, traffic-free hamlet of Porthdinllaen, which arcs around a sheltered, sandy bay and is backed by a verdant headland. At Caban Griff, the Trust's interpretation centre, you can learn about the shipbuilding and fishing industries that once flourished here, and how close Porthdinllaen came in the early nineteenth century to becoming the main port for the proposed London to Dublin railway (in the end, the government opted for the road route via Holyhead). Bring swimming

Below: Porthdinllaen

The Tŷ Coch Inn has the beach on its doorstep. Drink a pint with the sand between your toes.

gear, as beyond the lifeboat station (re-built in 2013) are two small, sandy coves, ideal for bathing. Warm up afterwards at the Trust-owned pub, the Tŷ Coch Inn. This small hostelry (voted the world's third-best beach bar in a 2013 survey) serves locally brewed ales, along with sandwiches.

2 Walk the squeaking sands of Porthor

The remote beach at Porthor gains its evocative English name, Whistling Sands, from the strange, squeaking sound the sand makes when you walk upon it. (This is, apparently, due to the uncommon size of the grains.) Stamp or slide your feet on dry sections of shore to get the best effect. There's more to do here, though – from rock pooling to seal and dolphin spotting – and in summer, there are wildlife adventure packs available for children from the National Trust cabin. Stroll along the Coast Path towards the two islets of Dinas Mawr and Dinas Bach (both of which were fortified during the Iron Age). Or pick up refreshments at the café, housed in a former coal shed – a relic of Porthor's past incarnation as a busy port, importing lime and fuel (closed in winter). For more information see www.nationaltrust.org.uk/llyn-peninsula.

3 Look out for choughs at Mynydd Mawr

For a bird's-eye view of this rugged coastline, climb to the summit of Mynydd Mawr, near Aberdaron, on the outer edge of the Llŷn Peninsula. From here, you gain a near-cartographic perspective of the region, with Cardigan Bay arching south and Bardsey Island offshore; on a clear day, you might even see Ireland. On the hill's lower slopes, have a go at spotting the rare chough – a member of the crow family, which has a stronghold here. You'll recognise them by their scarlet bill and legs, and the aerobatic swoops and dives they perform when on the wing and their distinctive 'kee-ow' calls. For tips on where to look, call in at the coastguard hut, manned by National Trust volunteers. For more information see www.nationaltrust.org.uk/llyn-peninsula.

Left: Bardsey Island

The island in the winter sunshine. It is owned and managed by the charity, Bardsey Island Trust.

4 Stand among the saints at Bardsey Island

The Celtic cross on Bardsey Island – a sacred outpost 2 miles off the Llŷn Peninsula – marks the 20,000 saints believed to have been buried here during the Middle Ages. Since the founding of a monastery in 516 by St Cadfan, the island has been a place of pilgrimage, a practice that still continues to this day. Visitors also flock to this designated National Nature Reserve and Site of Special Scientific Interest to see the abundant wildlife, such as grey seals and Manx shearwaters, or to be inspired creatively (an artists-in-residence scheme has run since 1999). Day trips are available during summer – see www.bardseyboattrips.com and www.enllicharter.co.uk. Or, for a longer sojourn, there are nine cottages to let through the Bardsey Island Trust. For more information see www.bardsey.org.

5 Go sea-cliff climbing on Anglesey

North Wales is one of the UK's top destinations for sea-cliff climbing – and the white-grey quartzite (transformed from sandstone by heat and pressure) crags of Anglesey's Gogarth, to the west of the island, are legendary, with hundreds of routes available (best suited to experienced climbers). Holyhead Mountain, meanwhile, offers more accessible terrain and opportunities for bouldering, or low-level climbing. If you're a novice, and would like to get to grips with this thrillingly vertiginous sport, there are several local providers running courses. To get the hang of things, book a few hours' tuition at your local climbing wall beforehand.

6 Go star gazing on Penbryn Beach

Little beats a night-time walk on a starlit beach for an atmospheric and memorable experience. The spacious, mile-long beach at Penbryn in Ceredigion is one of the best places to enjoy vast, dark skies studded with stars and, if you time it right, the silver orb of the moon. Go at dusk and you might also see seals, barn owls and, if you are very lucky, bottlenose dolphins. Park at the Trust car park at Llanborth Farm, then walk through the woods and a fern-clad valley to the beach. For a star-gazing walk see www.nationaltrust.org.uk.

Are your boots made for walking?

There are many wonderful walks along the Welsh Coast Path – there are a couple in this book – but if you are keen to find more, go to www.nationaltrust.org.uk/visit/activities/walking. There you will discover suggestions and routes for different interests and for all levels of ability. Choose from car-free walks, seasonal strolls, those that are dog-friendly, and walks suitable for children. There are also details of guided walks and two-day walks.

And for more about the joys of walking the coastal path, read Christopher Somerville's essay on pages 296-297.

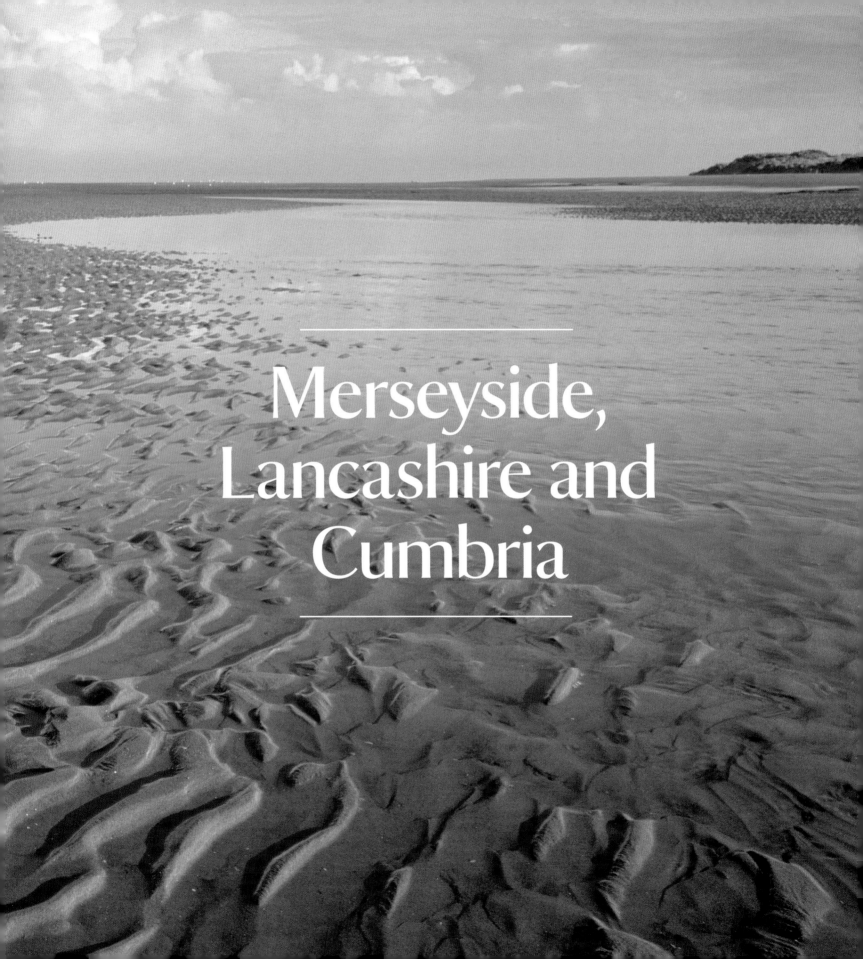

Merseyside, Lancashire and Cumbria

How do you stabilise acres of sand dunes as they are relentlessly assaulted? This is the challenge facing the National Trust at Formby Point, Merseyside, where the dunes are rolling inland, as well as being eroded by the sea. Working with the local council, the National Trust is planting marram grass, to knit the dunes together and make the system stronger and, for the longer term, key infrastructure is being moved out of harm's way.

From the beach at Crosby, sands stretch flat and wide in an arc to the Ribble Estuary and on via Blackpool, to Heysham and Morecambe Bay, and to the sand flats of the Duddon Estuary. The long sandy beaches between the dunes and the sea are the places to head to clear the head, fly a kite or canter a racehorse (Red Rum trained on the sands at Southport in the 1970s), but they are not the places to linger: the sea can come in fast and catch the unwary.

The North West coast is also about old-fashioned seaside fun. Blackpool has entertained holidaymakers since the railway reached it in 1846. Fortunes have also been made from this mineral-rich coastline, especially from coal, around which the towns of Whitehaven and Maryport were built.

The North West: vast shifting dunes and footprints in the sand

Overshadowed by its neighbours – the North Wales coastline and the impressive city of Liverpool – the Wirral Peninsula is easy to ignore. Which is a shame as this rectangular patch of green, sandwiched between the estuaries of the Rivers Dee and Mersey, offers a bucolic respite amid miles of industrial shoreline.

The Wirral's 25-mile coastline can be explored on foot or bike on the Wirral Circular Trail which traverses its perimeter. This will take you to the seaside resort of West Kirby from where, at low tide, it is possible to visit the tidal islands Hilbre, Middle Eye and Little Eye, designated as Local Nature Reserves and popular stopovers for migratory birds. West Kirby also has an impressive 13-hectare (32-acre) marine lake favoured by boating enthusiasts, and is the centre of the Wirral Country Park. This has 12 miles of trails for walkers, runners, cyclists and horse riders, which run along the route of a former railway line. (Look out for Hadlow Road Station which has been restored to how it was in the 1950s.) Nearby, Thurstaston Hill, a wild and rocky outcrop, has views of the mountains of North Wales and Trust-owned Heswall Fields (see page 334).

New Brighton at the tip of the peninsula, across the Mersey from Liverpool, has been a prosperous resort – its New Brighton Tower, built around 1898, was once the tallest structure in Britain. The town fell on hard times and subsequent neglect, however, with the Tower being demolished in 1921, and the pier where ferries brought holidaymakers from Liverpool and Lancashire's industrial towns, was dismantled in 1971. But regeneration has begun with a new leisure complex and concert hall adding to the town's existing attractions, which include a splendid Art Deco amusement arcade that has a suggestion of Miami about it, and miles of sandy beach.

Nearby, Port Sunlight, has survived almost intact, probably because it was conceived as a piece in 1888 by Lord Leverhulme who wanted to create a garden village for his workers. Named after the soap that made him rich, it is a model of town planning. At its centre is the Lady Lever Art Gallery, which has a fine collection of Pre-Raphaelite paintings and Wedgwood jasperware, among other delightful things.

The Wirral's main town, Birkenhead, which sits on the banks of the Mersey, has a bright future, with a £4.5 billion regeneration scheme, Wirral Waters, promising to turn 500 acres of unused docks into apartments, bars and restaurants. This is also the place to catch the famous ferry across the Mersey to Liverpool on the opposite bank.

Right: Marine lake

A red sailing boat on the marine lake at West Kirby, the Wirral, with people walking around the lake wall in the background.

Below: 'Another Place'

Antony Gormley's haunting installation on Crosby Beach, Liverpool, consists of 100 cast-iron, life-size figures.

Above: Blackpool Tower

Inspired by the Eiffel Tower in Paris, this iconic
tourist attraction is 158m tall and has incredible
views along the length of the promenade.

A great mercantile city

Which brings us to Liverpool with its magnificent waterfront of
imposing mercantile buildings, regenerated docks and bold new
developments. The waterfront won UNESCO World Status in 2004
because it is a 'supreme example of a commercial port at the time
of Britain's greatest global significance'. And indeed at the end of
the nineteenth century it was one of the biggest ports in the world
with 7 miles of docks lining the banks of the Mersey. These days the
waterfront throngs with visitors lured by the many attractions in
its four distinct areas: Princes Dock, where cruise liners come and
go; Pier Head where the Three Graces – the Royal Liver Building
crowned by the mythical Liver Birds, the Port of Liverpool Building
offices and the Cunard Building – sit beside the ultra-modern
Museum of Liverpool; Albert Dock which was regenerated in the
1980s and where Tate Liverpool, the International Slavery Museum
and The Beatles Story can be found; and Kings Dock with its new

arena, big wheel and a convention centre. A short distance along
the coast is Crosby, now more famous for artist Antony Gormley's
'Another Place' – 100 cast-iron life-size figures dotted along 1.8 miles
of shoreline staring out to sea – than for its mercantile past and
Regency houses.

The 12 miles of coastline between the estuaries of the Mersey and the
Ribble is known as the Sefton Coast and is noteworthy for its complex
of sand flats and sand dunes – the largest in England. A Site of Special
Scientific Interest, this evolving landscape is rich in wild flowers and
wildlife – the 202 hectares (500 acres) of Trust-managed Formby,
a welcome patch of wilderness after the urban sprawl of Liverpool,
boasts grey seals, red squirrels and natterjack toads (see page 334).

With its wide, tree-lined streets and ornate Victorian buildings trimmed
with wrought-ironwork and glass verandahs, Southport still retains
much of the flavour of a fashionable watering place. Right from its
beginnings in the late eighteenth century when a local innkeeper built
the first bathing house, landowners prohibited the building of factories,
and power cables were buried beneath the ground. This restrained
and well-behaved approach to urban development combined with a
massive inland lake, miles of expansive beach and the second longest
pier in the UK, all add up to a most elegant seaside resort.

The pleasure-seeker's shoreline

The west coast of the Fylde Peninsula, which extends from the Ribble
Estuary to Morecambe Bay, is almost entirely devoted to pleasure.
Seaside resorts run bumper-to-bumper along the shore, offering
no end of hedonistic attractions. Chief among these resorts is, of
course, Blackpool, which has been the playground of the North
since the railway arrived in 1846. A series of attractions: the North
Pier (1863); the Winter Gardens (1876) and Blackpool Tower (1894)
ensured that holidaymakers and daytrippers continued to come,
and they still do, these days drawn by new seductions such as the
Pepsi Max Big One (a whopping roller coaster on the Pleasure Beach),
and the annual Illuminations on the seafront. The Tower has had a
refresh, too, retaining its ballroom with its elaborate plasterwork and
gilding, and its circus with its grand water finale, and adding a 4D
cinema experience and ride to the top where a floor-to-ceiling glass
observation window delivers tremendous views and wobbly-knees.

Trams run along the seafront from Blackpool to the port of Fleetwood
where deep-sea trawlers were replaced by container ships after the

cod wars obliterated its fishing industry. Lytham St Annes, a quiet alternative to Blackpool, is best known for its Royal Lytham and St Annes Golf Club which hosts the British Open. Non-golfers are catered for, too. Fairhaven Lake is a popular boating spot and the broad stretch of beach appeals to sand-yacht racers, Frisbee-throwers and ramblers.

Fleetwood overlooks the yawning mouth of Morecambe Bay, more than 120 square miles of water which recedes at low tide to reveal a seemingly never-ending expanse of sand. Although the shimmering sand looks beguiling, beware – this is one of the most dangerous places in Britain. Rivers and hidden streams wriggle through and under the sand, creating quicksand and hidden pits. The tide comes in at a cracking pace and the unwary can easily become marooned. The only safe way to cross is in the company of the official Guide to the Sands, a position that has existed since the 1500s and is currently held by Cedric Robinson, who by drawing on a thorough knowledge of the terrain and a stick to test the depths, leads parties of walkers safely across. The sands teem with marine life: mussels, shrimps and marine worms provide food for wading birds such as godwits, oystercatchers and knots. Cockles are also abundant, clinging to rocks under the sands.

Above: Jack Scout Crag

A view of Morecambe Bay from the top of the sea cliff in Silverdale, Cumbria.

The sea-bathing craze

Blackpool first attracted visitors in the eighteenth century as sea bathing became popularised by medics convinced of the sea's curative properties. Fashion-conscious (and hypochondriacal) Lancashire gentry, accustomed to visiting the mineral springs at Buxton, headed to the town's shoreline to seek cures for all manner of ailments. There they found the first guest house – a cottage – which opened in 1735. Thirty years later Blackpool had four hotels and four alehouses and major roads had been built. The enthusiasm for sea bathing was stoked by Dr Richard Russell's 'Dissertation on the Use of Sea-Water in the diseases of the glands' (1750), which drew wealthy health-seekers to his new surgery in Brighton. King George III boosted the fashion for dips in the sea when he bathed at Weymouth in 1789.

Other eighteenth-century sea-bathing resorts: Margate, Brighton, Weymouth, Scarborough.

Left: St Patrick's Chapel

The ruins of the chapel sit on Heysham Head overlooking Morecambe Bay with the vast estuarial flats stretching into the distance at low tide.

Victorian resorts and a mining legacy

Morecambe's 4-mile promenade bows into Morecambe Bay and provides the perfect place to stroll as you gaze towards Piel Island and the Lakeland hills. Echoing the shape of the promenade is the Midland Hotel, a 1933 Streamline Moderne building whose crisp curved outline had become severely battered before undergoing a £7 million restoration by Manchester company Urban Splash. Now guests can enjoy Eric Gill's restored sea-themed sculpture, which decorates the front and interior of the building, and walk out on to the terrace to enjoy those views. Also on the seafront is a statue of comedian Eric Morecambe (who took his name from the town) in a pose familiar to all who watched the TV programmes he appeared in with Ernie Wise.

At the other side of the bay, at the start of the Carmel Peninsula, is Grange-over-Sands a lushly vegetated Victorian resort whose climate benefits from its sheltered position. Semi-tropical plants and shrubs thrive here, not only in the ornamental gardens around the lake but on the mile-long promenade which brims with ever-changing planting. This is not the place for bathing, however: at extreme low tides the sea is a strenuous 10-mile walk away.

Cumbria's southern coastline is easily bypassed in the haste to get to the Lake District but its estuaries and islands are well worth exploring. The Isle of Walney stretches for 12 miles, curling protectively around Barrow-in-Furness creating a natural harbour. This pulsed with activity during the eighteenth, nineteenth and early twentieth centuries when Barrow's steelworks were the biggest in the world, exports flourished, and submarines and ocean liners were made in Vicker's shipyard. Today the focus has shifted to energy generation with three wind farms located off the Isle of Walney boasting the highest concentration of turbines in the world.

The River Duddon broadens to a wide estuary as it extends southwards towards the sea. Low tide reveals great stretches of sand (2 miles wide at some points) backed by dune systems tufted with marram grass, and mudflats hopping with wading birds. Sandscale Haws National Nature Reserve overlooks the estuary and is a good place to spot natterjack toads and unusual butterflies (see page 339).

Sellafield nuclear fuel reprocessing plant presides over the coast towards St Bees, casting a shadow over the sandy beaches. The beach gives way to fissured red sandstone cliffs at the RSPB reserve St Bees Head (an outcrop of Lower Triassic sandstone and the only cliffs on the Cumbrian coast), home to colonies of seabirds including the only nesting black guillemots in the UK. St Bees is also the starting point of the Coast to Coast walk which runs for 190 miles to Robin Hood's Bay on the North Yorkshire coast and takes 12 to 14 days to complete. For those who prefer to cycle, Sustrans has developed a Sea to Sea (C2C) trail which follows a similar route.

Developed by the Lowther family as a port to export coal, Whitehaven is considered one of the most complete examples of planned Georgian architecture in Europe (its grid pattern has even been touted as the inspiration for New York). By 1730 the town was a major port and shipbuilding centre (over 1,000 ships were built here) driven by the export of coal to Dublin. This grew as connections were made with the colonies, and tobacco, spices and rum were traded with India, Madagascar and the West Indies until the late eighteenth century. But it was coal that had the most influence on the town: its three Scheduled Ancient Monuments are all about mining (see page 339), and the town depended on it for employment. Since the mines closed, the holiday trade has grown in importance and following a £11.3 million harbour rejuvenation, the marina is filled with leisure craft, and a dramatic Wave light sculpture ricochets along the harbour wall, changing colour with the tide. During the biannual Maritime Festival tall ships come to the harbour.

A curious thing … limestone pavements

The limestone landscape at Arnside and Silverdale was formed about 330 million years ago by deposits of marine sediments laid down in layers. The 'pavement', with its large blocks of exposed limestone, was created when the joints and cracks in exposed areas of horizontally bedded limestone were dissolved and enlarged by water creating slabs ('clints') separated by fissures ('grikes'). If grikes are straight and clints are uniform, they resemble paving slabs.

Left: Whitehaven

A view over Whitehaven Harbour, which was once one of the UK's biggest ports.

Explore National Trust places on the Merseyside, Lancashire and Cumbria coast

Heswall Fields, the Wirral Peninsula

Leafy, meandering footpaths lead to a stretch of beach overlooking the mudflats of the Dee Estuary backed by low, crumbling clay cliffs. Heswall Fields is one of the Trust's places under the banner 'The Wirral Countryside', which also includes Caldy Hill, a sandstone outcrop with views over heath and woodland to the mouth of the Dee Estuary and the Irish Sea, and Harrock Wood, Irby Hill, Thurstaston Common and Burton Wood. Between them they cover most permutations of countryside, including heath, farmland, coastal cliffs and dense canopy woodland.

Formby, near Liverpool

The National Trust manages 202 hectares (500 acres) of beach and pine woodland at Formby. The flat sandy beach with its miles of dunes is perfect for picnics, walking, kite flying, wave jumping and for letting dogs run and play (it is one of the few places on the Sefton Coast without dog-access restrictions). It is also where 220 trails of prehistoric human footprints have been revealed by shifting sands – it is believed they date back to the late Mesolithic to Neolithic eras 7,500–4,500 years ago. There are also footprints of a number of animal and bird species, including red deer, wolf, crane and aurochs, the ancestor of the modern cow. As you walk through the woodland, keep an eye out for red squirrels who have made their home here, and look in the dunes for natterjack toads who gather at the edge of shallow pools and sing to attract a mate. If you can't see them, you will probably hear them: their distinctive song is the loudest of any European amphibian and rings out at twilight during the mating season. (Also see natterjacks at Sandscale Haws, page 339.) **Victoria Road, near Formby, Liverpool, L37 1LJ**

Left: Formby footprints

A man and his dog examine 5,000-year-old human footprints in the Holocene sediment at Formby Point, Liverpool.

A day in the life of ... *Kate Martin, Coastal Ranger, Formby*

'My favourite days as a Ranger are lovely, cold crisp winter days in late January or early February. The first job is feeding the red squirrels. Armed with a homemade feed distributor (a plastic beaker stuck to the end of an extendable DIY pole) and a bucket full of sunflower seeds and peanuts, I fill the seven feeders whilst chatting to local dog walkers.

'Once squirrel breakfast is served, I take a quick turn around the site to check that everything is as it should be – emptying full bins and picking up litter. After this, I catch up with the rest of the Ranger team and our dedicated volunteers and head up on to the sand dunes to do some dune restoration – Formby style.

'For nearly a decade at Formby we have used recycled Christmas trees to help restore our internationally important sand dunes which have become damaged through erosion. In the last two years, we have dug in over 10,000 old Christmas trees into the dunes by hand. This can be a back-breaking job but it has its merits – when you need

a bit of an uplift, you can turn around and look over the beach to the full expanse of Liverpool Bay. I particularly love this view on either a stormy day with the big breakers crashing on to the shore, or on days when the sea is like a mill pond and you can see the heads of grey seals bobbing just offshore.

'After lunch, if I fancy a bit of a break, I head over to our natterjack toad breeding pools to do some pond and vegetation clearance. These pools were constructed in 2011 and we have had successful spawning in them every year. It is a real privilege to be able to give this rare and iconic species a helping hand, knowing that we are helping to sustain it on the Sefton Coast for years to come.

'Finally, after a long and rewarding days' work, it's back to base to put away the tools. It is a great feeling going home at the end of the day tired but knowing that I have done a little bit more to help protect this beautiful and fragile area of the coast and that through my efforts it will be enjoyed for ever, by everyone.'

Heysham Head, Lancashire

Heysham's sandstone headland overlooks the expansive sweep of Morecambe Bay, as do six body-shaped rock-cut graves. Hewn from a single outcrop of rock and dating from the eleventh century, these graves are probably the final resting places of some high-status individuals, which is why they have such a commanding position. (They also feature on the cover of Black Sabbath's album *The Best of Black Sabbath*.) Nearby are the ruins of St Patrick's Chapel, dating from the eighth century and now a Scheduled Ancient Monument, and notable for its Anglo-Saxon doorway, and a pre-Roman labyrinth carved into stone. After the gothic drama of the headland, nearby sea cliffs, the Barrows, offer more pastoral pleasures with coastal grassland and woodland that were once a garden and support rare cliff heather heath, two uncommon ferns and sea spleenwort. **Heysham village, near Morecambe, Lancashire**

Above: Heysham Head

Exposed trench graves in a slab of rock near the ruins of St Patrick's Chapel. They have been dated as pre-Norman and are unique in Britain.

Left: Arnside Knott

Spectacular view of Silverdale and Morecambe Bay from one of the viewpoints around the hill.

Below: Dalton Castle

The castle is a mid fourteenth-century pele tower, formerly of four storeys, but now of just two.

Arnside and Silverdale, Cumbria

This Area of Outstanding Natural Beauty on the edge of Morecambe Bay is notable for its limestone pavement (see feature, page 333) at Holme Park Fell and on Arnside Knott. This habitat, which also includes wet meadow, scree and scrub, attracts insects and butterflies and many species of wild flowers that grow in the pavement's cracks and crevices. It is also a good place to hunt for fossils: look out for brachiopods at Arnside Knott. The Lots is a grassy area in the middle of Silverdale and leads down to the shore at the Cove. Head to Jack Scout, one of two cliffs in the area, for great sunsets and to see the Arnside Bore, a monthly tidal wave. Caused by the combination of a high tidal range and the shape of the bay, which narrows at Arnside, the wave ranges in size from a few centimetres to almost a metre and is biggest when there is a spring tide. **Arnside, Cumbria**

Dalton Castle, Cumbria

This fourteenth-century pele tower in the centre of Dalton-in-Furness was constructed by the monks of Furness Abbey and was where the

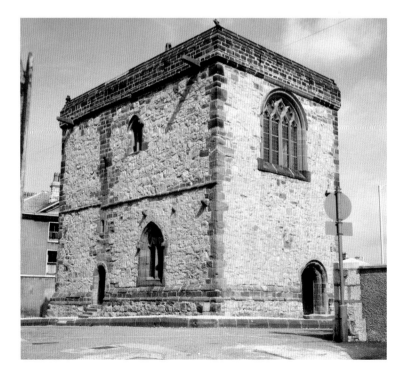

'Flint flakes and a polishing stone have been found at Sandscale Haws, evidence of flint tools being worked here during the Palaeolithic Period.'

abbot held manorial courts and administered justice. The building would have contained a court room, plus a gaol, guardrooms and stores. After the dissolution of the abbey, the castle continued as a courthouse for over 300 years, owned first by the Crown and then by the Dukes of Albemarle and the Dukes of Montagu. It was eventually given to the National Trust by the 8th Duke of Buccleuch in 1965. **Market Place, Dalton-in-Furness, Cumbria, LA15 8AX**

Sandscale Haws National Nature Reserve

This huge dune habitat on a sandy estuary of the River Duddon is a Site of Special Scientific Interest largely because of the incredible range of wildlife it attracts and the varying ages of the dunes. Rare natterjack toads thrive in its freshwater pools beside the car park boardwalk; wading birds feed in the estuary; the mudflats and sand banks hop with terns, oystercatchers and turnstones; numerous butterfly species fly among the sand hills and over 600 plant species have been recorded growing in the 283-hectare (700-acre) reserve. To maintain this, grazing is essential. Some small fenced enclosures in the slacks, erected in the 1970s, illustrate what would happen if grazing ceased. Flint flakes and a polishing stone have been found at Sandscale Haws, evidence of flint tools being worked here during the Palaeolithic Period. **Roanhead, Hawthwaite Lane, near Barrow-in-Furness, Cumbria, LA14 4QJ (01229 462855)**

The Whitehaven Coast

The coastline between St Bees and Whitehaven, known as the Colourful Coast because of its red sandstone cliffs and flora displays, has been shaped by its rich mineral deposits: coal, stone, alabaster and anhydrite have all been mined here, with over 70 mines in the area. Saltom Pit, sunk in 1729 and closed in 1848, was the first undersea coal mine in England and was a hub of industrial innovation with steam engines, dynamite, child workers and dangerous gasses to deal with. At the Spedding Steel Mill, a forerunner of the safety lamp was developed, and split oval shaft and air coursing was used to make conditions safer. Steam winding led to the mines moving to the cliff tops nearby with King Pit – the deepest man-made hole on earth at 160 fathoms – opening in 1750. Haig Pit still houses two winding engines with workings that reached 4½ miles under the Irish Sea. The coastline was black from coal but the low-nutrient soils this created, plus fallow areas left after decline in industrial activity, brought about ideal conditions for wildlife. Wild flowers and butterflies have reclaimed the area with the National Trust working to protect and enhance these habitats. On St Bees Head,

Left: Sandscale Haws

Grasses and willowherb at Sandscale Haws with the Duddon Estuary beyond and wind turbines visible on the hills.

Above: Whitehaven

The winding engine, part of the remains of the Haig Pit, an early twentieth-century colliery at Whitehaven.

colonies of seabirds thrive with England's only breeding colony of black guillemots. **Access to Saltom Pit is currently prohibited. Access is permitted to Wellington Pit, Duke Pit fan house and King Pit Cairn. Haig Colliery Mining Museum has re-opened with a visitor centre.**

Shore-spotter's Guide

'The rare nocturnal **natterjack toad** (*Bufo calamita/Epidalea calamita*) can be found breeding in shallow pools within the sand dunes at Formby. The adults are mainly visible during the breeding season and the call of the male toad can be heard over 1km away giving them their local name of the "Birkdale nightingale",' says Kate Martin, ranger at Formby. 'The adults are between 60cm and 80cm in length (females are bigger than males) and can be distinguished from the common toad by the yellow stripe that runs down their back.' (Also seen at Sandscale Haws National Nature Reserve.)

'The **northern dune tiger beetle** (*Cicindela hybrida*) is found in only two locations in Britain, with the Sefton Coast housing approximately 75 per cent of the British population. Look out for a smallish beetle of about 15mm in length, which is mainly red with a greenish sheen on top and then green underneath. The reason it gets its name 'tiger' is because it has incomplete horizontal yellow strips across its wing case. This rare beetle can be seen scurrying across the bare sand between marram grass clumps on the frontal dunes at Formby and is most visible in the summer months.'

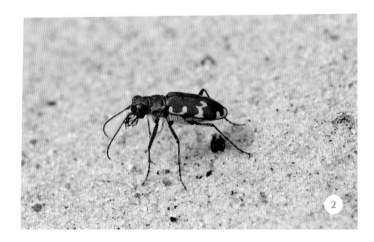

Several moths can be seen fluttering about the dunes at Sandscale Haws, including the brightly coloured black-and-red **cinnabar moth** (*Tyria jacobaeae*), which is active from April to September, and feeds on ragwort and groundsel. Its caterpillar is also brightly coloured with black and gold stripes. The colouration of both moth and caterpillar warns birds and other predators that it is unpleasant to eat.

'The small (approx. 20cm long) seabird, **leach's petrel** (*Oceanodroma leucorhoa*), can be seen off the Sefton Coast from late summer through autumn as it passes from its breeding sites in the North Atlantic to its wintering seas further south. It is a difficult one to spot and birdwatchers come from all over the UK to the Sefton Coast to see it. The best time to see one here is when westerly winds blow it closer in to the shore, making it easier to spot.'

5

The **Atlantic grey seal** (*Halichoerus grypus*) can be seen frequently off the beach at Formby all year round when the sea state is calm. Although they rarely haul out on the beach, their heads can be seen bobbing up and down just offshore. They are probably the same animals that haul out off Hilbre Island in the Dee Estuary to the south of Formby.'

6

'**Red squirrel** (*Sciurus vulgaris*) are also one of National Trust Formby's unique selling points. The pine woodlands are home to this rare native mammal, and the woodlands of the Sefton Coast are the most southerly of 17 red squirrel strongholds in the north of England. The best time to see them is during the breeding season in early spring and then in autumn as they get themselves ready for winter.'

Undiscovered Formby walk

MODERATE GRADE

Distance: 3 miles (4.8km)

Time: 1 hour 45 minutes

Discover Formby's hidden secrets, past and present on a walk that takes you through pine woodlands and along the beach.

Terrain

Varies throughout the walk and includes stone, compacted earth, sandy and grassy paths as well as a long section of beach walking. This walk also contains some short, steep climbs over sand dunes. Please check the tide times and heights before undertaking this walk as during high spring tides the beach section may be impassable.

Directions

① Cross the road and take the path (marked Cornerstone path) to the left of the toilets, heading down a ramp into the woodland. Follow this clear, broad path with its white and purple marker posts through the woodland until you meet another path at a T-junction with a set of large wooden chimes on your left-hand side. The pine woodlands were planted from the late 1800s by the Weld Blundell family, whose estate covered this area. Before the trees were planted the habitat would have been fixed sand dunes covered in grassland – if you look closely you can still make out the shape of the dunes underneath the trees.

' … if you look closely you can still make out the shape of the dunes underneath the trees.'

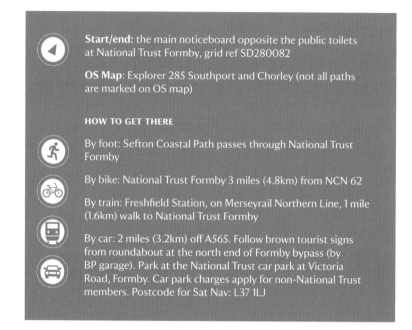

Start/end: the main noticeboard opposite the public toilets at National Trust Formby, grid ref SD280082

OS Map: Explorer 285 Southport and Chorley (not all paths are marked on OS map)

HOW TO GET THERE

By foot: Sefton Coastal Path passes through National Trust Formby

By bike: National Trust Formby 3 miles (4.8km) from NCN 62

By train: Freshfield Station, on Merseyrail Northern Line, 1 mile (1.6km) walk to National Trust Formby

By car: 2 miles (3.2km) off A565. Follow brown tourist signs from roundabout at the north end of Formby bypass (by BP garage). Park at the National Trust car park at Victoria Road, Formby. Car park charges apply for non-National Trust members. Postcode for Sat Nav: L37 1LJ

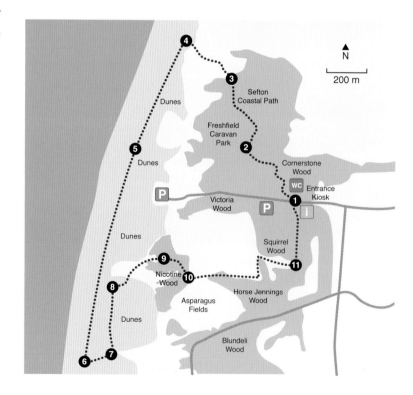

Above: Formby sand dunes

The walk takes you along the beach past the sand dunes, where coastal erosion reveals rubble from the former caravan site and car park.

2 Turn right and follow the wide stone path. As you come out into an open glade, look through the trees on your left-hand side to catch a glimpse of Freshfield Caravan Park. Continue along this path following waymarkers for the Sefton Coastal Path (yellow arrows on a white and grey background). This is the second location that the caravan park has inhabited since the National Trust took over this property in 1967. The first was abandoned due to coastal erosion in the early 1980s and you will see the legacy left by the old caravan site further along this walk.

3 You will eventually leave the woodland and head out into the open dunes. The path passes through a small cut in the dunes and passes an old natterjack toad pool on the right. At this point the path bends to the left and at a path junction by a bench leave the Sefton Coastal Path and take the path straight ahead, over the dunes and on to the beach.

4 Turn left and, keeping the dunes on your left, continue along the beach. You will notice as you go that there are marker posts along the beach denoting the main paths over the dunes. On a number

of days throughout the year, silt beds are exposed beneath the sand, approximately 100–150m from the base of the dunes, which hold human and animal footprints (see pages 334 and 346).

5 As you continue along the beach you may notice rubble and debris that is falling out of the dunes. This is the remnants of the old caravan site and car park that stood here. During the late 1970s to early 1980s the original caravan site and car park succumbed to the sands.

6 After approximately ¾ mile (1.2km) you will reach the Blundell Path marker. Turn left and leave the beach via the path over the dunes.

7 As you come over the dunes you will see a clear path going off to the left through a thickly vegetated area. Take this path and follow it as it passes along the landward base of the sand dunes.

8 Continue along the path as it makes a sharp right bend before going up a slope. When the path descends take the clear path on the right heading into a woodland of gnarled black poplar trees.

9 At a fork, take the right path which leads out onto a T-junction with a wide stone path. Turn right at this junction. After a short distance the path curves round to the right and at this point take the sandy path to the left which leads between two fenced fields.

10 Continue on and follow the fence on your left until the end of the field. At this point turn left along a grass/sand path until it meets a sandy path at a T-junction. Turn right and pass through a small area of woodland before coming out onto a grassy field. Continue straight ahead. Formby is famous for its asparagus. The areas of flat land and fields that you see throughout the site are not natural but are areas where the land has been levelled in the past to grow asparagus. Since the end of asparagus production in the 1990s, these fields have been left to grass over, however the remnants of the asparagus cultivation can still be seen today as ridges and furrows.

11 At the end of the field take the sandy path on the left that ascends a short steep slope into the pine woodland. Continue until you reach a fenced path at a crossroads with a bench on your right. Go straight ahead at this junction and follow the fenced path as it makes a left-hand bend. Shortly after the bend there is a path going off to the right. Take this path to return to the start of the walk.

Discovered in the sand

Beachcombing offers windows into different worlds, whether it's the deep past, the mysteries of the ocean, or the lives of other cultures, says poet **Jean Sprackland**, who spent a year scouring the beaches of the North West.

When I think of my adventures on the beaches of north-west England, the word 'beachcombing' doesn't quite seem to describe them. It suggests a more purposeful and methodical practice than my own, which consisted largely of wandering and stumbling across things by accident. To comb a place is to search it systematically for a particular missing someone or something, like detectives on hands and knees at a crime scene, conducting a fingertip search.

Since *Strands* [Jean's book about her year of discoveries on Ainsdale Sand Dunes] was published, I've had letters from beachcombers who do bring that kind of rigour to their activities. Some go out with GPS and camera and logbook, record their finds meticulously, photograph them in situ and enter them on maps and spread sheets. Others gather extensive collections that threaten to take over their homes and perhaps even their relationships. 'My husband hates my driftwood collection,' confided one of my correspondents. 'He says the house smells like rotten fish all the time.'

You have to feel for the husband. But I understand how beachcombing can become an obsession. I'm not by nature a collector, so I've hung on to very few of the things I've found. My own experiences have been less about acquisition and more about my love of randomness and chance discovery. Still, it obsessed me in other ways. By going back to the same beach again and again, in all seasons and all weathers, I developed a passionate relationship with that place, and gradually became attuned to its changing rhythms.

Above: Shipwreck

The skeletal remains of a boat sticking out of the sandy beach of Rhossili Bay on the Gower Peninsula.

Opposite: Formy Beach

The forces of wind and tide mean that the beach never looks the same, occasionally revealing and then concealing pre-historic footprints.

'By going back to the same beach again and again, in all seasons and all weathers, I developed a passionate relationship with that place, and gradually became attuned to its changing rhythms.'

It was like a long love affair which bucks the trend by growing in intensity rather than fading; my heart would beat faster every time I walked the path through the dunes, wondering what would greet me when I emerged onto the beach. I couldn't even rely on the landscape to look familiar – beaches are mercurial places, and the forces of wind and waves are so powerful that the topography can change from day to day.

Strangeness and beauty

There's no guessing what the tide might have left behind, either. A large proportion of my time on that beach was spent crouching on the sand, peering intently at something and wondering what on earth it could be. Beachcombing is the ideal pastime for those of us who love the cryptic and the mysterious, who enjoy wondering as much as finding out. It's good to be put in touch with our own ignorance, and to be reminded that the world is still, in spite of everything, an endlessly rich and interesting place. In the course of my research I learned so much about the beautiful and curious life that inhabits our shores. Mermaid's purses and sea potatoes, brittle stars and sea gooseberries. The sea mouse, which has been well known to natural historians since ancient times, but was new to me. It isn't seen all that often, because it leads a secretive life burrowing in the sea bed. When I saw one washed up on the beach, fringed with iridescent fur in shades of green and bronze, it was so unfamiliar in appearance I thought at first someone had lost a piece of vintage jewellery.

There's a dark side to all this. It's impossible to walk along a beach these days without seeing discarded plastic. Plastic is qualitatively different from other kinds of litter, because it takes hundreds or even thousands of years to degrade. At this very moment, every piece of plastic which has ever found its way into the ocean is out there, somewhere, travelling the currents, circling in the gyres, washed up on some remote beach or other and then swallowed again by the next tide. But there can be strangeness and beauty even in rubbish. The bottles and cans and crates I found in the tideline bore the names of distant cities, and carried instructions and warnings in as many different languages as I can hear on the streets and buses in the part of London where I live now. All the world turns up on a beach.

Glimpses of the past

If beaches are cosmopolitan places, they can also be like time machines. At Formby, which is managed and protected by the National Trust, it's possible to see the footprints of prehistoric people and animals, exposed by one tide and erased by the next: a fleeting glimpse of the deep past. Nearby, coastal erosion is revealing the evidence of more recent history, such as tobacco dumping and asparagus cultivation. And not far from there I made my most heady discovery: a china teacup from one of the Cunard ships of the 1950s. What made this find so special was that it instantly linked the here-and-now with the past, and with the journeys those great transatlantic liners used to make between Liverpool and New York. Who knows where that cup had been all those years, before it arrived on the shore for me to find? Was it tumbling about in the sea, or buried under the sand? I found it lying demurely on the surface, which that morning was as smooth as a tablecloth. It looked as if it had been left there half an hour ago, by a party of picnickers who had packed up in a hurry and forgotten it.

It's the restlessness of the elements which makes beachcombing exciting. The sea and the sand, always on the move, each with its particular talent for concealment and revelation. Things turn up here; things go missing. After a storm, it's as if the world has turned itself inside out, and all the hidden things are showing. In the intertidal zone near Formby, there are several old shipwrecks which come and go, rising out of their sandy graves to take the air for a few days before sinking back beneath the surface. I secretly hoped, whenever I visited one of these hoary old survivors, to find some small token of life on board in the days or weeks before the catastrophe. Some personal possession: a comb, perhaps, a coin or a button. It must be there, somewhere. But digging in wet sand is a fool's errand. I knew that if I ever found such a thing, it would have to be by chance.

Jean Sprackland is a poet and author. Her third collection of poems Tilt *won the 2007 Costa Poetry Award.* Strands, *her series of meditations prompted by walking the estuaries between Blackpool and Liverpool, was published in 2012 by Jonathan Cape.*

6 OF THE BEST

Seaside things to do in Merseyside, Lancashire and Cumbria

① Follow ancient footsteps at Formby – and cycle to 'Another Place'

Though Merseyside is better known for the port city of Liverpool and its attendant industries, there are beautiful beaches here, too, along the Sefton Coast between Crosby and Southport. Among these unsung treasures is Formby – a soul-soothing ribbon of sand, edged by tussocky dunes and pine woods. Formby has a fascinating history, as the site of the first ever lifeboat station in the UK (established in 1776). And signs of earlier habitation – human and animal footprints dating back 7,000 years – have been uncovered by sand erosion at Formby Point. You can find out what these tracks reveal about our ancestors, and look out for traces yourself, on a guided walk led by one of the Trust's archaeology experts. Alternatively, to see more of the Sefton Coast, join a National Trust bike ride from Formby to Crosby Beach, the site of Antony Gormley's installation, 'Another Place'. Find out more about cycling routes in National Trust countryside at www.nationaltrust.org.uk.

② Enjoy old-fashioned seaside fun in Blackpool

No visit to the North West coast would be complete without a stroll along the prom at Blackpool, where many of the traditional totems of the British seaside holiday are in evidence: pleasure piers, a vast funfair, donkey rides (from Easter to November) and sticks of rock. Much has been done in recent years to modernise the resort's appeal: take a look at the prom's 'Comedy Carpet', which is the UK's biggest piece of public art at 2,200m², featuring 850 jokes by British comics. Or visit the refurbished Blackpool Tower Eye viewing platform (replete with glass floor), for panoramic views of the Fylde coast. See if you can complete the day with an afternoon tea dance at the spectacular Tower Ballroom.

Below left: Ancient footprints

Visitors learning about the footprints found in silt beds on the shoreline at Formby.

Below: Blackpool North Pier

Designed by Eugenius Birch (see page 137), Blackpool's oldest pier opened on 21 May 1863. Its amusements include a theatre, carousel ride and the Sun Lounge.

③ Follow a photographer around Liverpool

Follow in the footsteps of photographer Edward Chambré Hardman from his house at 59 Rodney Street on three short walks that take you past some of the sights and scenes he photographed. The routes will take you through the city centre, past the cathedrals, the station, the pier head and the docks and can be downloaded from www.nationaltrust.org.uk/hardmans-house. Each includes images of Hardman's photographs of similar scenes, so it's fun to take along your own camera and compare yours with his. Then upload them to the National Trust's Facebook or Twitter feed so we can all see them.

④ Watch the sunset from Jack Scout

This, one of only two cliffs between Silverdale and Arnside, overlooks Morecambe Bay and is a great destination for an evening walk. A short stroll from the road across wild flower-rich meadows brings you to the rocky headland. At dusk, the daytime walkers have gone home and all is quiet. Listen out for birds including oystercatchers and curlews on the sand below, and warblers and blackbirds around you as the sun sets. Or watch the spectacle from the pebble beach below, a short scramble down a path through the bushes.

⑤ Wild paddle on the Isle of Man

The Isle of Man, with its plunging cliffs, sheltered bays and sea caves, is a natural adventure playground for fans of adrenaline and water sports, offering ideal terrain for coasteering, climbing, abseiling, sea kayaking and a range of wilderness experiences. On sea-kayaking trips with local course providers (not National Trust) it's possible to enjoy twilight (or night) expeditions and overnight camping in remote locations – or even to circumnavigate the whole island (85 miles) over four to five days, if you're an experienced paddler.

⑥ Go on a technological treasure hunt

If you haven't discovered geocaching yet, now is the time! This treasure hunt for the digital age is becoming increasingly popular and you can take part in it at numerous Trust properties, including the dunes and woods at Formby. First find a cache on www.geocaching.com (you will need to sign up), then enter the co-ordinates into your GPS device or smart phone app (try Garmin's OpenCaching). Follow your GPS towards the spot to find the cache. Once discovered, open it up and fill out the logbook. Sometimes people also leave messages and small objects to swap. By now you will have caught the bug and will be looking for your next cache.

Northern
Ireland

The 120-mile Causeway Coastal Route that winds around the North Antrim coast from Londonderry to Belfast has been called one of the world's best coast road trips. This may seem exaggerated until you realise that it passes a UNESCO World Heritage site (Giant's Causeway), a rope bridge that connects an island to the mainland (Carrick-a-Rede), the ruins of a romantic castle (Dunluce), miles of sand, dunes, cliffs and mountains, and scenic golf courses.

Foremost of these attractions is the National Trust-owned Giant's Causeway, which is not only geologically spectacular but is wrapped in legend: it is where giant Fion MacCumhail (Finn McCool) built his bridge to Scotland. Northern Ireland's dramatic coastline of cliffs, bays, glens and mountains, and its many prehistoric dolmen and burial chambers, lends itself to the generation of myths like this, and still stokes the imagination of writers and film-makers – *Game of Thrones* was filmed here.

Further south, Strangford Lough, the largest sea lough in the British Isles, is enclosed by the Ards Peninsula and is a landscape rich in variety, including islands, marsh and beaches, which attract large amounts of wildlife including 2,000 species of marine wildlife and 2,000 species of birds.

Previous pages: The Mourne Mountains from Murlough National Nature Reserve, County Down.

Left: An abandoned boat lying on the foreshore of Ballymorran Bay in Strangford Lough, County Down.

Northern Ireland: giants, loughs, and mountains that sweep down to the sea

Leaving the walled city of Londonderry behind, the road travels beside Lough Foyle to Benone Strand, one of Ireland's longest stretches of sand. A European Blue Flag beach (based on water quality and environmental management), the 7 miles of beach backed by cliffs are a popular destination for anglers, body boarders, power kiters and anyone who likes wide-open spaces, stretches of clean, flat sand, and the sound of rolling surf.

The sands continue to Downhill, which is sandwiched between the sea and high basalt cliffs which mark the northern flank of the Binevenagh Mountains. The beach is safe for bathing and surfing; picnickers in search of a lunch spot with a view, should head for Gortmore Picnic Site, 272m above sea level with views across Lough Foyle to Donegal and the Scottish islands. Overlooking the beach on the edge of the cliff is the precariously perched local landmark Mussenden Temple, and the imposing remains of Downhill House, built by Frederick Hervey, Earl-Bishop in 1768 (see page 362). The small resort of Castlerock has the first of this coastline's many championship golf courses and also Trust-owned Hezlett House, one of Ireland's oldest examples of domestic vernacular architecture (see page 362).

Left: Downhill House

The south front of the ruins of Downhill House, County Londonderry. The house was built around 1774 for the Earl-Bishop Frederick Hervey.

Right: Mussenden Temple

The temple, seen from from Downhill Beach, is part of the Downhill Demesne Estate.

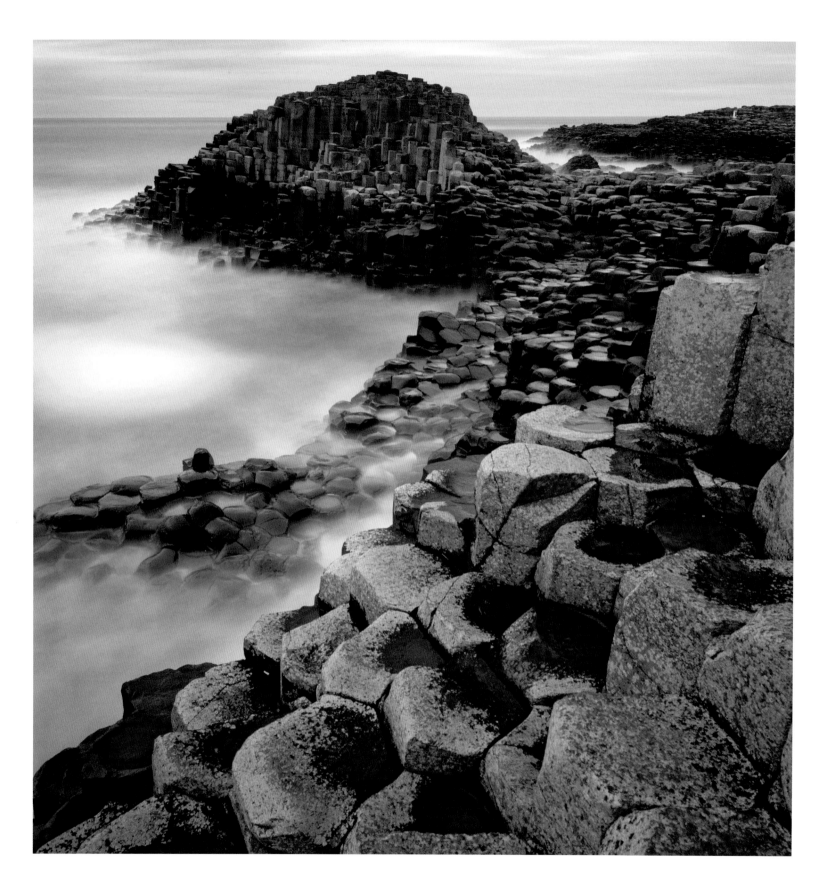

In the giant's footsteps

Waymarked footpaths crosshatch the North Antrim coast. The 33-mile Causeway Coast Way follows the shoreline tightly from Portstewart to Ballycastle, talking walkers past the spectacular Giant's Causeway and the adrenaline-boosting Carrick-a-Rede rope bridge (see pages 364 and 365). A pleasant, leisurely alternative to walking is to take a 2-mile ride on the Giant's Causeway and Bushmills Railway, a narrow-gauge steam train that connects the world's oldest licensed whiskey distillery in Bushmills with the World Heritage site that is the Giant's Causeway.

Portstewart is an interesting Victorian resort with a two-tiered promenade, a picturesque harbour and a much-loved beach, Portstewart Strand (see page 362). Three miles further on, the popular resort and harbour of Portrush, is sheltered by the mile-long peninsula of Ramore Head and bustles with entertainment options and places to eat. The greens of the Royal Portrush golf course are scattered among the dunes with views of the sea cliffs and the Skerries, a chain of islands rich in fossils and seabirds.

Between Portrush and Portballintrae, the romantic turrets and towers of fourteenth-century Dunluce Castle are silhouetted against the stormy sea. Teetering over a precipitous basalt outcrop, it is accessible via a bridge that connects it to the mainland. Once the headquarters of the McDonnell clan, the castle was constantly besieged until part of it fell into the sea during a storm in 1639, when it was finally abandoned.

White Park Bay, which stretches between the better-known destinations, Giant's Causeway and Carrick-a-Rede, is significant in the history of the National Trust, as it was the first piece of coast the Trust took ownership of in Northern Ireland. The Trust bought it in 1938 with support from the Pilgrim Trust, a charity particularly interested in saving unspoilt coastline, and the Youth Hostel Association. It is a wide, sandy beach bookended by headlands and backed by botanically rich dunes and species-rich chalk grassland. This habitat attracts butterfly species, including small

Left: Giant's Causeway

The unusual rock formations at Giant's Causeway, County Antrim are seeped in myth and legend.

Right: White Park Bay

Organic cattle on the beach at White Park Bay on the North Antrim coast.

Salmon fishing in Northern Ireland

Catching wild salmon from the sea around Northern Ireland was once a thriving industry. In the nineteenth century, 21 salmon fishermen worked in the parish of Ballintoy and catches of up to 300 salmon a day were common. This lasted until the 1960s when a combination of over-fishing and pollution led to the industry's decline. Atlantic salmon were fished for almost 400 years off Carrick-a-Rede: the last fish was caught in 2002 by Aki Colgan who had worked there for 25 years. To get an idea of what life was like for the salmon fishermen, the National Trust has restored Aki's cottage on Carrick-a-Rede (reached by crossing the famous rope bridge) complete with all the paraphernalia associated with the work. Look out for the lifting gear used to raise the boats and salmon fishing nets. For more information see www.nationaltrust.org.uk/carrick-a-rede.

copper and orange tip, and birds such as fulmars, meadow pipits
and ringed plovers, plus at least nine different species of orchid have
naturalised here. The bay obviously suited Neolithic man: evidence
of a settlement is constantly being discovered and there are three
passage tombs on high points surrounding the bay, the most striking
of which is known as the Druid's Altar. The beach is also a good place
to search for fossils such as belemnites, ammonites and gryphaea.

White Park Bay has fine views of Rathlin Island, Northern Island's
only inhabited offshore island (about 70 people live there). Reached
by ferry from Ballycastle, it is also home to a colony of seals and
an RSPB Seabird Centre which teems with puffins, guillemots,
razorbills and kittiwakes in the summer months.

Natural wonders and a sinking ship

Enthusiasts of Portmeirion in North Wales (see page 317) should visit
Cushendun, at the mouth of the River Dun, which was designed by
the same architect, Clough Williams Ellis. Like the more fanciful Welsh
village, this is a 'borrowed' architecture: Cushendun was designed to
resemble a Cornish village to please landowner Baron Cushendun's

Penzance-born wife, Maud. The parkland around Glenmona House,
the Baron's neo-Georgian home to the north is Trust-owned.

The McDonnell family, occupants of Dunluce Castle until 1639 when
it began its tumble into the sea, now lives in Glenarm Castle. Its
Walled Garden is open to the public from May to September and is
cleverly planted with year-round interest. To the north of the seaport
of Larne, lie the Nine Glens of Antrim, valleys which radiate from the
volcanic Antrim plateau to the coast. Each has its own name and
character and, like much of the surrounding country, is veiled
in myth.

Running parallel with the coast between Larne and Whitehead,
Islandmagee is a sparsely populated peninsula packed with natural
wonders. Foremost of these is the Gobbins, a series of limestone
cliffs reaching over 60m high and stretching for 4 miles. A derelict
cliff path cut through the rock linking rocky outcrops with suspended
walkways and bridges, built by Victorian entrepreneur Berkeley Dean
Wise, is in the process of being rebuilt in pre-fabricated steel by
Larne Council. A less adrenaline-fuelled way to enjoy the peninsula

Above: Belfast Lough

Birdlife on Ballymacormick Point, an area of coastal heath on the shore of Belfast Lough.

is to walk from the sandy beach at Brown's Bay to its southern tip at Skernaghan Point through rolling fields and quiet villages. One of these, Portmuck, a harbour on the northwest coastline, has an ancient monastery and castle and good views of the pig-shaped Island of Muck and its many seabirds.

It seems almost inevitable that the fortunes of the city of Belfast would be built from shipbuilding. Located at the western end of Belfast Lough and at the mouth of the River Lagan, it was ideally situated. At its height, the city's main shipbuilders, Harland and Wolff, was the most productive in the world and constructed that most famous of ships, the *Titanic*, in 1911–12. The fortune of that ill-fated liner and the shipyards are told in a museum, Titanic Belfast, which has been built beside the docks where she was constructed.

A great body of water

Strangford Lough, which at 58 square miles is the largest sea lough or inlet in the British Isles, is enclosed by the Ards Peninsula, which folds around it leaving one small opening, the Narrows, to the Irish Sea. ('Strangford' is derived from the Norse for 'strong fjord', a reference to the fast currents that power through here creating energy now harnessed by a tidal stream power station (see feature, opposite).

Above: Strangford Lough

View of the lough from Castle Ward Bay.
Audley's Castle, a fifteenth-century tower
house, can just be seen on the left.

Although various bodies own different parts of the foreshore, the National Trust manages 4,000 hectares (9,884 acres) of coast and countryside in and around Strangford Lough and the Ards Peninsula, and looks after two properties, Mount Stewart (see page 366) and Castle Ward (see page 369). The landscape and habitats on the seabed and shoreline are rich and varied – marshes, rocky outcrops, bays, islands, beaches – and provide homes for many different creatures, including 2,000 species of marine wildlife and 2,000 species of birds. Large numbers of duck and goose including wigeon, shelduck and pale-bellied Brent geese (see page 370) overwinter here, and wading birds including oystercatcher, lapwing, golden plover, curlew, redshank, dunlin and knot feed in the mudflats.

The Lough is one of an increasing number of Marine Protected Areas (MPAs). The emergence of MPAs around the UK coast reflects the growing awareness towards ensuring that there is adequate protection of the marine environment. The Lough has at least 100 islands, a number of which are owned by the National Trust. On the west shore, these include Innisharoan and Darragh Island off Whiterock; Island Taggart to the north of Killyleagh; Green Island, Salt Island (which is accessible to the public by boat has bothy-style accommodation), Launches Long and Little to the south of Killyleagh; and Gibb's Island 2 miles south of Killyleagh which is linked to the mainland by a causeway.

Tidal power, Strandford Lough

The currents in the Narrows channel connecting Strangford Lough to the Irish Sea, flow at a rate up to 4m/sec. In 2008, recognising the potential power of the tides, Siemens-owned Marine Current Turbine bolted a commercial tidal stream power station, SeaGen, on to the seabed at the Lough's mouth. The position was perfect: near enough to the shore for maintenance but still exposed to the full rigours of the tides as they power in and out of the Lough. 1.2 megawatts of electricity – enough to power around 1,500 homes – is now generated via two massive underwater propellers. This initiative, which is part of Northern Ireland's Environment and Renewable Energy Fund, is set to create renewable energy that poses no threat to wildlife.

The National Trust has worked with the local community to protect the Ards Peninsula, particularly McCutcheon's Field, which it saved from development in 2000. Nearby, the National Trust owns about a mile of coastline at Orlock Point: a short circular walk takes visitors past a Second World War lookout and tunnel and along part of a nineteenth-century coach road said to have been used by smugglers.

Below: Orlock Point

Coastal path at Orlock Point, an area of
unspoilt land with interesting flora and fauna.

Left: Ballyquintin Farm

A volunteer warden takes his favourite pig for a walk along a country lane near the farm.

The sandy beach of Ballyholme Bay is reached down a narrow track through Ballymacormick Point and is a wild and unvisited place. Lighthouse Island, one of the Copeland islands 2 miles off Donaghadee has a breeding colony of 3,000 pairs of Manx shearwater.

At the tip of the peninsula on Outer Ards, Kearney Village was the National Trust's first purchase in Northern Ireland through the Enterprise Neptune scheme in 1965. The National Trust restored the village based on the 1834 Ordnance Survey to replicate the flourishing fishing village it once was. All the houses are now occupied and life has been restored to what had become a forlorn spot. The 47-hectare (116-acre) farm at Ballyquintin up the road (or dirt track) has been in the Trust's care since 2000 and is farmed using environmentally friendly methods specifically to provide habitats to encourage wildlife.

'A network of paths and boardwalks runs through the dune heath'

It is a lovely place with views of the Isle of Man and the Mourne Mountains providing a backdrop for the antics of the Irish hare and the yellowhammer.

Mountains, dunes and a seaweed bath

Climb to the summit of Slieve Donard, one of the Mourne Mountains, and you are rewarded with a glorious view of the County Down coast. The seaside town of Newcastle sits below, uniquely situated between the mountains and the curl of its beach (and the inspiration for the song lyric 'where the mountains of Mourne sweep down to the sea'). Little wonder that it is so popular with walkers who set off from its centre to climb the Mournes or ramble along the Mourne Coast Path to Dundrum Bay. Others come to play a round at the Royal County Down Golf Club, go pony trekking or take a leisurely stroll along its refurbished prom. There are even seaweed baths.

To the north of Newcastle is Murlough National Nature Reserve, a 6,000-year-old dune system that runs for nearly 4 miles. Its unusually high dunes built up across the head of Dundrum Bay at the end of the last Ice Age. Owned since 1967 and managed by the National Trust as Ireland's first Nature Reserve, it is a beautiful place to walk, bird watch and generally escape the frenzy of daily life.

A network of paths and boardwalks runs through the dune heath (considered to be the best in Ireland), which in the summer is lively with 620 species of butterflies and moths, and the common lizard which preys on them. Its raised shingle storm beach is 4 miles long and an important feeding place for summer birds and over-wintering waders and wildfowl. There are also healthy populations of common and grey seals.

The coastline of Northern Ireland ends in some style at Carlingford Lough, a glacial inlet that forms part of the border with the Republic of Ireland. The Lough, its shoreline and surrounding mountains have been popular tourist destinations since Victorian times and still attract the adventurous drawn by possibilities of canoeing, sailing, rock climbing and windsurfing. The more sedentary will also find plenty of opportunities to simply stand and stare.

Above: Murlough Nature Reserve

View of the Mourne Mountains from Murlough National Nature Reserve.

Explore National Trust places on the Northern Irish coast

Downhill House, Mussenden Temple, Hezlett House, County Londonderry

Although in ruins, it is still possible to get an idea of the scale and grandeur of Downhill House. Built for globe-trotting Frederick Hervey, 4th Earl of Bristol after he was made Bishop of Derry in 1768, it had a three-storeyed front, two wings topped with domes and facing an inner courtyard, and two curving basalt bastions overlooking Downhill Strand. Inside, the Earl-Bishop (as he was known) furnished the many rooms with paintings and statues gathered on his travels. Unfortunately the house was almost entirely gutted by fire in 1851 and despite being rebuilt in the 1870s by John Lanyon, it fell into disrepair after the Second World War during which it was used to billet RAF servicemen and women. The National Trust acquired it in 1980.

On the cliff top nearby is local landmark Mussenden Temple, a small domed rotunda modelled on the Temple of Vesta in Tivoli, Italy. Originally built as a library, it became a memorial to Hervey's niece Frideswide Mussenden after her death in 1785. Erosion has brought the temple close to the edge of the basalt cliff on which it perches and the Trust has carried out cliff stabilisation to prevent its loss.

At the crossroads of Castlerock village is Hezlett House, which was built around 1691 as a rectory or farmhouse. The Trust has restored this thatched cottage, one of the oldest vernacular domestic buildings in Northern Ireland, telling the story of the house through the experiences of the people who lived there.
Mussenden Road, Castlerock, County Londonderry, BT51 4RP

Portstewart Strand and the Bann Estuary, County Londonderry

It is easy to see why Portstewart Strand is one of Northern Ireland's most popular beaches. At the height of summer its 2-mile stretch of sand is busy with kite flyers, ramblers and children building sandcastles, all enjoying its golden beach, clear water and hummocky dunes. And it couldn't be easier to reach: cars have permission to drive on to the beach, a long-standing tradition that the Trust has allowed to continue (although there is a car-free zone in operation from July to August). Its attractions, however, are year-round: the magnificent dunes – some are up to 30m high – provide a perfect habitat for wild flowers and butterflies and can be enjoyed on a number of waymarked nature trails. For the more ambitious walker, this is also the starting point for the 33-mile Causeway Coast Way walk

Right: Portstewart Strand

A family explores one of the magnificent dunes on the beach at Portstewart.

Below: Mussenden Temple

The Earl-Bishop Frederick Hervey began to create the house, estate and temple at Downhill in 1772. The temple was built between 1783 and 1785 by Michael Shanahan, and was originally intended as a library.

that ends at Ballycastle. The saltmarsh of the Bann Estuary nearby attracts migrant waterfowl and wading birds which can be observed in the bird hide in Barmouth. **118 Strand Road, Portstewart, County Londonderry, BT55 7PG (028 7083 6396)**

Giant's Causeway, County Antrim

It's little wonder that myths have grown up around the Giant's Causeway. Its ranks of polygonal basalt columns rising from the North Atlantic Ocean startle not just because of their uniqueness but also because of their regularity. It's almost believable that the giant Fion MacCumhail (Finn McCool) did construct it as a paved bridge across the Irish Sea to reach his Scottish rival Benandonner. But the reality is just as marvellous. Over 60 million years ago the North American plate began to split from the Eurasia plate, creating the Atlantic Ocean. There was intense volcanic activity along the line of separation causing magma to spew up from the Earth's core. As it cooled and shrank, horizontal contraction created vertical cracks, leaving pillar-like structures that created the 40,000 honeycombed columns we see today. The size of the columns was determined by the speed at which the lava cooled.

Such is the importance of this natural phenomenon that it was designated a World Heritage Site by UNESCO in 1986. The National Trust has cared for the Giant's Causeway since 1961 (it opened to the public in 1962), and opened the 10 miles of the North Antrim Coast Path alongside it in 1964. In July 2012 the Trust opened a new visitor centre, with a restaurant serving seasonal food and a shop. Ever mindful of the environment and the surroundings, the Trust built the centre with sustainability in mind: it has a green roof (grown from seed collected in neighbouring fields), the basalt on the exterior was quarried locally and 95 per cent of all waste is recycled.

The Giant's Causeway is also home to a variety of wildlife including fulmars which nest here, peregrine falcons, buzzards and choughs, and lizards who bask on the rocks. **44 Causeway Road, Bushmills, County Antrim, BT57 8SU**

Left: Giant's Causeway

A child investigates a pool within the rocks, against a backdrop of the bay and the pillars at the World Heritage Site in County Antrim.

Carrick-a-Rede, near Ballintoy, County Antrim

Constructed by salmon fishermen in 1755, the rope swing bridge connecting the mainland and the volcanic plug, Carrick-a-Rede, was intended to make access to their fishing nets easier. Carrick-a-Rede is Gaelic for 'rock in the road', the route taken by salmon each year. These days the bridge, which spans a chasm 30m deep and 20m wide, is one of Northern Ireland's most visited attractions. The National Trust replaced the original single-hand rope rail with a two-handed one, but a walk across is still not for the faint hearted: below rocks are lashed by the sea and the bridge has been known to sway in high winds. Once on the island, visitors can join guillemots, razorbills, kittiwakes and fulmars, and try and spot basking sharks, dolphins and porpoise in the ocean below. Nearby, Larrybane was a working quarry until the mid-1970s and a walk through there makes a scenic approach to the bridge. There are also good views of Sheep Island and Rathlin Island from the rocky headland of Fair Head 4½ miles offshore from here, but binoculars will be needed to spot the tens of thousands of seabirds that inhabit it alongside a population of 100 people. **119a Whitepark Road, Ballintoy, County Antrim, BT54 6LS (028 2076 9839)**

 Holiday Cottage

Carrick-a-Rede, Balllintoy, County Antrim. Watch the sun set over Rathlin Island and the Isle of Mull from the front of this handsome house near the village of Ballintoy. The small courtyard at the back gets the benefit of full sun in the morning and is the perfect place to eat breakfast before a short walk to the Carrick-a-Rede rope

'It's little wonder that myths have grown up around the Giant's Causway.'

Paddle power

You get a totally different perspective of the coast when you approach it in a kayak or a canoe. Slipping quietly through the water, the boat takes you to hidden coves and secret beaches often not accessible from the shore. Strangford Lough with its sheltered waters and many islands to explore, is ideal for this sort of boating. The adventurous can even follow the Strangford Lough Canoe Trail and stay overnight at the bothy on Salt Island. For canoe trail details visit www.canoeni.com. To book the bothy or to camp overnight contact the National Trust at Mount Stewart on 018 4278 8387.

Other National Trust coastal places to paddle: Mullion Harbour, Cornwall; the Fal river, Cornwall; Fowey Estuary, Cornwall; Salcombe, Devon; Studland Bay, Dorset; Stackpole, Wales.

bridge nearby. Free entry to all National Trust sites on the North Coast (including the rope bridge) are included in the price of the accommodation. Inside, the house is comfortably furnished with a roll-top bath, winged armchairs and a real fire in the living room. **For more information see www.nationaltrustcottages.co.uk**

Mount Stewart House, Garden and Temple of the Winds

The lavish gardens at Mount Stewart, recently voted among the Top 10 in the world, were created by 7th Marchioness, Edith, Lady Londonderry, in the early twentieth century. The National Trust has owned the gardens since 1957 (and the house since 1977) and carefully manages Lady Londonderry's series of Mediterranean-style gardens, distinguished by their unusual plant varieties and sculptural topiary. The Temple of the Winds – an octagonal former banqueting hall – overlooks Strangford Lough and was inspired by the Grand Tour taken by the 1st Marquess. Tours of the neoclassical house (currently undergoing conservation) take place hourly, 12–3pm, during open season, while garden tours are available at weekends. **Portaferry Road, Newtownards, County Down, BT22 2AD**

Opposite: Mount Stewart

The Italian Garden at Mount Stewart runs across the entire length of the front of the house.

Right: Temple of the Winds

This neoclassical gem in the grounds of Mount Stewart was used by the family as an informal retreat.

'The Mourne Mountains in County Down are the highest in Northern Ireland.'

Castle Ward, County Down

A conflict of architectural taste between Bernard Ward, 1st Viscount Bangor, and his wife, Lady Ann Bligh, resulted in a unique eighteenth-century mansion being built on the shores of Strangford Lough, with classical features dominating on one side and a gothic influence on the other. Find out more on a guided tour (daily, mid-June to end August – call ahead to confirm), or explore the 332-hectare (820-acre) estate, where attractions range from the formal parterre planting of the Sunken Garden to miles of multipurpose trails (for walking, cycling and horse riding) through woods, parkland and along the lough shore. Children will enjoy indoor and outdoor play areas, plus the chance to meet farmyard animals. **Strangford, Downpatrick, County Down, BT30 7LS**

The Mournes, County Down

The Mourne Mountains in County Down are the highest in Northern Ireland (Slieve Donard, the tallest of the 12 summits, reaches 852m) and their picturesque 'sweep down to the sea' was immortalised in the 1896 song by Percy French. There are various hiking routes to choose from, including the Mourne Coastal Path, which allows visitors to walk on otherwise inaccessible coastline. Take in features such as the Mourne Wall, built by the Belfast Water Commissioners in the 1900s, or the 'Bloody Bridge', site of a massacre during the 1641 rebellion. Views extend across Newcastle town, the Murlough dunes and to mainland Britain. **Near Newcastle, County Down**

Left: Coal Quay

The 200-year-old quay at the Castle Ward Estate on the edge of Strangford Lough.

Right: Castle Ward

This view shows the classical Palladian front of the mansion. This side is in complete contrast to the Gothic façade on the other side of the house.

Shore-spotter's Guide

1

There are over 2,000 different types of marine creatures living in Strangford Lough, including the **common starfish** (*Asterias rubens*), which you may be able to see resting on rock along the shore, where it feeds on molluscs and other invertebrates. Growing up to 30cm across, it has five arms and is usually orange or brown.

2

The **oysterplant** (*Mertensia maritima*) grows on exposed shingle beaches at the Giant's Causeway. Like other coastal plants such as the yellow-horned poppy, it requires some disturbance to maintain its open shingle habitat but is threatened by extreme storms, coastal squeeze, too much recreational activity and shingle being removed from beaches. As a result, it is now nationally scarce. However, there is hope: as its seeds can be dispersed over long distances by the sea, there is the potential for it to spread and colonise new sites.

3

The **pale-bellied Brent goose** (*Branta bernicla hrota*) breeds in Svalbard in the Artic Ocean, and Arctic Canada, and winters in Ireland and Denmark, flying over the Greenland ice cap at heights of almost 2 miles. Look out for a small goose with a short, stubby bill on Strangford Lough in October when 75 per cent of the entire population make the journey from north eastern Canada.

'This semi-feral horse now lives on the islands in Strangford Lough'

Strong and stocky with a small head, the **konik** pony (*Equus ferus caballus*) originated in Poland where it was an important transport animal for Russian and German troops in the First World War. This small semi-feral horse now lives on the islands in Strangford Lough where the National Trust has introduced it as a grazing herd.

The **marsh fritillary** butterfly (*Euphydryas aurinia*) is a rapidly declining species in Europe, found mainly in western Britain. It is still quite widespread in Northern Ireland, with a stronghold around Crom in County Fermanagh. At Murlough National Nature Reserve, on the County Down coast, it is often abundant, breeding in inland dune slacks and flying alongside the cryptic wood white (*Leptidea juvernica*), a butterfly only recently recognised as being a separate species to the similar-looking Réal's wood white.

The **ringed plover** (*Charadrius hiaticula*) breeds on the pebbly beaches at White Park Bay, County Antrim – a valuable site for conservation. Small and dumpy with an orange bill (tipped with black) and orange legs, it is a Species of Conservation Concern, as is the fulmar and meadow pipit, also seen at White Park Bay in County Antrim.

Runkerry trail, near Giant's Causeway, walk

MODERATE GRADE

Distance: 2 miles (3.2km)

Time: 1 hour 30 minutes

Wouldn't it be fantastic to enjoy the often-crowded Giant's Causeway in tranquillity even during main visitor hours? We can offer such a thing. Take a walk around Runkerry, located just next to the Causeway with views of the stones and on most days to Scotland and the Inishowen Peninsula in Ireland, too. A cliff walk takes you along Trust land which has significant numbers of breeding skylark, stonechat, linnet and the occasional chough. Parts of this walk also follow the route of the Bushmills Heritage Railway.

Terrain

Gravel path, steep in places, wooden steps and Tarmac road.

Directions

1 Start at the Causeway Hotel, where there's a path on the left side of the building leading towards the cliff path. Turn left and follow the path around Runkerry Head. On your right side you will have fantastic views of the Causeway stones and the chimney tops. On a clear day you can also see right across to Scotland, which is just 26 miles (41.8km) away. The island of Islay can be seen on most days and sometimes the air is so clear that even the Paps of Jura (three distinctive mountains on the southern half of the island) on the Inner Hebrides are visible.

'... you will have fantastic views of the Causeway stones and the chimney tops.'

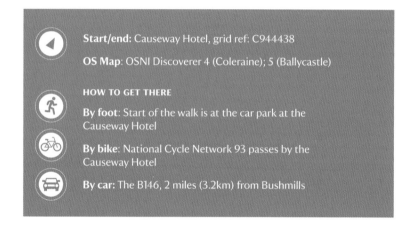

Start/end: Causeway Hotel, grid ref: C944438

OS Map: OSNI Discoverer 4 (Coleraine); 5 (Ballycastle)

HOW TO GET THERE

By foot: Start of the walk is at the car park at the Causeway Hotel

By bike: National Cycle Network 93 passes by the Causeway Hotel

By car: The B146, 2 miles (3.2km) from Bushmills

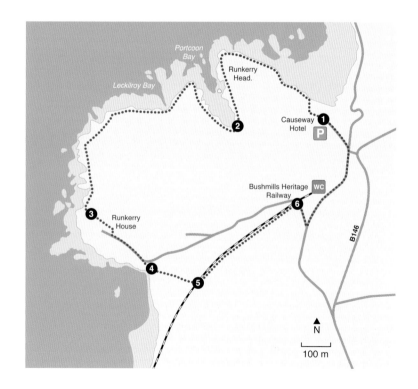

2 Leaving the headland behind, you come to a little bay called Portcoon. Continue on the cliff path around the second headland.

3 When the path goes downhill you can see the first signs of Runkerry House and Portballintrae. Look out for dolphins and porpoises; they like swimming at Bushfoot Strand. Once there were working salmon fisheries everywhere along the North Coast but that time is long gone. All that's left are deserted buildings and rusting fishing gear.

4 When you reach a small wooden bridge now, follow the path up the hill until you come to a railway.

Above: Basalt columns

Visitors walking on the basalt columns at the Giant's Causeway, seen at the start of the walk.

5 Carefully cross the railway and turn left on to the Tarmac path with the railway on your left side. This track will lead you to the small station of the Bushmills Heritage Railway.

6 From here you can see the Causeway Hotel again. Walk up the hill but be aware of traffic. Weir's Snout cottage offers a great view over Runkerry and the walk you've just done.

Seaside things to do in Northern Ireland

❶ Go on a sea safari on Strangford Lough

For an otter's-eye view of the largest sea lough in the British Isles – home to 100 islands and 2,000 species of marine wildlife – take to the water. The Strangford Lough Canoe Trail is supported by the National Trust, and the 21-mile Sketrick-Killyleagh route includes an overnight stay in bothy accommodation on Salt Island. Regular 'Sea Safaris' depart from Strangford Village, packing in the lough's top-ranking sights: the Angus Rock Lighthouse, the SS *Empire* shipwreck, the whirlpools at Routen Wheel and the resident colonies of grey and common seals.

❷ Walk the Carrick-a-Rede rope bridge

Not for the faint hearted, the rope bridge at Carrick-a-Rede is an exhilarating skywalk experience, which now attracts 250,000 visitors a year to this part of the North Antrim coast, where a 400-year-old salmon fishery once thrived. Find out more about the island's fishing heritage, look out for wild orchids and nesting fulmars, guillemots and razorbills, or lap up the views across to Rathlin and the Scottish islands from the Weighbridge Tea Room. Still hungry for adventure? Then walk the 11-mile coastal trail from here to the Giant's Causeway.

❸ Ride a Segway around Downhill Demesne

Downhill Demesne has much to ensnare the visitor's fascination – from the eighteenth-century mansion ruins and the cliff-edge Mussenden Temple to a sheltered Bog Garden and rugged headland, leading down to 7 miles of sand. There are self-guided trails for walkers through the estate, but for something a bit different, why not hire a Segway® (a two-wheeled, electric personal transporter) and glide your way around the

Right: Brave the rope bridge

Striding out across the rope bridge between the mainland cliffs and the island of Carrick-a-Rede.

Left: Scrabo Tower

Scrabo Tower, west of Newtownards, stands atop a volcanic plug and was built as a memorial to Charles Stewart, 3rd Marquess of Londonderry.

site. The Trust has teamed up with local company, Segway Express, to provide a 4- to 5-mile tour of Downhill Demesne, including the gardens and Mussenden Temple. There is also a Segway tour available of neighbouring Benone Strand, which has one of the largest dune systems in the UK and Ireland, plus spellbinding views of the North Coast. For more information see www.segwayexpress.co.uk.

④ Look out for Murlough's magical wildlife

Have binoculars at the ready when visiting Murlough National Nature Reserve, near Dundrum Bay – a site of international importance for overwintering wildfowl and waders, such as pale-bellied Brent geese and oystercatchers, and inhabited by rare species of moth including the black rustic and pink-barred sallow and 23 species of butterfly including the endangered marsh fritillary. There are two nature trails leading through the 6,000-year-old dune system (tracker packs and kids' activity leaflets are also available). On your way around, savour the scenic backdrop of Dundrum Castle and the Mournes, and the outlook across meditative sands towards the Isle of Man. Also, see if you can identify evidence of earlier human occupation dotted around the reserve, such as prehistoric standing stones and a Second World War rifle range.

⑤ Climb to the top of Scrabo Tower

One of Northern Ireland's most celebrated landmarks – and visible for miles around – Scrabo Tower, near the northern shore of Strangford Lough, was built by local people in 1857, in memory of Charles Stewart, 3rd Marquess of Londonderry, for his kindness towards his tenants during the potato famine. (You can find out more about the building's history via the exhibition inside.) Standing on a volcanic plug 165m above sea level, the turreted monument is 38m tall and rewards visitors who climb all 122 steps to the top with a vast panorama encompassing Strangford Lough, the Mourne Mountains and the Scottish coast.

⑥ Try out a trail at Castle Ward

The National Trust has upgraded the 22-mile network of multi-use trails around the grounds at Castle Ward with 12 miles of new trails. Whether you enjoy walking, cycling or horse riding, there is something for every ability on one of the five different routes. Be sure to look around you as you go: the trails offer some of the best views of the estate and the surrounding area and will take you through woodland, beside the lake and over rolling hills. There is cycle parking on the site for those who want to enjoy a car-free day.

How we've looked after the coast

1895 Creation of the National Trust. The first ever piece of land acquired by the Trust was Dinas Oleu, a small area of coastal cliff in north-west Wales.

1912 Blakeney Point on the north Norfolk coast acquired by the National Trust – its first sizable stretch of coastline.

1925 The much-loved Farne Islands, off the Northumberland coast, comes into the care of the National Trust.

1962 The geologically stunning Giant's Causeway in Northern Ireland is acquired by the National Trust.

1965 **Enterprise Neptune** is launched when the National Trust owns 192 miles of coastline. The Treasury pledges £250,000 towards the appeal.

First Neptune Site acquired – Whiteford Burrows on Gower, South Wales.

1966 R. C. Sheriff, author of *Journey's End*, gives Down House Farm on the Dorset Coast to the National Trust.

Dunwich Heath, Suffolk, is bought by the National Trust thanks to the support of Heinz.

1967 The world-famous Rhossili beach and Down on Gower in South Wales is acquired thanks to Neptune funding.

The dramatic Carrick-A-Rede is purchased on the Antrim coast.

1968 Murlough National Nature Reserve, the first National Nature Reserve in Ireland, on the County Down coast, is acquired by the National Trust. Subsequent acquisition is made possible by Neptune funds.

1969 Lundy Island comes on to the market and Sir Jack Hayward steps in to help the National Trust buy this unique place.

First 100 miles of coastline purchased with Neptune Funds.

1970 15,000 members of the Devon WI hold a sponsored walk to help buy Little Dartmouth Farm in South Devon, which runs 1.5 miles westward from the entrance to Dartmouth Harbour.

1973 By November Enterprise Neptune funds meet the original target of £2m; 338 miles of coast are now owned by the National Trust.

1975 The Needles on the Isle of Wight, known and loved by millions, is purchased by the Trust.

1976 8 miles of magical coastline around Stackpole in Pembrokeshire comes into the care of the National Trust.

A start is made on the Yorkshire coast with 5 hectares of Robin Hood's Bay in October.

1981 The 5,000-hectare Kingston Lacey and Corfe Castle Estates are left to the National Trust under the will of Mr H. J. R. Bankes. Previous Trust purchase of Ballard Down means that the entire coastline between Swanage and the mouth of Poole Harbour are now protected.

1987 Gift of Cape Cornwall from Heinz through their 'Guardians of the Countryside' scheme with the WWF.

First acquisition in Tyne and Wear takes place in April when South Tyneside Borough Council hands over the Leas along with funds to cover the running for 50 years.

1988 14 September 2014, Enterprise Neptune celebrates the 500th mile of coastline to come under National Trust Protection, at Warren House Gill and Foxhole Dene, County Durham. The land came from British coal for a nominal sum – this stretch of coastline is also known as the black beaches.

1990   Neptune's Silver Anniversary. £2million is raised through the generosity of supporters.

Souter Lighthouse, sited on the cliffs at Whitburn, South Shields, is bought with the help of various funds including a European Regional Development Fund grant.

1993   A 5-mile stretch of internationally rare and extremely fragile coastal vegetated shingle coastline, backed by 6,000 hectares at Orford Ness in Suffolk, is acquired from the Ministry of Defence.

1994   Nestling on the Llŷn Peninsula in north-west Wales, funding from Neptune helped make the acquisition of Porthdinllaen possible.

1998   Sutton Hoo, Suffolk, of significant nature conservation interest, is acquired by the National Trust and comprises almost 100 hectares of land at the southern end of the Suffolk Sandlings and alongside the River Deben.

2000   Greenway House has been an important Devonshire home on the Dart Estuary for at least five centuries. One of its most famous owners was the crime writer Agatha Christie, who purchased Greenway as a holiday home from 1938 to 1954. Since 2000 the Trust has owned and managed the estate after it was given by the Hicks family. The estate was secured by funds from the Neptune Coastline Campaign.

2002   Brean Down Fort overlooking the Bristol Channel is acquired by the Trust. The fort was originally constructed in about 1865 as part of the protection of Bristol Channel ports devised by Lord Palmerston and extensively modified for anti-shipping operations and as a test area for the Department of Experimental Weapons in the Second World War.

2004   Wembury Point in South Devon is acquired from the Ministry of Defence. Tens of thousands of people help to raise three times the amount needed to acquire this important stretch of coastline east of Plymouth.

2005   40-year anniversary of Neptune. The National Trust now owns almost one-tenth of the coastline in England, Wales and Northern Ireland.

Shifting shores research commissioned to assess how the coastline is likely to change over the next 100 years. The results suggest that many of the Trust's important sites are at risk from coastal erosion and flooding. Learning from experience, Trust policy now favours adaptation, giving time and space to change with the coast and work with the forces of nature.

'The Coast Exposed', an exhibition run in partnership with Magnum Photos to capture the changing nature of the coast and the people that live and work on the coastline.

Ten coastal walks become the first downloadable walks on the Trust website.

2010   The National Trust is offered the opportunity to save a stretch of coastline at Henfaes and Porth Simdde on the Llŷn Peninsula, North Wales. Supporters help to raise over £450,000 for this beautiful part of the Welsh coast.

2012   Successful White Cliffs of Dover Appeal. Money is raised through public donations to buy a strip of land in front of South Foreland Lighthouse to safeguard this landmark for generations to come.

2013/14   Winter storms and a tidal surge hits National Trust sites hard from Blakeney Point in Norfolk to South Milton Sands in south Devon and Murlough National Nature Reserve in Northern Ireland. Many places see years' worth of change in a few weeks or even an afternoon. The Trust publishes an updated 'Shifting Shores' report focusing on the need to have a clear adaptation policy on the coast.

2015   The Trust marks 50 years of Neptune.

These pages from left to right

Dartmouth Estuary, White Cliff of Dover, Cape Cornwall.

Index

Picture credits

FLPA

© FLPA / C Castelijns, NiS/Minden 292 (top left); © FLPA / R Becker 161 (bottom); © FLPA / Biosphoto 265 (top); © FLPA / J Brandenburg/Minden 265 (bottom); © FLPA / H Clark 107 (middle); © FLPA / B Coster 131 (right); © FLPA / F De Nooyer/Minden 160 (bottom right), 193 (top), 292 (top right), 371 (bottom); © FLPA / H Doernhoff, BIA 61 (middle); © FLPA / D Duckett 318 (bottom); © FLPA / M Durham 318 (top); © FLPA / G Ferrari 264 (bottom), 319 (top), 340 (bottom); © FLPA / A Forsyth 292 (bottom left); © FLPA / P Friskorn, NiS/Minden 60 (middle); © FLPA / B Gibbons 265 (middle), 370 (middle), 371 (top); © FLPA / J Hawkins 227 (bottom); © FLPA / J Herder/Minden 193 (bottom); © FLPA / T Hinsche/Minden 292 (bottom right); © FLPA / P Hobson 37 (lower right), 293 (bottom); © FLPA / D Hosking 37 (top middle), 130 (top right), 192 (middle); © FLPA / Imagebroker 37 (left), 106 (middle), 264 (middle), 318 (middle), 340 (middle); © FLPA / S Jonasson 341 (top); © FLPA / M Lane 61 (top), 226 (top), 264 (top), 319 (bottom); © FLPA / N Van Kappel/Minden 130 (top left); © FLPA / C Marshall 319 (middle); © T Marent/Minden 130 (bottom left), 227 (top), 371 (middle); © FLPA / C Mattiion 340 (top); © FLPA / P McClean 226 (middle); © FLPA / P Miguel 60 (bottom); © FLPA / E Olsen 84 (bottom left); © FLPA / P Sawer 37 (top right), 60 (top), 341 (middle); © FLPA / D Schoonhoven/Minden 131 (left); © FLPA / M Schulyl 131 (top); © FLPA / G K Smith 106 (bottom), 160 (bottom left); © FLPA / C Stenger/Minden 107 (top); © FLPA / K Szulecka 36; © FLPA / S Trewhella 61 (bottom), 84 (top right), 130 (bottom right), 227 (middle), 293 (top), 370 (top); © FLPA / P Van Rij/Minden 84 (top left); © FLPA / P Verhoog/Minden 106 (top); © FLPA / J Vink, NiS/Minden 84 © (bottom right); © FLPA / J Watkins 370 (bottom); © FLPA / T Wharton 161 (middle); © FLPA / D Williams/Minden 85 (top); © FLPA / W Wisniewski/Minden 161 (top); © FLPA / M Woike, NiS/Minden 192 (top and bottom).

Alamy

© Alamy / Lyndon Beddoe 137 (right); © Alamy / Kevin Britland 217; © Alamy / Andrew Chisholm 170; © Alamy / Ian Dagnall 142, 330; © Alamy / Nigel Dickenson 317 (top); © Alamy / Andrew Duke 171; © Alamy / Greg Balfour Evans 143; © Alamy / flab 55; © Alamy / tony french 54; © Alamy / geogphotos 176; © Alamy / Jeff Gilbert 99; © Alamy / Paul Hobart 111; © Alamy / Holmes Garden Photos 309; © Alamy / imageBROKER 375; © Alamy / C W Images 310; © Alamy / Peter Jordan_NE 63; © Alamy / Mike Kipling 53; © Alamy / Marianthi Lainas 329; © Alamy / Tony Lilley 5; © Alamy / Raymond Long 149; © Alamy / Geoff Marshall 118; © Alamy / Robert Maynard 120; © Alamy / MkStock 304; © Alamy / Christopher Nicholson 230; © Alamy / Alan Novelli 311; © Alamy / Andrew Paterson 52; © Alamy / Robert Harding Picture Library Ltd 117; (left), 299, 346 (right) © Alamy / Robert Harding World Imagery 137; © Alamy / Billy Stock 275; © Alamy / Geoffrey Taunton 97; © Alamy / William Thorne 328; © Alamy / T.M.O. Buildings 72; © Alamy/ T.M.O. News 73; © Alamy / Steve Vidler 165; © Alamy / Tony Watson 147; © Alamy / Robert Wilkinson 159.

National Trust Photo Library

© National Trust Images / Matthew Antrobus 188 (bottom), 189, 316 (bottom), 359 (top), 369; © National Trust Images / Peter Aprahamian 366 (bottom); © National Trust Images / David Armstrong 358; © National Trust Images / Don Bishop 210; © National Trust Images / Andrew Butler 218 (top), 222 (top), 225, 239, 254, 255 (left and right), 258; © National Trust Images / Neil Campbell-Sharp 177; © National Trust Images / Brian & Nina Chapple 65, 229; © National Trust Images / Stuart Chorley 90; © National Trust Images / Joe Cornish 8–9, 11, 22, 27, 29, 30, 33, 34, 35, 36 (top and bottom left), 39 (top), 41, 42, 43 (right), 44–5, 46, 49, 50, 56, 57, 58, 64, 66–7, 68, 82, 83, 85, 88, 96, 100, 102, 146, 152, 155, 174, 179, 180, 181, 183, 185, 186, 196, 197, 202, 208, 214, 215, 237, 241, 245, 250, 252, 261, 270–1, 272, 277, 279, 280, 282, 283, 284 (top and bottom), 285, 295, 298, 302, 305, 306, 307, 308 (top and bottom), 321, 322, 324–5, 326, 332, 333 (top and bottom), 334, 335, 338, 339, 341, 345, 348–9, 350, 354, 355 (top), 356, 357, 360, 361, 364, 365, 366 (top), 377; © National Trust Images / Derek Croucher 232–3, 247, 289 (top); © National Trust Images / John Darley 246; © National Trust Images / David Dixon 344; © National Trust Images / Carole Drake 223, 224, 260; © National Trust Images / Graham Eaton 323; © National Trust Images / Rod Edwards 10, 20–1,70, 74, 75, 76, 77, 374; © National Trust Images / Andreas von Einseidel 207, 315, 347 (right); © National Trust Images / Phillip Fenton/ Lightwork 175; © National Trust Images / Simon Fraser 15; © National Trust Images / Dennis Gilbert 148; © National Trust Images / Fay Godwin 195; © National Trust Images / Naomi Goggin 373; © National Trust Images / Steve Gosling 25; © National Trust Images / Nick Guttridge 376 (bottom); © National Trust Images / John Hammond 32, 218–9 (bottom); © National Trust Images / John Hannavy 337; © National Trust Images / Paul Harris, 89, 346 (left); © National Trust Images / Ross Hoddinott 3–4, 133, 178, 205, 206, 211 (bottom), 216, 242, 243 (top), 267; © National Trust Images / Chris Lacy 13, 187, 198, 253, 256; © National Trust Images / James C Laver 243 (bottom); © National Trust Images / David Levenson 16 (top), 222 (bottom); © National Trust Images / Leo Mason 140, 153, 157; © National Trust Images / Nick Meers 166–7, 314; © National Trust Images / John Millar 12, 26 (bottom), 80, 128, 129, 138–9, 144, 145, 156, 163 (top and bottom), 164, 172, 173, 188 (top), 212, 231, 236, 249, 251, 257, 259, 269, 276, 363, 379 (right); © National Trust Images / John Miller 16 (bottom), 78, 121, 122, 125, 127, 135, 154, 376 (top); © National Trust Images / Andrew Montgomery 289; © National Trust Images / Geoff Morgan 79; © National Trust Images / Tudor Morgan-Owen 95; © National Trust Images / Robert Morris 87 (top and bottom), 287 (top and bottom), 352, 353, 362; © National Trust Images / David Noton 112, 126, 184, 200–1, 209, 213, 221, 234, 238, 244, 267 (left), 291, 331, 337 (top); © National Trust Images / Erik Pelham 286; © National Trust Images / Alex Ramsey 367; © National Trust Images / David Sellman 127 (top), 297; © National Trust Images / Ben Selway 19, 168, 220, 226 (bottom), 240, 248, 262 (left and right), 263, 268, 378, 379 (left); © National Trust Images / Arnhel de Serra 24, 31, 39 (bottom), 92, 103, 190, 191, 312, 347 (left); © National Trust Images / Ian Shaw 18 (left), 313, 316 (top), 355 (bottom); © National Trust Images / William Shaw 300–1, 317 (bottom); © National Trust Images / Solent News and Photography Agency 104, 109 (left and right), 110; © National Trust Images / Jemma Street 343; © National Trust Images / Colin Sturges 36 (bottom right), 43 (left), 123; © National Trust Images / Claire Takacs 119; © National Trust Images / Megan Taylor, 144; © National Trust Images / Simon Tranter 7; © National Trust Images / Martin Trelawny 151; © National Trust Images / Rupert Truman 204; © National Trust Images / Paul Wakefield, 71, 81, 211 (left), 278, 290; © National Trust Images / Derek Widdicombe 59; © National Trust Images / Mike Williams 26 (top), 368; © National Trust Images / Jennie Woodcock 288; © National Trust Images / Tony Wright 336.